D1547979

THE HISTORY OF CANADIAN ROCK 'N' ROLL

THE
HISTORY
OF
CANADIAN
ROCK 'N' ROLL

Bob Mersereau

Backbeat
Books

AN IMPRINT OF HAL LEONARD CORPORATION

Published in 2015 by Backbeat Books
An Imprint of Hal Leonard Corporation
7777 West Bluemound Road
Milwaukee, WI 53213

Trade Book Division Editorial Offices
33 Plymouth St., Montclair, NJ 07042

Printed in the United States of America

Book design by Michael Kellner

Library of Congress Cataloging-in-Publication Data is available upon request.

ISBN 978-1-4803-6711-1

www.backbeatbooks.com

Contents

CONTENTS

Foreword

A Life in Canadian Rock

It must have been the summer of 1964, so I was going on twelve. A group of four or five families from our neighborhood was living in a ragtag cluster of tents at Morgan's Point, on the Ontario shore of Lake Erie. We were all camping there together for a few weeks that summer, while our dads commuted to St. Catharines for work. It was a boyhood ambience of sunburns, mosquito bites, campfires, a warm, shallow lake with a threatened undertow, playing *coureurs de bois* in the woods, and a first kiss under the sumacs.

One evening some of us kids were gathered outside the dance pavilion. We were too young to go in, and couldn't have paid anyway (to have a quarter of your own was a big deal then), but stood nearby to listen. Who can now imagine such a remote time, pre-*everything*, when a man could remember the first time he ever heard rock music?

(And if that makes me "old," I'm comfortable with it—proud of it. If a youngster tells me he was born in any later decade, my only response is sympathy: "You missed so much.")

According to the posters, they were called The Morticians. They were pictured in long-tailed suits and top hats, and the battered hearse they and their gear traveled in was parked outside. My first impression of live rock music was that it was *loud*—surprise. They probably had a bunch of fifty-watt amps, but I'd only ever heard Dad's hi-fi, the car radio's single speaker, and the little transistor pressed up to my ear at night. The guitars were brash, jangly and warbly, voices echoey and unintelligible, something low was rumbling the walls, and I couldn't understand why the drums sounded so *metallic*—not knowing what cymbals were. But the drumming sure galvanized my attention.

So did the noise . . .

It was the time of the British Invasion, and soon there were rock bands *everywhere*—in every dance hall, and in every second garage. In those years I often spent school holidays with my Blackwell grandparents in Georgetown, Ontario. By an accident of familial timing, my uncle Richard was just a year older than me, so more like a cousin. He played drums in a band called The Outcasts, emulating the "blue-eyed soul" trend that was *everything* in nearby Toronto.

Even as I took up playing drums myself (well, practice pad and magazines on the bed for the first year), the musical education that was being *delivered* to me in little old St. Catharines was, in retrospect, astounding.

It is probably safe to say, from this twenty-first-century vantage point, that there was no better decade in which to be a kid than the '50s, and no better decade to be a teenager—especially an aspiring musician—than the '60s. Discuss . . .

(If you missed it, see above sympathy.)

It was not radio or television or even word of mouth that introduced me to the music I came to love—it was cover bands. While I very much appreciated the R&B that influenced the "Toronto sound," and played it in some of my earliest bands (still identifiable in my playing today), the first music that really *electrified* me was the "second wave" of the British Invasion. That was when rock 'n' roll became *rock*, I guess—edgy, aggressive-sounding bands like The Who, The Kinks, and The Hollies. I did not hear that kind of music on Top-40 radio, not then, but I heard it played by Graeme and The Wafers. They were a mod-style band from the Prairies who took up residence in the Niagara Peninsula one summer—and rocked my world.

The bands I saw at high schools, the roller rink, and the Castle ("A Knight Club for Teenagers") included local heroes like The Modbeats, The Evil, The Ragged Edges, The Veltones (still remember their mournful single on CHOW radio from their hometown of Welland, "Just Another Face in the Crowd"), and dozens more, plus so many truly *excellent* bands from Toronto.

A few records trickled out from there, too, and we all liked the singles and albums by Mandala and The Ugly Ducklings. (One of my earliest conversations with bandmate Alex was about that album *Somewhere Outside*—including "Gaslight," a single that ought to have been a huge hit everywhere—and Alex laughed when I played the staggered drum figure that opened "Just in Case You Wonder.")

And the drummers! Anyone trying to lay down funky beats for those blue-eyed-soul bands simply *had* to have more chops than a surf-rock drummer. So they were all at least *good*, and some were masters whose playing still echoes in this eternal youngster's inner transistor. Whitey Glan with Mandala, Skip Prokop with Lighthouse, Graham Lear with George Olliver's Natural Gas, Danny Taylor with Nucleus, Dave Cairns with Leigh Ashford, and many more—all playing in my hometown on a weekly basis. Every drummer did a solo—it was simply expected—so even just standing in the audience, no young drummer ever had it so good.

Further afield, it was an adolescent thrill to see The Guess Who at a county fair in Caledonia, then again at the psychedelic youth pavilion called "Time Being" (1967, of course, the Summer of Love—still not fifteen, I was a little young for all that, but sure *wanted* to be part of it!) at the Canadian National Exhibition in Toronto. The next time I saw The Guess Who was at a pop festival at Brock University in 1969, with Mashmakhan (Jerry Mercer another great drummer) and a number of local bands—including my first band with a handful of original songs, J. R. Flood. In front of ten thousand people, I played a drum solo in Santana's "Soul Sacrifice," just as Michael Shrieve had done at Woodstock, and it received a life-affirming reaction.

My head didn't swell, but my ambition did. . . .

In later years I would be privileged to become *part* of the history of Canadian rock, achieving unimagined success and accolades with my bandmates ("the Guys at Work") Alex and Geddy.

Even that road was illuminated by touring with other Canadian bands—crossing paths early on with The Stampeders, April Wine, and the great Downchild Blues Band, as we all struggled as opening acts and playing rock clubs around the U.S.

This book spotlights the pivotal role played by Ronnie Hawkins in early Canadian rock, and he had his part in Rush's history, too. Our *Moving Pictures* album was written in the summer of 1980 at his farm near Peterborough—the same farm that hosted John and Yoko a decade earlier.

When Rush started to headline, we were able to bring other Canadian bands, like Max Webster and FM, on our U.S. tours. We even brought Max on a European tour—but even then they never caught on in the way we, as fans, expected they would. That "divide" remains a mystery—why so many great bands, from the '60s and up through the '70s and '80s, failed to make that connection with American (or European) audiences. (That is to say, even when they had the *opportunity*.)

The Tragically Hip are another puzzling example. As a longtime fan of theirs, singing their praises, I sometimes describe them to unaware

FOREWORD

Americans as "the Canadian Pearl Jam." In some aspects, notably lyrics and arguably songwriting in general, The Hip are the superior in that comparison—but again, by and large, Americans didn't "get" them. I don't get that.

Seeing them play at the House of Blues in West Hollywood one time in the early 2000s, I had rarely seen an audience more *engaged* with a band's songs. But alas, there weren't as many *in* that audience as there might have been. . . .

The rest of the story can be left to the book you are about to commence reading. It is enough to say that the history Bob has researched so lovingly, and woven so deftly into an entertaining story, reflects a vitality, a creativity, and a power that is profoundly worth celebrating.

It begins at a time when the only native rock was . . . the Canadian Shield and the Rocky Mountains. . . .

Neil Peart, 2015

Acknowledgments

Over the years of reporting on music, I have had the chance to interview and speak to thousands of Canadian musicians, and most of them approach their art with an appreciation and acknowledgment of the country's talent that has come before them. They also never fail to remark on how much exists in the country to inspire them. No matter how small the town and how far away it is from the next musical hotbed, there's a shared kinship. Once those musicians start touring, that's what sustains them—knowing that in the next place, they'll find a couple of friends into the same kind of music, ready to share a meal, a place on the sofa, and to show up at the gig. They also speak with reverence about the trailblazers before them and have a deep knowledge of the Canadian music history, at least the part that interests them. It's always a pleasure to speak to them; there's rarely an ego involved, mostly a fun conversation with another music fan. Much thanks goes to all of them who have passed this first-hand knowledge on to me, as it makes up the bulk of what is collected here. A special thanks for this volume goes to Skip Prokop and David Clayton-Thomas, two major par-

ACKNOWLEDGMENTS

ticipants and pivotal eyewitnesses, who gave generously of their time in conversations.

A thanks to the staff of Backbeat Books and Hal Leonard Corporation who worked on this book, especially Associate Editor Bernadette Malavarca, who patiently dealt with my aversion to proper formats and most rules and accepted protocols of publishing. The same suffering must have been felt by copyeditor Gary Sunshine, who also had to stickhandle (an appropriate hockey metaphor) around all my Canadian spellings and terms. Thanks also to Robert Lecker of the Robert Lecker Agency for approaching me with the project. And to Sara Parks, who read chapters with friendly excitement, ignoring the small issues and letting me know if the big picture was in focus. Thanks, once again, to Winnipeg's music historian and the fine writer John Einarson for valuable input on this project and continued friendship and encouragement. Much thanks to Neil Peart for the wonderful memories in the foreword and for his support and contributions in three books now.

Once again, as with previous books, I am indebted to my patient children. Evan, Aidan, and Ben never complain about my late hours or lack of attention to their lives during these writing projects. Nor do they ever suggest I should perhaps spend as much time improving my cooking skills as I do on writing. They are proper gents, good friends all of them, and great company when I do get home. Finally, this is for Susan, who also showed remarkable patience as I spent most of my time writing, helping me set a rigid schedule of work and sticking to it. She never complained and only encouraged me all the way. Her words were inspiring at times when my energy was flagging. Her companionship made it all worthwhile and was what I looked forward to at the end.

Introduction

Here's a pop quiz for you, about pop music. Most of these questions are a bit hard, so give yourself a pat on the back for each one you get right. But it will be even more impressive if you figure out what each group or artist has in common, once the answers are revealed.

1. Who wrote the classic cowboy anthems "Cool Water" and "Tumbling Tumbleweeds"?
2. What was the top rock band from 2000–2009?
3. What is the best-selling country album of all time?
4. What was the best-selling rock album of the 1990s?
5. Who welcomed in the New Year from New York City on radio and television for forty-eight consecutive years?
6. Who holds the record for most consecutive weeks at number one on the British charts?
7. What was the number one chart single of 1960?
8. Which singer's debut single sold ten million copies in 1957, at the time second only to "White Christmas"?

INTRODUCTION

These are some big achievements, and certainly we're looking at some pop culture milestones with these questions. Let's find out the people responsible, starting back in the 1930s.

1. "Cool Water" and "Tumbling Tumbleweeds" were two of the best-loved songs by those singing cowboys, The Sons of the Pioneers. The original group featured Leonard Slye, who became better known as Roy Rogers once he started acting in films as well. But Roy wasn't the writer; that was singer and bass player Bob Nolan, a true Prairie son born in Winnipeg, Manitoba.

2. The 2000s belonged to Nickelback, in the rock world. They sold some fifty million albums, and had the top rock song of the decade, "How You Remind Me." Adding up all their chart numbers, *Billboard* magazine declared them the top rock group of the decade.

3. Shania Twain's 1997 album *Come On Over* has sold over forty million copies around the world, making it the top-selling country album of all time. Of its sixteen tracks, eleven became hit singles, including the chart-topping "Love Gets Me Every Time," "You're Still the One," and "Honey, I'm Home." By crossing over to the pop world, Twain continued to set records, and eventually *Come On Over* became the best-selling album by a female artist in any genre.

4. Twain had the best seller of the '90s, but rock also held its own in the decade. Bands such as Nirvana, Pearl Jam, and Metallica led the way for harder rock, while Santana, Hootie & The Blowfish, and Matchbox Twenty matched them in moving well over ten million copies each. But when the decade ended, it was Alanis Moris-

sette who took the crown with her 1995 release *Jagged Little Pill*. You oughtta know it sold over thirty million copies.

5. You want to say Dick Clark, but the *Rockin' New Year's Eve* host didn't hit Times Square until 1973, and his final broadcast was in 2012, a mere thirty-nine years. The record goes to Guy Lombardo, who began in 1928, and continued until 1976. With his big band The Royal Canadians, Lombardo was beamed first via radio and then TV from the ballroom of the Waldorf-Astoria Hotel. His program included the famous ball drop in Times Square, and Clark's program was merely a competitor at first, trying to capture a more youthful audience.

6. Ho-hum, just another number one for Bryan Adams in 1991, with "(Everything I Do) I Do It for You," a soundtrack job for the film *Robin Hood: Prince of Thieves* (the Kevin Costner one). The power ballad was certainly a sizeable hit, the number one single of the year in the U.S., and number one for nine weeks at home in Canada. But in England, they went nuts for it. The song stayed on top for a record sixteen consecutive weeks, and ran roughshod across the continent as well, hitting the top spot in most European countries. Like Hannibal in reverse, Adams then crossed the Alps, becoming India's biggest English-language star and conquering much of South and East Asia as well.

7. Elvis warned "It's Now or Never," The Everly Brothers sang of "Cathy's Clown," Brenda Lee said "I'm Sorry," and Ray Charles had "Georgia on My Mind." But none of those number one hits could match a little movie

mood music called "Theme from a Summer Place,"
used in the 1959 film starring Sandra Dee and Troy
Donahue. It was re-recorded by Percy Faith, and his
version shot to the top for nine consecutive weeks, a
record at that time. It also won the Grammy for Record
of the Year, and it is still the number one instrumental
of all-time on the *Billboard* charts. The easy listening
orchestra leader Faith was from Toronto.

8. Paul Anka was only fifteen when he went alone from
Ottawa to New York to get a record deal and become
a pop star. That was exactly why he went, and exactly
what happened. One of the very first teen idols, Anka
sold an astounding ten million copies of the song he
wrote, "Diana." It outdid anything by Elvis, including
"All Shook Up," on the charts at the same time, and easily bested Jerry Lee Lewis's "Whole Lotta Shakin' Goin'
On" and Buddy Holly's "That'll Be the Day." Adding in
the millions of copies sold in other countries where it
grabbed the top spot, including England, Canada, and
Australia, only the immortal "White Christmas" was
figured to have sold more copies.

Okay, that's enough. You get the point I'm sure. These, and many other
chart records and fascinating facts in popular music feature a Canadian connection. Pop, rock, country, jazz, then and now, you name it,
there's a Canadian or two or twenty as an important part of the story.
Some of them are superstars, known around the globe, such as Adams, Neil Young, Leonard Cohen, and Joni Mitchell. Others are just
super-talented, maybe known better in their home country, but their
art has touched millions. Take Gene MacLellan as one example. The
shy songwriter from Prince Edward Island managed to get himself on

CBC television thanks to a demo tape of exceptional material. His fellow performer Anne Murray knew a great song when she heard it, and her 1970 version of MacLellan's "Snowbird" became the most widely played song in the world, according to Broadcast Music Inc. (BMI). In 1971, another Canadian group, Ocean, grabbed a second MacLellan song and had an even bigger chart hit with it, called "Put Your Hand in the Hand."

Now here's where things become what might be considered unfair for Canadians in pop music. If you were a songwriter in 1970 with a couple of huge hits to your credit for others, say a Randy Newman or Jimmy Webb–type, you would be the toast of L.A. or Nashville. Artists, producers, and record labels would be scrambling for your songs and lining up at your door. But they couldn't find that door far away on P.E.I., and MacLellan was just as happy to stay away from the limelight. Still, there should be credit where credit is due, and you rarely see his name in any list of great songwriters. The more you look, the Canadian conundrum keeps coming up. Back to Paul Anka; after "Diana," the hits didn't dry up. He became one of the very biggest acts of the early rock 'n' roll era, tallying a very impressive thirty-three Top 40 hits on the *Billboard* charts, including three at number one. By the numbers, that is more than Little Richard, Jerry Lee Lewis, Frankie Lymon & The Teenagers, Richie Valens, Eddie Cochran, Gene Vincent, Bo Diddley, and Carl Perkins. Combined. Yet all of those other artists are in the Rock and Roll Hall of Fame. Anka is not. Of course, you can argue that Anka went on to more Vegas-style material, and wasn't really rock 'n' roll, but he was in 1957 when he sold ten million copies of "Diana," and one hit alone (Valens, Bo Diddley, Perkins) was enough to get others in.

Canadians just don't seem to get their due in the accepted history of rock 'n' roll. They get left out, marginalized, or worse still, assimilated. Rock histories place Mitchell and Young as part of the California sound,

INTRODUCTION

just because they moved there. Yet musicians often move to the bigger recording centers of the day, whether it's Memphis, New York, Nashville or L.A., London, or Kingston, Jamaica. When Young sang about a town in north Ontario, that wasn't a California reference, and when Mitchell wished she had a river she could skate away on, it probably wasn't the Sacramento. Nobody is trying to shut Canadians out. It's simply that the history books have been written by those in the bigger countries, the U.S. and the U.K. They dwarf Canada in population, and it's only natural if you are writing about your own country, you pay attention to the scenes and sounds there. The mythology was created and accepted years ago. Rock 'n' roll was invented in the U.S., and England gets let in the club thanks to the incredible success of The Beatles, The Stones, The Who, and The Kinks. Then it's as if the doors were slammed shut. It has to be Detroit or New Orleans, London, or Liverpool. You'll read lots about the folk scene in Greenwich Village, but nothing about the coffeehouses in Toronto that spawned Ian & Sylvia and Gordon Lightfoot. Much is made about EMI's Abbey Road, or Chess in Chicago, but in Montreal sits one of the most important recording studios in the world, the RCA Victor plant that Emile Berliner himself built, a company that gave the world Wilf Carter and Hank Snow's recordings, the first records of Oscar Peterson, and the fascinating, distinct, and thriving world of French Canadian music. In 1964, every second teenager in the U.S. grabbed up a guitar and started a garage rock band thanks to The Beatles on *Ed Sullivan*, but Canada's Capitol Records had released the band's records a year before that. And when Elvis went in the army, Buddy Holly's plane went down, and Jerry Lee Lewis and Chuck Berry got into legal trouble with very young women, conventional rock 'n' roll history says the music died, at least for a few years. Don't tell that to Conway Twitty, then a full-fledged rockabilly cat who found a huge scene in and around Hamilton and Toronto and invited his Arkansas buddy Ronnie Hawkins along to liven up the party.

INTRODUCTION

Is this some kind of secret history of rock 'n' roll? Not really, and certainly not in Canada. But it's not all that well known either. The formation stories, the background, the trivia, the stuff that makes up music history books, hasn't been passed on that often, and you won't find that much on the Internet either. And if the artist is Canadian, it's often not really considered very important. It's only when you start adding up all the accomplishments, the talent, the landmark recordings, and the milestone developments that you realize the country is pulling way above its weight in the music department. Hopefully, you'll find all of that in this volume. It won't have every great Canadian band or performer, as there is a lot of ground to cover. There's rock, pop, folk and jazz, country, soul and rap, alternative and electronica, dance and metal, all of it in French as well. It won't try to figure out what sets the national music of the rock era apart; great swaths of Canadian forest have been felled to print essays on our songwriters, their relationship to nature, the cold climate, the wide expanse of land and the long empty spaces between cities, the traditions brought via immigration, and even how polite Canadians can be. None of the theories fully explains how the country can produce such different artists as Barenaked Ladies, Drake, Arcade Fire, Justin Bieber, Rush, Anvil, Bachman-Turner Overdrive, Loverboy, and Celine Dion. Yet they are all obviously and could only be Canadian. Here then is the history of music in the rock 'n' roll years from a different angle: the Canadian story. We'll stick to the rock 'n' roll era, from the mid-1950s on, and look at the most popular music as the decades progressed.

MOMENTS TO REMEMBER

Canada's First Rock 'n' Roll Hits

I f there was ever a nasty, brutish, ugly mutt of music, it was rock 'n' roll. There was no way you could identify its parents. This mongrel was made up of rhythm and blues, country and western, some jazz, gospel, old folk, and sweet harmonies. And don't even try to put a date on the birth of rock 'n' roll. Dozens of songs, from the '30s and '40s up until "Rock Around the Clock" in 1954, get credited as the start. Or maybe it was a moment, such as Sam Phillips opening Sun Studio in 1950, or DJ Alan Freed popularizing the phrase "rock 'n' roll" on the radio in Cleveland. Lots of braggarts over the years have claimed to be the daddy or mama. There's no clear moment when the rock era began—music slowly changed over several years until it became obvious by 1955 that rock 'n' roll was big.

The years leading up to 1955 saw many artists edging the music along, most notably rhythm and blues performers. They were, in everything but name, rockin' and rollin', as jump blues and boogie-woogie were getting more and more electric. But music was still largely segregated, especially on the radio, and there were few stations playing R&B.

Eventually, some white artists started to pick up a bit of the sound, making it a lot more popular and mainstream. That's as good a place as any to trace Canada's entrance into the rock 'n' roll era, with some transitional groups that were among the first to gain wide success with the changing sounds.

So we begin not in some wild juke joint, with ear-piercing guitar and sweaty bodies packing the dance floor, or on the makeshift stage of a county fair, as a good ol' country boy shakes his hips in a most lascivious manner. No, this is Canada, and Toronto in particular, which is nothing if not polite. At that time, it was still known as Toronto the Good, a name derived from its Victorian morals and strict Days of Rest laws. So our rock 'n' roll story begins at St. Michael's Choir School, behind the imposing St. Michael's Cathedral, the 1840s Gothic Revival landmark. It was a private Catholic school, set up to supply St. Michael's Cathedral with a steady supply of voices for its boys' choir. Students would get the basic Catholic education of the day, and learn choral singing as well. Very well. The school is renowned for its performances, tours, and graduates, including opera singers, jazz vocalists, and one Barenaked Lady along the way.

In 1947, four boys at the school decided to form a vocal group. They were Bernie Toorish, Connie Codarini, Rudi Maugeri, and John Perkins, and unfortunately chose among other names The Otnorots (spell it backward). That wasn't going anywhere, and Maugeri and Perkins left to finish up high school at St. Michael's. We'll hear more from them later. Jimmy Arnold and Frank Busseri replaced them, and by 1950 the group was singing around the club circuit, and had become The Four Lads, specializing in squeaky-clean harmonies and popular hits of the day. It was the style that supper clubs loved, and word spread, landing them a lengthy residency at Le Ruban Bleu in New York, a mainstay in the city since 1937. All the right people stopped by, including Mitch Miller, the oboist and bandleader who had just started his new job as the head of Artists & Repertoire for Columbia Records. Miller liked what he heard and had a job in mind for the four Canadian lads.

The first the world heard of The Four Lads on record was the sound of four voices going "Ooo-wah, ooo-wah, ooo-WAAHH," before singer Johnnie Ray cooed his massive hit "Cry." Miller had teamed the quartet with a singer about to shake the music world. Ray's over-the-top warbling was an instant smash, as he poured more and more emotion into the lyrics, almost crying the words. Those rich harmonies of the Lads were big, too, influenced by a new vocal style. Ooo-wah's were all the rage, thanks to the street corner sounds that would later be called doo-wop. It was a number one single, and number one on the R&B chart as well, although its tinkling xylophone and gentle pace weren't the R&B of John Lee Hooker's "I'm in the Mood," or B. B. King's "3 O'Clock Blues," also hits around that time. But the huge white audience was being introduced to a small bit of R&B with that song, and the Canadians received full billing on the cut, the label reading Johnnie Ray and The Four Lads. On the flip side as well, "The Little White Cloud That Cried" was almost as big a hit, making it to number two.

Hitching their ride to Ray's skyrocketing fame, The Four Lads recorded more sides with the singer in 1952, and then got their own deal from Miller. By 1953 they were in the Top 10 with "Istanbul (Not Constantinople)," not rock 'n' roll but a fun novelty number. The group's big year was 1955. They scored back-to-back number two hits on the pop charts, with "Moments to Remember," and "No Not Much," and 1956 saw them hit with "Standing on the Corner" at number three. "Moments to Remember" became the group's signature song, with its unison opening lines soaring into dramatic harmonies. Decades later, it was always the highlight of PBS fundraising specials and vocal group reunion shows.

Meanwhile, those two old St. Michael's buddies, Rudi Maugeri and John Perkins, saw what was happening with the group they passed up.

When The Lads returned for a reunion concert, Maugeri ran into Perkins and decided they wanted back in the game. Drafting in Perkins's brother Ray and Pat Barrett, the quartet drifted around the club circuit for a couple of years before getting a break through a Cleveland TV show. Through it they connected with Bill Randle, considered the top DJ of the day in the U.S. His support got them a record contract with Mercury, and their new name, to match their haircuts.

After a couple of false starts, the group's first hit, 1954's "Crazy 'Bout Ya Baby," did have a bit of rock 'n' roll to it, with a few electric guitar licks and a walking bass line behind the big band brass. The vocals were still very clean-cut, even if they did swing a little. For 1954, it wasn't a bad effort, given that members Maugeri and Barrett wrote it themselves. When it hit number eight, The Crew-Cuts were brought back into the studio, but this time Mercury had a number in mind. Atlantic Records had a new R&B group, The Chords, with a song that was poised to be a hit. It was one of the earliest examples of doo-wop, "Sh-Boom." With its repetitive "Life could be a dream" theme, part scat vocals, and infectious sh-boom backing vocals, it conquered the rhythm and blues charts for the summer of '54, and also became one of the very first true R&B numbers to cross over to the pop charts, opening the ears of white teens even further. However, it was common practice in those days for other labels to grab on to a hit and try to steal the original's thunder with a cover version. The Crew-Cuts sent their version to pop stations a month after the The Chords had first hit the charts. The more sanitized version was the bigger hit, soon a number one.

The differences are obvious. The original by The Chords is driven by drums, bass, and electric guitar, plus a great honking sax solo. The Crew-Cuts use an orchestra. The Chords' vocals soar, with lots of energy, and the harmonies are rooted in gospel singing. The Crew-Cuts' singing is precise, and it sounds like they are back in St. Michael's. That's how the great early race debate of rock 'n' roll began. Were The

Crew-Cuts (and more to the point, the band's record label) stealing the money, fame, and artistry of The Chords? Or, were they doing the opposite, leveling the playing field, and bringing R&B to bigger and bigger audiences? The Chords never had another hit, but Fats Domino was thrilled with the royalties that poured in when Pat Boone covered "Ain't That a Shame." Boone is the best known of the cover artists, but The Crew-Cuts were, for better or worse, the first to score a big hit, and turn it into a career.

The Crew-Cuts followed "Sh-Boom" with another tune lifted from the doo-wop school, "Earth Angel," originally by The Penguins. The lovely ballad followed virtually the same trajectory as "Sh-Boom": The Penguins' version went to number one R&B, crossed over to the Top 10 in pop, and a few weeks later, in swooped The Crew-Cuts. They outsold the original, and had the bigger hit, a number three. Again, the original is the best, just piano, drums, harmonies, and Cleveland Duncan's remarkable, pained lead. This time, The Crew-Cuts aren't as unhip as the "Sh-Boom" effort, but still, orchestrated horns take over, and no one is hurting in the vocal performance.

The Crew-Cuts would continue to cover R&B songs through the rest of the '50s, gaining one more Top 10 hit with a version of Otis Williams & The Charms' "Gum Drop." The band did do more originals along the way, and even a little country, with Sonny James's "Young Love." They also learned to rock a little; in 1957 they charted with a cover of Dale Hawkins's immortal "Susie Q," which included a distorted guitar solo.

Another Canadian vocal group were a little more rock 'n' roll than The Crew-Cuts and The Four Lads, probably because they didn't learn their chops in a cathedral. The Diamonds, originally Tedd Kowalski, Phil Levitt, Bill Reed, and Dave Somerville, got together in Toronto a little further into the '50s, when the rock 'n' roll era was beginning. They did learn from The Crew-Cuts' example though; getting a gig in Cleveland, they attracted Bill Randle, still a powerhouse DJ, and once again he worked his contacts, lining up a tryout with Mercury Records. Randle had a copy of a new record by Frankie Lymon & The Teenagers, "Why Do Fools Fall in Love," and suggested to all that a cover of that would be a smash. The Diamonds' version was rush-released in January of 1956, following the Teenagers' 45 by only a few days. For once, the cover didn't match the huge success of the original, but it did put The Diamonds into the Top 10, and started the ball rolling.

The rest of 1956 saw The Diamonds continuing to cover R&B numbers by such groups as The Willows and The Clovers, to some minor chart success. Everything changed in 1957. An obscure group, The Gladiolas, had a minor hit brewing. But for a change, the original R&B version wasn't that hot. The song itself was great but the production was sloppy, cluttered, and the vocalists weren't the most talented, certainly not as strong singers as The Diamonds. The song was "Little Darlin'," a bold slice of doo-wop written by Maurice Williams, who would later score with his group The Zodiacs and the classic "Stay." But his Gladiolas weren't bothering the pop charts and "Little Darlin'"wasn't even a major R&B hit. A month later, The Diamonds' version became one of the best-known songs of the early rock 'n' roll era.

The arrangement was stolen from the original, from the clickity-clack percussion of the claves at the start, to the spoken-word interlude. But The Diamonds added more and stronger doo-wop parts, and had much more spark, so that the song jumped out of the radio. The vocals start much earlier on The Diamonds' version, an exciting "Ah-ya-ya-ya-ya," whereas The Gladiolas' lacks urgency. Even most R&B purists admit The Diamonds had greatly improved the song, and left their mark in the heady early rock 'n' roll days.

It wasn't just R&B groups that were getting one-upped by Canada's vocal kings. Even the great Buddy Holly saw one of his classics snatched away, "Words of Love." The Diamonds' version, the group's follow-up to "Little Darlin'," came out a month before Holly's own. Theirs was very different, starting with doo-wop bass vocals, soaring oh-oh-oh's, and was much speedier. They also turned the second verse into a spoken-word segment, to mimic "Little Darlin'." Finally, they added a twangy rock 'n' roll guitar solo, a coup de grace that took the song to number thirteen. When Holly's version arrived, it didn't even chart. Up next was a carbon copy of The Rays' current hit "Silhouettes," identical right down to the B-side, "Daddy Cool." This time, it was Top 10 for both, although The Rays won, number three to number ten.

Being on Mercury Records provided The Diamonds with another huge hit, thanks to label executive/songwriter Clyde Otis. One fall afternoon in 1957 the group was watching TV, and saw some kids doing a line dance they called The Stroll. There was no song to go along with it, so the group asked Otis to come up with one. The slow, sexy strut was a number four hit for The Diamonds, and one of their most raw, with a bleating sax and honky-tonk piano, and became their second million-seller after "Little Darlin'." Of all the so-called cover acts of the '50s, The Diamonds won the most respect, for their authentic doo-wop and R&B chops, and their run of hits.

The '50s saw musicians who had specialized in one of the older forms of music being drawn into the new, exciting rock 'n' roll field. Many young country singers followed Elvis and hopped on the rockabilly bandwagon. The sound coming out of Sun Studios led the way, with Carl Perkins, Jerry Lee Lewis, and Johnny Cash among the many. Gene Vincent, Wanda Jackson, and Dorsey and Johnny Burnette all played the wild music too. The rock histories always focus on those players, and rockabilly is generally regarded as a Southern and Western sound. So once again, a Canadian has been forgotten, one of the biggest stars of that era.

Jack Scott was an odd mix for that time, or any. Born in Windsor, Ontario, he was an Italian in love with hillbilly music, especially Hank Williams. Scott was born Giovanni Scafone Jr. his father a recent immigrant from Italy to Canada. In the late '40s when he was ten, the family moved right across the border from Windsor to a Detroit-area town. Like so many others, Scott became a devotee of the sounds he heard beaming up on high-powered radio stations from the South, especially *Louisiana Hayride* and the Grand Ole Opry. In the early '50s he started playing country dances, and after a couple of years the influence of Elvis was being felt in Detroit. Young people at the shows were asking for rock 'n' roll, too, and Scott adapted. He was good at that, as we'll see.

By 1957, Scott had developed a significant local following and a rockabilly sound, with a big bass fiddle, rockin' electric lead guitar, and some sax. He was big enough to get a record deal and score a couple of local hits. His year was 1958, though, starting with a tune he wrote about a local troublemaker he knew who had just been sent to jail for assault. He called it "Greaseball," and perfectly channeled the James Dean–rebel identity of the times. The slapback echo made Scott sound huge and menacing. There was just one problem: "Greaseball" wasn't the nicest of titles. His new record label insisted on a change, and the song became "Leroy." It headed up the charts to number eleven in the U.S.

There was more to that 45, though. Scott had written a love ballad for the flip side, and along the way, a DJ started playing that as well as "Leroy." "My True Love" was more of a doo-wop number, a slow weeper highlighted by a vocal much different from "Leroy." Scott had a terrific range, and that ability to adapt. Singing down low for "My True Love," he was joined by a vocal group he had found over the border in Ontario, The Chantones, who would go on to back him on many of his hits. "My True Love" had perfect timing, as ballads were becoming the big sound of '58. It wound up being the bigger hit than "Leroy," peaking at number three and giving Scott his first Gold record.

"With Your Love" came next, another slow ballad with The Chantones, and with another bass vocal lead, copying the formula. It was a medium hit, but then "Goodbye Baby" took him back to the Top 10, with a return to rockabilly. The other side was interesting, too, a gospel tune called "Save My Soul," done in rockabilly style, The Chantones in full flight, Scott with a hiccup vocal and some pretty good histrionics on the chorus. It had a lot more fire than Elvis's gospel sides of the day. Plus, it, too, got into the charts, another double-sided hit.

A short stint in the army slowed things down, Scott honorably discharged for an ulcer, and 1959 brought him only one major hit, "The Way I Walk." It was a classic sound, all echo and vocal and acoustic guitar for the first verse, before The Chantones join in with the de-oo-ee-oo-wops. Scott growls, "Talk to me," cueing the sax solo. It's one of the best examples of rockabilly, and one of the very last from its heyday. Safe pop singers and nice ballads were taking over. Scott wasn't done yet though. Ever able to adapt, he brought back the ballads in 1960 and landed right back in the Top 10, first with "What in the World's Come Over You," and then the strings-and-syrup number "Burning Bridges," matching his biggest hit at number three. While that was happening on the pop charts, Scott released an LP of country, called *I Remember Hank Williams*, for his early idol.

Scott's career continued long after that, but somehow his music faded over the years in North America. The ballads, his biggest hits, haven't aged that well, but his rockabilly and country material are as strong as that of any of the major stars of that time. Maybe it was because he could do it all and could sound like several different singers. Or maybe rockabilly stars aren't supposed to be Italian hillbillies from Windsor-Detroit.

Maybe pop stars aren't supposed to come from Ottawa either. There wasn't any particular music tradition in Canada's capital, and no connection to recording studios or music labels or radio and TV networks. Paul Anka had to make it his way. Not only was he alone, he was also ridiculously young. He formed his first group at thirteen. At fourteen, he won a contest at his local IGA grocery store by collecting Campbell's Soup labels, which took him to New York. At fifteen, he left for L.A., trying to excite people with his music. He got a single out of it, which failed, and back home convinced his father to let him go back to New York for one last shot. If that didn't work, he agreed to return home. This time he found the right man, with ABC-Paramount's Don Costa listening to him play his original songs on piano, including one called "Diana," about a girl in his church he liked. Anka didn't have to return to his father; instead the elder Anka had to come to New York to sign the contract for his son, still a minor.

To say that "Diana" was a hit is a massive understatement. It's difficult to describe the enormity of its success. It was number one, not just in the U.S., but in England, where it sold over a million copies, in Australia, and of course in Canada. As the sales figures started to add up, records began to fall. Now that Anka was sixteen, his self-written song had become the biggest-selling single of the year, the decade, and in pop music history, with only the immortal "White Christmas" ranking higher. Anka was immediately a huge star and a teen idol as well. Screaming teens kept him hidden away in hotel rooms on tour, and it quickly became a hard and lonely life. Anka poured those feelings of isolation into his songs, autobiographical hits such as "Lonely Boy," "Put Your Head on My Shoulder," and "Puppy Love." He was also branching out, offering his songs to other artists. Buddy Holly asked Anka for a song when the two met on tour. Holly wanted something with strings, a different sound for him. Anka gave him the broken-hearted number "It Doesn't Matter Anymore," which Holly recorded at his last-ever recording date, with Anka present. It was to be Holly's last hit, as he died in a plane crash in February of 1959. Anka could have been on the flight as well, but his manager made him stay back, as he was supposed to keep an eye on Anka for his father. After his friend's death, Anka decided to give his royalty rights to Holly's widow, Maria.

MOMENTS TO REMEMBER

Branching out was a brilliant career strategy for the still-young performer. Anka was able to work in TV and film, acting and composing. He did both in the 1962 film *The Longest Day*. He played an Army ranger in the Academy Award-winner and wrote the movie's theme song as well. It was another theme song that really secured his future as a songwriter, thanks to its three-decade payday. A song Anka wrote in 1959 called "Toot Sweet" took a roundabout route to end up as one of the most famous themes in TV history. Anka's instrumental, a pleasant little number with a harpsichord playing the melody at the start was recorded by bandleader Tutti Camarata. Camarata happened to also produce Mouseketeer Annette Funicello's records, and he asked Anka for a batch of songs for the *Annette Sings Anka* album (they were famously dating at the time). "Toot Sweet" was given lyrics, and a new name, "It's Really Love." That same year, Anka recorded it as well for a French movie, *Faibles Femmes*. In 1962, the famous *Tonight Show* was undergoing a major change, welcoming Johnny Carson as its new host. Carson and his live band would need a theme song, and he approached Anka. The old "Toot Sweet" was dusted off, given a dynamic drum opening and pulsing horns where the harpsichord had once been, and it never left the airwaves until Carson retired. Night after night, Anka got paid with every play, a considerable fortune.

As Anka left his teen years, he changed his style and image and left his teenage audience behind as well. He started appearing on the Vegas and supper club stages, and his days on the pop charts ended, seemingly for good. Not that he needed the hits; when his label dropped him in favor of new stars, he shrewdly bought back his master recordings, another move worth millions in future earnings. Still much younger than the rest of the Vegas performers, he became a junior member of the Rat Pack, on good terms with Frank, Dean, and Sammy. Sinatra was in a blue mood and told Anka he was going to retire. He wanted to do one more album, and reminded The Kid, as he called him, that he was supposed to write him a song. Months later, Anka was going over a song from France, a melody he loved and to which he had purchased the publishing rights. It was called "Comme d'habitude," and sitting at his piano, Anka reflected on Sinatra's desire to quit. He imagined himself as the embattled Chairman of the Board, bitterly leaving the stage, facing his "final curtain." In a night, Anka had written new lyrics for what became "My Way." It revitalized Sinatra's career, and became a worldwide hit. There was no more talk of retirement. "My Way" spent an incredible 124 weeks on the U.K. singles chart starting in 1969, more than doubling the record previously held by Bill Haley's "Rock Around the Clock," and still untouched to this day.

Anka had the magic touch and the craftsman's perseverance. Tom Jones was another who came calling for a hit, and got one in 1971, with "She's a Lady," the biggest song of his career, and a million-seller. To make the deal sweeter for Anka, the B-side was Jones's version of "My Way." Finally, the way was paved for Anka himself to return to the top of the charts. Anka and his wife, Anne, had five children, all girls, and as a loving tribute, he wrote "(You're) Having My Baby" in 1974. It was syrupy, a bit outdated, and criticized on a number of levels, but it also found a huge sentimental audience, and brought Anka back to number one. It started another run of Top 40 hits for Anka that lasted the decade.

Anka continued to be sought out by stars in need of his hit-making talents. He'd long known The Jackson 5 and family, and in the early '80s, he sat down with Michael to work on material. The idea was to find a duet track for an Anka album, and the pair cowrote several songs over the course of a month. The tracks weren't used at the time, as Jackson's *Thriller* album exploded. But after Jackson's death, executors announced a new single and album, both called *This Is It*. The track used was from the Anka sessions, and another called "Love Never Felt So Good" was used on the 2014 album *Xscape*. It broke into the Top 10, a mere fifty-seven years after Anka's initial hit with "Diana."

In the new rock 'n' roll landscape, Canada's biggest successes had come from performers leaving their home and native land. There wasn't a star system in place for the new music. There was no national hits chart, no chains of radio stations playing the same songs. The national broadcaster, CBC, was still leery of the music, and had little programming time for it. The infrastructure wasn't there. There were very few recording facilities, labels, and business professionals. It was difficult to tour and spread the word. The cities were too far apart, the travel was expensive and dangerous in the winter. So the rock 'n' roll scenes were building in each community with local stars, but very few that were heard outside their own cities. There were exceptions; Montreal's Jimmy James and The Candy Kanes got a deal with the new Columbia Records of Canada in 1958, and managed to get their rockabilly hit "Baby Sitter Rock" on the charts at CHUM Radio in Toronto. But more than likely, if your star was starting to shine at home, you'd be attracted to a bigger U.S. center.

That was the route for one Leonald Gauthier of Rouyn, Quebec. The country singer had started in logging camps, but soon was playing shows in town as well. At one of his concerts he met another singer, Ginger Heppel, in town from Ontario for a gig. She liked him, he joined her band, and they teamed up, personally and professionally. They soon had a stage show in Montreal and upstate New York. Leonald changed his name, and they became Hal and Ginger Willis. Country great Webb Pierce caught their act, and convinced them to move to Nashville. That led to the Grand Ole Opry, but Elvis had broken big by then, and rock 'n' roll worked its way into their set too. Their signature song was "My Pink Cadillac." Colonel Parker picked them to tour with Elvis, and others picked them for their songwriting, everyone from Patsy Cline ("Walkin' Dream") to Flatt and Scruggs, Ernest Tubbs to Jim Reeves. Willis eventually hit the big time with the autobiographical country hit "The Lumberjack" in 1964, which sold 1.5 million copies.

Quebec's music scene was one of the most vibrant on the continent in the late '50s. Montreal especially had plenty of clubs, from show bars to cabarets to teen dances. Touring acts were plentiful, including most U.S. stars at the time. African-Americans had long favored playing Montreal (and Canada in general) thanks to better race relations, and there was a constant flow of the best jazz, blues, and R&B artists. There was also a unique Francophone music scene beginning, something completely different from rock 'n' roll. Folk and traditional music had long been an important part of Quebecois culture, and the chanson was adapting to modern times. Singer-songwriters, or chansonnier, would soon become important voices for a political and cultural explosion in Quebec in the 1960s known as the Quiet Revolution. The roots of that movement were established by Félix Leclerc, a playwright, poet, actor, and songwriter. Moving to Paris in 1950, he became a superstar in Europe and a hero back home. He returned to Quebec in 1953, and his writing, in all its forms, had a great influence on the growing attitude of change in the province. His songs were direct, the work of the poet-songwriter, with themes of nature, love, death, the elements, God, and country. Leclerc set the model for the chansonnier to come, with his acoustic guitar, passion, and his connection to the land and people, a nationalist. The song and the words were everything, the show business meant as little as possible.

Somehow Leclerc and those who followed, including those from the Quebec rock 'n' roll world that developed, managed to survive the crush of English culture all around them. Not just English Canada, but that of the U.S. as well, bordering Quebec to the south. The province numbered about five million people in 1960, fighting off the barrage of media, and star systems from Hollywood, New York, and Nashville. Lots of Quebec people loved Elvis of course, but they had their own hit artists and TV stars, and a self-supporting music industry way before English Canada.

The biggest stars in early Canadian rock 'n' roll music had made their names by leaving the country, but there were plenty of rockers at home. Young people were actually crazy for it—there were bands everywhere, just not much of a chance to make records and make it big. But if you wanted to play rock 'n' roll, and were good at it, there was a market, and money to be made. It was actually a couple of Americans who recognized that first and helped start a rock 'n' roll movement that soon went around the world, Canadian roots that are still a big part of music today. The Hawk was ready to soar.

FOUR STRONG WINDS

Canada Blows into the Folk and Rock Worlds of the Early '60s

R ock 'n' roll was in trouble in 1958. Not with the kids, mind you. They were still wild for the beat, but their parents weren't that thrilled with it. Even though teenagers had started to flex their financial muscles, buying up hamburgers, souping up cars, going to movies, and buying 45s, adults weren't letting them control the marketplace yet. Columbia Records' Mitch Miller summed up the larger music industry's feelings, saying of rock 'n' roll, "It's not music, it's a disease." It's bordering on a conspiracy theory to suggest that there was some kind of collusion to wipe out rock 'n' roll, but when Elvis went in the army in March, the dominoes started to fall. In May, Jerry Lee Lewis caused a scandal when it was revealed he had married his thirteen-year-old first cousin once removed. After a bad plane flight in Australia, Little Richard promised God he'd clean up his act. When he saw the Sputnik satellite, he figured it was a sign and vowed to quit rocking. His last big hit was "Good Golly, Miss Molly" in the spring of '58. What started replacing rock 'n' roll at the top of charts were more ballads, teen idols, and even old-style pop vocalists. The top song of the year was "Volare" by Domenico Modugno. Dean Martin and Perry Como had big hits, and easy listening tunes such as "He's Got the Whole World in His Hands" and "It's All in the Game" ruled.

Ballads, the rock 'n' roll singers were told, were where it was at. All the rockabilly stuff was supposedly out. That had an effect on Harold Jenkins's career. After playing in a band while doing Army duty in Japan, Jenkins had hit Memphis when he got out, thanks to all the excitement around Elvis. He even started recording at Sun Studios, and changed his name to Conway Twitty. And he wasn't the Conway Twitty of country music fame back then, he was a rockabilly cat who hadn't come close to a hit yet. He'd had a couple of singles out, but nothing much was happening. However, he had found what he felt was the Promised Land for rock 'n' roll singers. He'd moved to Canada, where they couldn't get enough of rockabilly. There was quite a scene in the southern Ontario area, in and around Toronto, over to London, and down to Windsor, where the bands would cross the border to Detroit.

Twitty was booked into a long-term gig at the Flamingo Lounge in Hamilton by agent Harold Kudlets. During a break one night, drummer Jack Nance started fooling around on the piano and called Twitty over, thinking he had something. They quickly worked up the song "It's Only Make Believe," a dramatic ballad. Issued by MGM Records, the company first pushed the tune "I'll Try" as the A-side, but disc jockeys soon went for the ballad on the back instead. "It's Only Make Believe" went to number one in the U.S., Canada, and England. There was just one problem: there was no way Conway could stay in Hamilton to honor his commitments to Kudlets. Twitty was given his blessing to go, but with the caveat that he find somebody just as good to take his place.

Twitty knew a great one. Ronnie Hawkins came from Arkansas, and although he wasn't famous, those who did know him thought he was one of the best, including many musical peers. The early rock 'n' roll guys said only Elvis and Jerry Lee could match him, and his stage moves were legendary. Hawkins was a phys. ed. grad from the University of Arkansas, and a gymnast, and put that to great use onstage. He'd run up the side of a wall, and do a backflip back onto the stage. It was primal rock 'n' roll, Hawkins like an animal barely held back by the microphone chord. A young Robbie Robertson, still a kid and a fan, called it the fastest and most violent music he had ever seen, very exciting and very explosive. Hawkins had also developed his version of the camel walk, which became his signature dance move, similar to James Brown's steps, and made popular again in the 1980s when Michael Jackson renamed it the moonwalk. Still, Hawkins was struggling for bookings in the South, as the money was poor and the club owners just as liable to cheat you as pay you. He decided to take a chance on what to him was a very foreign territory. "We didn't know nothin' about Canada, we thought it was a wildnerness country," he recalled. "Levon's dad, who'd never been out of Arkansas, said, 'Them Canadians, they'll stick a knife in ya for a dime.'" Kudlets soon had Hawkins working clubs all around, first at the Golden Rail in Hamilton, later at the Grange, the Brass Rail in London, Ontario, and then into Toronto, at the Le Coq d'Or on Yonge Street. He was a huge success, becoming the king of the Yonge Street Strip.

Hawkins loved Canada, and started setting up shop. For a while, he would go back and forth to the U.S. between Ontario gigs, replenishing the ranks of The Hawks, his backup group. Drummer Levon Helm was his second-in-command ("Stick with me son," he told Helm. "Soon you'll be fartin' through silk."). Kudlets was hugely impressed by Hawkins, and took him to New York, arranging a contract with Roulette Records' Morris Levy. Levy was convinced he'd found the next Elvis and thought he could fill the void left with the King in the army. Hawkins appeared to be heading that way, too. His "Forty Days" and "Mary Lou" in 1959 both hit the U.S. Top 50, and Hawkins appeared on *The Dick Clark Saturday Night Beechnut Show* May 9 of that year doing "Forty Days," leaping onto the stage with the first notes, pushing the piano across the floor while Willard "Pop" Jones played a wild solo. But Hawkins had decided on making Canada home, and headed back north, much to Levy's dismay.

Hawkins had an uncanny eye for talent and wisely kept musicians coming into the band. Hot players such as Telecaster king Roy Buchanan and future Nashville session ace Fred Carter Jr. came into the fold, both hired away from Hawkins's cousin Dale ("Susie-Q"). But the Americans were hard to keep in Canada, and one by one they left. Hawkins had a kind of farm team operation in Toronto, always on the lookout for the best local players. As he often explained, "When you've got as little talent as I have, you've got to surround yourself with the biggies." His work ethic was challenging. The band was playing six or seven nights a week, and then was required to rehearse after, learning new material and honing their chops. Hawkins was notoriously tough to please. But as much as they worked, they partied as well. The stories are legend, sometimes funny, sometimes bordering on depravity. Hawkins has always been an excellent storyteller, and his own best mythmaker, so it's hard to tell which are real, but there are plenty of witnesses to back up a lot of them.

A kid who had been following him around since 1958 was finally let in the band, first as a roadie at age sixteen. Robbie Robertson had been playing guitar with several local bands, including The Consuls (later to become Toronto hit makers Little Caesar & The Consuls, still active today). His first onstage job was playing bass, and soon Carter was instructed to train him up on guitar. Gradually more locals came in the fold, including bassist Rick Danko and pianist Richard Manuel. Another player they wanted badly was keyboardist Garth Hudson, a classically trained musician who could read music and was considered a bit above the rest of the group. Hudson was eventually hired with the understanding he'd also be giving music lessons to the other players, which made it seem more acceptable to him and his parents. There was some truth to it as well, as Hawkins had hired Manuel more for his voice than piano chops, and Hudson was also able to work out intricate arrangements and harmonies. The Hawks were still a more fluid outfit than the above five musicians, with other players in and out of the group as needed, but by assembling this talented crew, Hawkins would change the course of rock music a few years down the road.

One of the young musicians who worked with The Hawks was David Clayton-Thomas. As a teen, he'd been in quite a bit of trouble, eventually ending up in reform school and then regular jail. But he could sing, with a mighty voice that impressed everyone from cellmates to Ronnie Hawkins. Even though he was the lead singer, Hawkins hired Clayton-Thomas, as a fill-in, understudy, and second singer. "I got my start on Yonge Street," says Clayton-Thomas. "I used to beg to sit in with the Ronnie Hawkins band, which of course later became The Band, and became very close with them. I eventually started my own little band on the side, know as The Shays.

"Ronnie never pretended to be a great singer, that's why he hired me to be in his band. 'Oh man, with your pipes, oh ya ya, you got a job.' That left him free to circulate around the club, be the genial master of ceremonies, the host, the party-giver, and that's what he was best at."

As for The Hawks, in their classic combination of Helms, Robertson, Manuel, Danko, and Hudson, David Clayton-Thomas pulls no punches: "They were the best rock 'n' roll band I've ever heard, today, before, or since. When they became The Band and put out that first album [*Music from Big Pink*], I threw a party and had all my friends come over, saying this is the album of the decade."

Hawkins had changed Toronto's Yonge Street Strip. Before, it had been show bars and country clubs, but now rock 'n' roll had taken over, in such spots as the Zanzibar, the Edison Hotel, Friar's Tavern, The Blue Note, and Steele's Tavern. The Colonial had the best jazz and later, blues. Rompin' Ronnie held court at the Le Coq d'Or most nights. It was a musical scene as vibrant as those in London and New York, or such later and better-publicized spots as the Haight-Ashbury district of San Francisco. You could see Bo Diddley, Bill Haley, Carl Perkins, Stevie Wonder, The Righteous Brothers, and of course a flowering of Toronto musicians, learning the ropes in one of the best proving grounds in the world. Big names such as Ray Charles would play Massey Hall or Maple Leaf Gardens, then wander down to the late-night and after-hours clubs of Yonge.

"It was a very exciting time here," says a still-excited David Clayton-Thomas,

> because all of the black artists in the '60s, the R&B artists from Detroit and Chicago and Memphis. They couldn't play in white clubs in the States, the color barrier was still very much in force. So they loved to come to Toronto. So us young, fledgling musicians, we were treated to seeing James Brown, Ike and Tina Turner, Muddy Waters, B. B. King, they all played on Yonge Street in the bars. They loved playing up here. That's why today, what's identified as the Toronto sound from then is very much R&B. When The Band first broke, everyone thought they were from the Deep South, they were so funky, nobody dreamed they were from Ontario. That's where we got our influences.
>
> I remember going to Club 88 in the Masonic Temple on Yonge Street, and saw The Ike and Tina Turner Review. Holy cow, that was big-time show business, it just blew me away. You could go out to the Roller Rink in Mimico, and see the James Brown band, and the bars on Yonge Street, I can't tell you how many nights I nursed a beer and watched the Muddy Waters band, I mean just one of the greatest blues bands ever.

And we also had a tremendous country influence, I first saw Johnny Cash at the Edison Hotel. But Ronnie Hawkins was really the godfather of that era. Wherever he was playing, that was the club to go to.

Eventually, Hawkins even opened his own club in the Le Coq d'Or, The Hawk's Nest.

Through it all, he kept spotting and attracting the best talent. Robbie Lane and The Disciples were one of Toronto's favorite bar bands, and doubled as The Hawks on Ronnie's gigs. Various '60s members split to become the beloved Crowbar, who would rule the R&B scene along with their buddy King Biscuit Boy, another Hawkins find. Yet another flock of Hawks was grabbed to become Janis Joplin's group, named The Full Tilt Boogie Band, after guitarist John Till. They worked on her last album, *Pearl*. There was Bearfoot, featuring Terry Danko, Rick's brother. Skylark had a huge hit in 1973 after leaving Hawkins, called "Wildflower," which reached the Top 10 in Canada and the U.S. That group featured the young David Foster from Victoria, B.C. on keys, before he became one of the most successful producers of all time. Hawkins had first hired him to drive his bus. Hawkins also spied hard-rockin', fast-playing guitarist Pat Travers, giving him his schooling in the early '70s before he became a star.

Meanwhile, Hawkins kept popping up, Zelig-like, at the right moment in rock history. When John Lennon and Yoko Ono arrived in Toronto in 1969 during their peace campaign, they pronounced themselves sick of hotel living. A mutual friend suggested Hawkins's nearby farm, and he agreed to host them. Soon pictures of Lennon riding a snowmobile and hanging out with prime minister Pierre Trudeau appeared around the world, Hawkins side by side with history. Lennon was fooling around with a song soon to be called "Imagine" while he stayed there. The Hawkinses got on famously with the Ono-Lennons, except for the matter of a transatlantic phone bill in the thousands of dollars that didn't get paid. However, the couple did do promotional praise for Hawkins's new album, featuring soon-to-be guitar hero Duane Allman. They also left artwork, Lennon's famous lithographs, clothing, even drug paraphernalia, which Hawkins just gave away to Beatles fans. It would have paid the phone bill many times over.

Hawkins saw himself becoming an unlikely actor in 1975. Bob Dylan, long a friend of sorts thanks to their mutual musician pals, asked him to appear in his rather incomprehensible film *Renaldo and Clara*. Hawkins played the role of Bob Dylan. Dylan was playing Renaldo, after all. In 1976, Hawkins nearly stole the show (and film) from his old group, as The Hawks (now The Band) invited him to perform in their famous finale and film, *The Last Waltz*. Digging out the old moves, Hawkins fanned Robertson's guitar, and a whole worldwide audience who'd never heard of him started digging The Hawk. His next major movie role was less successful and less viewed. His buddy Kris Kristofferson got him a role in the bomb *Heaven's Gate* in 1980, one of Hollywood's most colossal failures.

Along the way, Hawkins has been honored and appreciated at every turn. Greats of the 1950s such as Jerry Lee Lewis have been quick to point out his worthiness, Carl Perkins thought he was brilliant, and Elvis was reportedly a fan. In 1993, President Bill Clinton invited him to play at his inauguration ball, the Arkansas one named the Blue Jeans Bash. It turns out Clinton had first been turned on to The Hawk when he was attending the University of Arkansas. Typically, Hawkins saved the best and weirdest story for the last, or what was supposed to be the last. In 2002, Hawkins was diagnosed with pancreatic cancer. It proved inoperable, Hawkins declined chemotherapy, and he was given weeks to live. In typical Hawkins fashion, he decided to go out with a bang and proceeded to round up some like-minded friends and party his way to the grave. That included, he said, lots of powders, some that "even Bob

Dylan had never heard of." The tributes came in, and old pals such as Clinton, David Foster, and Paul Anka showed up to pay homage. Anka remembered the time they first met, Hawkins mistaking him for the hotel bellhop, when the youthful Anka was actually headlining the whole show.

After a while, something odd happened, or didn't happen. Hawkins was still around, and the cancer, if there had been cancer at all, was gone. The doctors felt it was some sort of medical miracle. It could have been all the medical marijuana, Hawkins suggested. Or, there was one other theory. At the time, a sixteen-year-old boy from Vancouver by the name of Adam read about Hawkins in a newspaper. Adam was a healer, and he contacted Hawkins's management. With nothing to lose, Hawkins agreed to the treatment. It involved Hawkins sitting quietly at his home in Ontario, while Adam peered at a photo of Hawkins back in Vancouver. He would visualize his pancreas, and the tumor, and enter his body. Over the course of several weeks, Adam would fight the cancer. He described it as distance healing, thanks to quantum mechanics. Hawkins described feeling pulses in his stomach, but was reluctant to give credit to the healing technique, instead saying he was still alive thanks to the Big Rocker in the sky.

Hawkins retires every few years, then shows up again, giving interviews and being the best storyteller alive. The stories change a little, usually getting better. Unlike others from the '50s or '60s, his reputation has stayed strong, thanks to his storied career, and that awesome appearance in *The Last Waltz*. Canadian musicians routinely credit him as the one who opened up the nation for rock 'n' roll, who pointed to the possibilities, and brought legitimacy to the country's homegrown scene. And Hawkins has never wavered in his praise for Canada's talent, and has been outspoken about the lack of appreciation it received home and abroad. He's one of the originals, one of the very few left. He's held the biggest rock 'n' roll party for sixty years and survived to tell the tale.

While the bars were flourishing on Yonge Street, another type of club was doing well, in Toronto and across Canada. Parallel to rock 'n' roll, folk music was also undergoing a boom time, a rebirth in its case, and coffeehouses were springing up everywhere. Most had no liquor licenses, so they were easy to start, cheap to run, and the musicians were plentiful, all hoping to play a couple of songs on acoustic guitar. Canada had a strong folk tradition, dating back to the melting pot of peoples that had settled the country over the centuries. Still-strong ethnic communities right across the country each provided their own regional music and traditions, and Canadians had grown up with fiddle star Don Messer on the radio and TV, Celtic singers and players, Western crooners, aboriginal drumming, Francophone folk music, Newfoundland seafaring songs, and much more. The folk tradition was informed by songs played in isolated lumber camps through the long winter months, on Prairie cattle ranches, in thousands of legions and Women's Institutes and community halls. And in kitchens; when it was too cold to do anything else, you could always have a party with a fiddle and guitar, and the kitchen was always the best place to do it.

Canadians were already keen to play folk music when it arrived back in the popular consciousness in the late '50s. With groups such as The Kingston Trio hitting the top of the charts, and Joan Baez debuting at the brand-new Newport Folk Festival in 1959, folk was spreading quickly as another hit sound for young people. Greenwich Village in New York became the epicenter, but the musicians had to start somewhere before they got there. Like Vancouver. That's where Ian Tyson made his debut in 1957, mostly playing rock 'n' roll of the day. Tyson had taught himself guitar as something to do when he was recovering from a bad ankle injury suffered in a rodeo accident. But it wasn't the cowboy life that was calling him at that point. He was actually an art student. When he graduated in 1958, he had trouble finding work, so he hitchhiked to Toronto, where there were far more jobs for commercial artists. He found that world, but he also found the coffeehouse scene.

So did Sylvia Fricker. She was younger, just eighteen in '58 but already a big folk fan. She liked the traditional stuff, British folk songs, spirituals, centuries-old melodies. From small-town Chatham, Ontario, she was keen to get to the big city. A mutual friend heard her singing in Chatham, and Tyson got in touch, inviting her to a show of his in Toronto, at the First Floor club. They clicked, and he told her to get into the city. In 1959, she moved to Toronto full-time, but Tyson had gone back out West for a spell, having caught the rodeo bug again. Fricker simply started singing on her own, getting gigs at the many coffeehouses that were popping up.

The chief area for the new scene was Yorkville Village. Originally a village on its own, it was now in a central part of Toronto, farther north on Yonge Street than the Strip, and west on Bloor Street. It was still relatively cheap real estate, with old Victorian houses, perfect for owners of small businesses who wanted to put in these new clubs. Really, it was just a transition from the beatnik days; jazz and chess and berets gave way to teenagers and hootenannies, and lots of coffee. With a drinking age of twenty-one, the kids couldn't go to the bars to see Ronnie Hawkins, but folk music was now just as popular.

Eventually Tyson came back, and started working at a new club in Yorkville, the Village Corner. Fricker was still playing solo, and she became a regular at the Bohemian Embassy, which was not part of the Village, instead farther south in the Gerrard Street area. It was an avant-garde, free-spirited spot that featured the best and brightest of Canada's poets and writers. On any given night you could find a young Margaret Atwood, Milton Acorn, Irving Layton, or Michael Ondaatje trying out new work. Bill Cosby would drop by to do some stand-up, Bob Dylan poked his nose in, and in 1960, Fricker was doing her songs in between some impressive talent. Tyson and Fricker hadn't forgotten their initial chemistry, though, and soon a partnership bloomed. What stood out was their excellent repertoire and their distinct vocal blend. Fricker liked to source out obscure traditional material, studying the collections of song-hunting musicologists. She even ventured into French Canadian material, and one of the duo's early favorites was the ballad "Un Canadien errant." As singing partners, it was one of those cases where two very different voices created a third, almost eerie sound. Tyson sang the melody, Fricker the harmony, but not conventional ones. Instead, she often used countermelodies, learned from her time in the choir in her teens. Tyson had that rodeo thing going on, singing old cowboy songs he knew from the West, while she brought the Olde English folk songs. He played guitar and she chimed in with the Autoharp; there was no one like them. There was romance in the air as well, which added to the mystery. The duo packed The Village Corner, and quickly moved to the bigger Village clubs, becoming the most in-demand folk performers in the city. "We were big dogs on the block at that time," remembers Tyson.

After 1959's Newport Folk Festival, folk music communities were galvanizing all over North America. Southern Ontario's scene was big enough to have its own gathering in 1961. Local fans had convinced the town of Orillia, 135 kilometers north of Toronto, to allow an arts festival to promote the area, and folk music was chosen. The name was picked from famed writer Stephen Leacock's fictionalized name for the town, Mariposa. The first Mariposa Folk Festival was held over two days in August of 1961, attracting four thousand people for its headlining night. It featured the darlings of the Canadian folk revival, Ian & Sylvia, and a young Toronto woman named Bonnie Dobson, who had written a remarkable song called "Morning Dew," which would eventually become an international favorite recorded by Fred Neil, The Grateful Dead, Jeff Beck, and Robert Plant. The headliners, though, were The Travellers. They had long been popular in the country, especially with their Canadianized version of "This Land Is Your Land," which had replaced Woody Guthrie's U.S. place names with Canadian ones. They had even formed at the instigation of Pete Seeger, who had met them at a Jewish summer camp in the 1950s. They had been regulars on CBC-TV for several years, and were well placed between the old and new folk movements.

Mariposa was considered a success, and an annual tradition began. By 1963, it was already too successful. It sold out its eight thousand tickets, and the town was swamped by rowdy fans, jamming the streets and overfilling the restaurants. Orillia got a court order blocking the festival, and it was forced to move into Toronto. That didn't stop the interest though. It had become the most desired folk music gig in the country. Over the next few years, Canadians such as Buffy Sainte-Marie, Joni Mitchell (then Joan Anderson), Leonard Cohen, Murray McLauchlan, Bruce Cockburn, Neil Young, and Gilles Vigneault all appeared. When the festival was opened to Americans, it was an immediate hit, attracting Phil Ochs, Pete Seeger, Howlin' Wolf, Tom Rush, Doc Watson, Tom Paxton, James Taylor, and many more. It has weathered rough patches over the years, changed venues often, been canceled, and then saved several times. But in 2000, the festival was invited back to Orillia, and it has flourished in the (now) city ever since. It celebrated its fiftieth anniversary in 2010, with the historic reunion of Ian & Sylvia.

Back at the first Mariposa in 1961, there had been one sour note. Orillia had a local boy who was keen to get on the program. But the organizers felt Gordon Lightfoot, and his then-partner Terry Whelan, weren't "of high enough caliber" to appear. They mentioned they sounded too much like The Everly Brothers. They did pass the audition for 1962. Once solo, Lightfoot would perform many times at Mariposa, including the fiftieth anniversary, and a surprise appearance in 2014.

Lightfoot had set his sights on performing as a teenager in the '50s, singing in local vocal groups in Orillia. He'd taken piano and voice lessons, performed in music festivals, taken up the drums, and even written his first song. In 1958, he took the major step to head to Los Angeles to study at the Westlake College of Music. Compared to most, he was already highly trained. Returning home, he got a job as a chorus member and dancer on the CBC-TV show *Country Hoedown* in Toronto in 1960. Lightfoot had fallen under the spell of folk music from The Weavers, and Chicago's Bob Gibson. He began performing, both solo and as a member of The Two Tones with Whelan. In 1962, he recorded the country-flavored "(Remember Me) I'm the One," which became a local Toronto hit. He'd been writing songs all this time, but he was not satisfied with the results. Lightfoot was still waiting for the muse to arrive. His fate would be tied to that of Ian & Sylvia.

The duo was ready for more. Intense perfectionists, they practiced their material, and felt ready to compete at a higher level than Yorkville could offer. By then, Greenwich Village had erupted with talent drawn to its important clubs and record labels, including Joan Baez; Peter, Paul & Mary; The Brothers Four; Judy Collins; The Clancy Brothers & Tommy Makem, and many others. Tyson, for one, was convinced they had the goods to be in that league. "We had a sound that was pretty unique, and we went to New York and we got a contract, it was that simple," he described. It was a little more complicated than that of course, but they were that good. They were well familiar with all the important names in Greenwich Village and were looking for the right bookings, and the right record label. They found all that in manager Albert Grossman. A cofounder of the Newport Folk Festival, he had run the Gate of Horn club in Chicago, and had recently put together the rising stars Peter, Paul & Mary. Grossman was able to land them a contract with Vanguard Records, the home of The Weavers and Joan Baez, and to Ian & Sylvia, recognition of their talent.

The duo thrived in Greenwich Village. As Canadians, they brought a different perspective to the folk revival ("The great Folk Scare," as Tyson has long joked), introducing many songs and some forms not heard in the clubs there before. Their classic good looks helped gain them more attention. Their repertoire and knowledge of traditional material was much envied by their peers, and soon they were considered among the elite of the folk music world. By this time, a circuit had developed on college campuses in the States, and Grossman was able to book the duo on those lucrative shows after their debut album came out on Vanguard. "We were just at the right place at the right time," Tyson downplays once again.

Grossman had also begun managing a scruffy guy well known to Tyson and Fricker. They had become friends with Bob Dylan and his girlfriend Suze Rotolo. They were under no illusions about Dylan. Fricker described him as a sponge, soaking up everyone's influences, but putting it together in his own way. Tyson saw him succeeding despite a guitar that was never in tune and a voice that was worse. Still, Rotolo and Fricker became good friends, and couples would hang out. As Tyson told CBC,

> We were all there on MacDougal Street, and nobody had any money, but we had a lot of fun, a good time. There was a little weed floating around Greenwich Village at the time, that was considered kind of exotic. Suze Rotolo was Bob Dylan's girlfriend at the time. Suze and Sylvia were real good friends. (In 2009) Suze's book came out, and in it, she says that I turned Bob Dylan on to pot. Now I have no memory of that, but it could have been true I guess. If it is, Bob Dylan turned on The Beatles, and I turned on Bob Dylan, that makes me the king.

More importantly, Dylan turned Tyson on to songwriting. That was something off-limits for all the young folk singers of Greenwich Village.

The purists who watched over folk music felt songwriters were people such as Woody Guthrie, or Lead Belly, or those who had come from centuries before. Even Tyson felt Dylan had no business writing his own material at first. But hearing Dylan's new "Blowin' in the Wind," the challenge was on. "I said, yeah, I can do that. So I started exploring it, and shortly after that I wrote 'Four Strong Winds.' It was a twenty-minute thing. That's not an uncommon phenomenon in this business. The first songs, you've got all that unused material to draw on."

Tyson had already lived a live worth writing about, and some of it came out in his first composition. He's described it as a song about itinerant workers who had to follow the jobs across Canada with the seasons, going out to Alberta where the weather is good in the fall. Just as clear is the broken relationship, the good times all gone. Later in the verses, he offers to send the fare for her to join him, but realizes there's nothing for her to do if she does come to be with him. In John Einarson's 2011 book *Four Strong Winds: Ian & Sylvia*, written with the pair, Tyson talks about his five-decade relationship with a woman named Evinia Pulos whom he had met in art school in Vancouver. Pulos is interviewed and reveals that she had long felt she was the inspiration for the lyric. That wasn't a surprise to Fricker, who called her "the third person in our marriage" and felt that she was the great love of Tyson's life.

"Four Strong Winds" was an immediate hit in the folk circles for Ian & Sylvia. They chose it as the title of their second Vanguard album, and it was released as a single. It didn't have an impact on radio in the U.S. but in Canada, it was a national hit. It made Top 10 charts at various radio stations and its status continued to grow over time. Ian & Sylvia's peers recognized its beauty, with The Kingston Trio, Joan Baez, Judy Collins, and even Dylan eventually recording versions. It did become a U.S. hit in 1965 on the country charts, when Bobby Bare took it to number three. Its best-known cover came from long-time fan Neil Young, who recorded it for his 1978 album *Comes a Time*. In Einarson's book, Young tells him "I've always loved it. It was the most beautiful record I'd heard in my life, and I could not get enough of it." CBC Radio listeners chose it as the greatest Canadian song of all time in 2005.

As Tyson had predicted, the rules had changed dramatically in Greenwich Village thanks to Dylan. Quickly, it was no longer enough to do old songs from other eras. You had to also write or cover new and original material. No one could keep pace with Dylan; most of them included his songs in their sets, and he even wrote one for Ian & Sylvia, "Tomorrow Is a Long Time," included on the *Four Strong Winds* album. Tyson only had a few originals, and it was Fricker who came up with the next hit. "You Were On My Mind" was a bit of folk fun, a traveling blues, and classic Ian & Sylvia, with acoustic interplay between six- and twelve-string guitars, and Fricker's Autoharp supplying a solo, plus those oddball harmonies. It was a single from their 1964 *Northern Journey* album, and once again supplied them with hit cover versions as well. In the U.S., the pop group We Five picked up the tempo, taking an almost-giddy version in the Top 5. In England, it did even better for Crispian St. Peters, landing at number two. Sylvia's foray into songwriting didn't surprise Tyson: "I knew she was a talented girl and had that very exciting and electric vibe that was going on. It would follow that a bright talent like her would write. It was the thing to do, we all started doing it." In 1964 the couple also made it official and married.

Even with two writers in the family, the duo was still looking for more originals to compete with the rest of the folk stars. They had always had an edge finding material thanks to their Canadian knowledge and connections, and once again that proved to be a powerful source. On a return trip to Toronto in '64, they were advised to check out Gordon Lightfoot. By then he had at residency at Steele's Tavern in Toronto, not in the more comfortable Yorkville Village, but down on the rowdy Strip. There he was playing country covers, unsure that his own material would go over with the bar crowd. "I used to have to work in around the hockey game," he remembers. He would play during the intermissions, but once the puck dropped, the TV came back on. "Saturday night, I would always let the hockey game go because I knew people wanted to see it." He had started writing his own material, inspired by Dylan and Ian & Sylvia, and eventually worked up the nerve to try it out. The next time Ian & Sylvia heard him at Steele's, they were immediately impressed with his songs. They included "For Lovin' Me," and "Early Morning Rain." The Tysons connected Lightfoot with Grossman's team, and worked hard to convince the songwriter to sign up. They went to bat for him, helped get him a good deal, convinced him to make the jump, and Lightfoot has always acknowledged the debt he owes them.

Grossman had already discovered the benefits of the many, many golden eggs his goose, Bob Dylan, was providing, thanks to songwriting royalties. His songs were everywhere, and Grossman started shopping Lightfoot's work around as well. That meant the Tysons didn't get to hold on to his work exclusively, but they did record "Early Morning Rain" and "For Lovin' Me" on their *Early Morning Rain* album of 1965, which also included several Tyson and Fricker compositions. Peter, Paul & Mary, another of Grossman's clients, recorded the same two songs, and made "For Lovin' Me" a Top 40 hit. Lightfoot was soon all over the charts: "Marty Robbins took that song 'Ribbon of Darkness' and turned it into a hit. Before we knew it, we had a whole list of cover recordings. Of course, the importance of all that sunk in later. Through that I got a contract with United Artists, so I had pretty good distribution with the *Lightfoot!* album (1966). When it sold a hundred thousand copies, I was actually quite shocked. I never believed that would be possible." In just over a year, he'd gone from Steele's Tavern to the top tier of the folk world. "I did feel that I had gotten into that particular club, yes."

In Quebec, Félix Leclerc's influence had inspired a whole movement of new performers, who would collectively become known as the *chansonniers*. His was the example, a writer-composer-performer, the solitary voice who accompanied himself on guitar. It was, at first, apolitical, a poetic and personal view of human values and the relationship with nature. The other major figure helping to establish the chansonniers was Raymond Lévesque. Like Leclerc, he had moved to Paris in the 1950s for a singing and broadcast career, although he wasn't such a recognized star there. He returned to Montreal in 1959, and helped establish a group called Les Bozos, named after Leclerc's song "Bozo." It was really just a loose band of chansonniers, who performed at *boîtes à chansons*. These were small, smoky, intimate rooms, with cheap furniture, maybe a checkered tablecloth, probably serving only coffee, and held only a few dozen people at best. They were pretty much the Quebec version of the coffeehouse, and Chez Bozo was possibly the first of them. Joining Lévesque were Jacques Blanchet, Hervé Brousseau, Clémence Desrochers, Jean-Pierre Ferland, and Claude Léveillée. It was, for all intents and purposes, the birth of the movement.

Ferland started appearing on television and released his first album in 1959. Along with the actress, singer, and monologist Desrochers, he appeared in a successful, yearlong show at the Anjou Theatre. There were distinct cultural differences in the artistic worlds of Quebec and English Canada and the U.S. Whereas folk singers in New York and Toronto and elsewhere would simply play their songs, and perhaps stop to explain some origins, the chansonniers could incorporate theatrical elements, spoken word, and create more of a performance. They would take up residency in a hall, small or big, depending on their draw. It's still felt today, and explains why Celine Dion would establish herself as a long-running performer in Las Vegas, while still capable of chart-topping hits and world tours. Ferland became known as one of the greatest romantic singers from Quebec, and his early career saw him perform in a casual, crooning style. He would win several major prizes, in Quebec and internationally, including the grand prize at the Gala internationale de la chanson in Brussels.

The other great singer of the time was Gilles Vigneault. Originally a poet, he began setting his work to music and getting other singers to perform the songs. Finally he was convinced to perform for the first time at a *boîte à chansons* in Quebec City in 1960 and made his first record in 1962. He was known for his poetry, sincerity, and the joy found in his work. In 1964, he composed the anthem "Mon pays," for a film. Its lyrics described Quebec as not so much a nation but as part of nature, roughly translated as "My country is not a country, it's winter." It's one of the first modern, poetic songs to use nature as a metaphor for life in Canada, although it is specifically a song of pride for Quebec. It became hugely popular and was adopted by many as an anthem for Quebec nationalism, although Vigneault has always denied that was its intent. The song was heard so much it was one of the few of the decade to trickle into the rest of Canadian society. Its familiar melody became much more famous in 1976 when Acadian singer Patsy Gallant borrowed it for her international English language disco hit "From New York to L.A."

The early 1960s had shown that Canadian talent was top-tier, and able to stand alongside the world's best, when given the chance. You still had to go to New York, or Los Angeles, or Paris to make it into the big time, but when the best did go, they were able to shine brightly. At home scenes were developing in certain cities, in coffeehouses and bars that were producing these great musicians. It was time for the rest of the country to get involved, and for the first stirrings of an actual industry to take root.

SHAKIN' ALL OVER

The Whole Country Joins in the Rock 'n' Roll Scene of the Mid-'60s

There is a town in North Ontario. Geographically, that's not quite correct, but it sounds good in the song "Helpless." The town Neil Young is singing of is called Omemee, and it's not far from Toronto, two hours north, and there's a whole lot of central after that before you really get to North Ontario. Omemee was one of the important spots in Young's early life, although not his birthplace, that was Toronto. It's where the family moved when he was four, and they spent the next seven years in the village of around seven hundred. There was fishing right down the road, a country store, ice cream, and happy times. There was a bout of polio, too, something that would haunt him his whole life. He'd have a lot of tough times, but Omemee was always there as an idyllic spot before innocence was lost.

The family moved to Pickering, Ontario, in 1956, and then back to Toronto in 1957, as Young's writer and journalist father Scott switched jobs. Radio fired Young's imagination, with all the rock 'n' roll sounds pouring out of his transistor radio. He got his first ukulele around then, before graduating to guitar. Toronto would later be an important mid-

'60s stop in his career, with its coffeehouses and clubs, but first he had one more move to make, a less happy one. His father and mother, Rassy, separated, and Neil joined his mother as she went back to her former home of Winnipeg, Manitoba, in August of 1960. Although he'd spend less than six years living in the city, they were pivotal, and Young would always consider himself a Winnipegger first. Although that town in North Ontario did get a major billing in a hugely popular song (from Crosby, Stills, Nash & Young's 1970 *Déjà Vu* album), Winnipeg has directly or indirectly been mentioned several times over the course of Young's career and was his vantage point for the reflective *Prairie Wind* album of 2005.

The point of all that is to show that Neil Young should, for our purposes, be considered a Winnipegger. At this time, Canada's rock 'n' roll history had been dominated by the scene in Toronto, and the one in Montreal. Of course, there were rock 'n' roll dreams beginning all over the country, as more and more towns and cities saw teen clubs and coffeehouses opening, and local singers were making hits for the hometown radio stations. The problem still remained though, with no national charts or methods of exposure for a regional record to start getting heard anywhere else. Only Toronto and Montreal had enough population, media, and clout to create major stars in the early '60s. However, the next wave was coming, and they were coming from far-flung places.

Winnipeg of the early 1960s was a pretty isolated spot, culturally. Although it was the main city of Canada's Prairies, and with its suburbs, approaching a half million in population, it was far off the beaten track for music tours. Bordering on North Dakota and Minnesota, 1,300 miles from Toronto and 1,400 miles from Vancouver, Manitoba saw few rock 'n' roll shows make their way to the province. Far from being rock 'n' roll starved, though, the teenagers of Winnipeg were crazed by it, thanks to radio and television, and the demand for live music was huge. The city had a unique situation, with a series of venues for bands and dances already in place, thanks to dozens of community clubs and school halls, in the downtown and into the suburbs. Community groups had begun building local centers back in the 1940s. Good citizens and parents would start a campaign to build a rink, along with a clubhouse, some even starting small in old railroad boxcars. As more money was raised, better buildings and more programs were added. Today, the Earl Grey Community Centre boasts Zumba and Bellyfit classes, youth meal programs and drop-in time for young mothers, as well as subsidized sports programs for low-income families. Back in the 1960s, there would be a teen dance at the Earl Grey featuring future Bachman-Turner Overdrive singer and bassist Fred Turner and his band, Pink Plumm.

These were sock hops, after-school shows or Saturday night socials, for kids who had no hope of getting into bars and clubs. Budding musicians with the nerve to play could easily get a show in their neighborhood community club, and sometimes guts and the ability to make a racket in a jacket was all that mattered. There was a pecking order of bands, and some musicians were more serious than others. The idea of a career in rock 'n' roll had even been floated. Randy Bachman had been talking about it since he was a kid, and had spent high school learning guitar directly from jazz prodigy Lenny Breau. His playing with area groups brought him to the attention of one Allan Kowbel, unfortunately not a drummer but the lead singer of Allan and The Silvertones. Kowbel drafted Bachman and his pal drummer Garry Peterson into the band, which also featured bass player Jim Kale and keyboard player Bob Ashley. In 1962, Kowbel changed his name to Chad Allan, the group became Chad Allan and The Reflections, and Winnipeg's best band was born.

The local groups featured all the hits of the day, but there was a Winnipeg twist in the mix as well, led by The Reflections. Instrumental bands were very popular in the city, and much of the set list could feature covers of numbers by The Ventures and Duane Eddy. Cliff Richard's backing group The Shadows was a particular favorite of Allan's, and The Reflections were even named in homage to the sounds of The Shadows. Thanks to Canada's membership in the British Commonwealth, there was always a stronger English influence on local radio stations. There were also young people with relatives back in the home country, and a few Anglophiles would get rare copies of up-and-coming English rock 'n' roll groups, pre-British Invasion. So the Winnipeg sound had room for Buddy Holly, Hank Marvin of The Shadows, and guitar instrumental favorites such as "Walk, Don't Run" and "Telstar."

As the top teen band in the city, Chad Allan and The Reflections were getting lots of bookings, from sporting events to movie theaters to local businesses trying to attract kids to their shops. They were getting gigs outside Winnipeg as well, such as high school dances west across the Prairies into Saskatchewan, or east into Northern Ontario. They kept returning to an important source for sounds others didn't have. A friend of Allan's regularly received reel-to-reel tapes from England, with all the latest pop hits. Allan and the group would hear the tapes, and get a chance to be the only area group that knew the songs. Months before The Beatles appeared on *The Ed Sullivan Show* in 1964, Chad Allan and The Reflections were leading their own British Invasion in Winnipeg, playing "Please Please Me" and more.

There was also enough happening in Winnipeg to attract record companies to the area. Allan got signed to the Canadian American label, for the 1962 cover of U.K. song "Tribute to Buddy Holly," and then got a deal with Canada's Quality Records. There was some regional action, but nothing approaching national attention, and Allan and The Reflections had to continue working the Winnipeg scene as hard as they could. By 1965, the group even had to change its name to The Expressions, after the Detroit group The Reflections had scored a decent hit with the song "(Just Like) Romeo and Juliet." Being in Winnipeg was still hurting the group, until Allan, Bachman, and company once again used the British connection to their advantage. One of the songs they had heard on the reel-to-reel tapes was "Shakin' All Over," by Johnny Kidd & The Pirates. It had been a big, number one hit in the U.K. in 1960, but was unknown in North America. The Expressions decided to try to record a cover, as the originals they'd done by Allan and Bachman had failed. Recorded in primitive conditions in a TV station, it was just the kind of raw, scorching guitar rock that Winnipeg loved and the rest of the continent was discovering as well: pure garage rock. The group did little to change it at the start, except adding piano, make it a little tougher, and a little more distorted thanks to the recording limitations. But then Allan started freaking out on some screams, and Bachman's guitar got increasingly stinging as the intensity built. This was miles away from the Merseybeat copycat song Bachman had written for the group as their last single, "Stop Teasin' Me," which sounded like Gerry and The Pacemakers. Now, they were nastier than The Rolling Stones.

This left Quality Records with a dilemma. Allan and The Reflections/ Expressions had little respect with disc jockeys outside of Winnipeg, and even "Stop Teasin' Me" had only managed to get to number thirty-five on the local hit parade. What came next is a legendary bit of promotional magic, a story told so many times the real version is now a bit murky. Here are some of the facts and some of the legend: The Quality people knew how hot the British Invasion still was, and they knew that the song was originally British. In order to hide the fact that this was just another Canadian band, and in fact the same old Chad Allan bunch they'd already been flogging, Quality sent promotional copies of the "Shakin' All Over" 45 out to Canadian radio without the band's name. The label copy just read, "Guess Who?" They were trying to trick radio into thinking it was one of the British groups, maybe even The Beatles themselves.

The ruse worked, and the record got played, and played. DJs loved it, so did listeners, in Winnipeg, Toronto, Montreal, Vancouver, and Halifax. It went to number one on the new *RPM* magazine national chart on March 22, 1965, replacing The Beatles' "Eight Days a Week," and stayed on top for three weeks. It was only the second time a Canadian song had topped the national chart, after *Bonanza* actor Lorne Greene's novelty country hit "Ringo" of the year before. It didn't stop there, as the track crossed the border, eventually making it to number twenty-two on *Billboard*, and even made the Top 30 in Australia. Every copy now had "Guess Who?" as the credit, and the group had no choice but to rechristen themselves.

That should have been a great new start for the group, but The Silvertones/Reflections/Expressions/Guess Who somehow always managed to find a unique way to snatch defeat from the jaws of victory, at least in the early days. Excited by the prospects of fame in the U.S., they answered the summons to New York, home of their American record label, Sceptor. Bachman often tells the story of driving straight to the Ed Sullivan Theater, thinking they were booked to perform, being convinced by a local agent he'd gotten them the TV show, only to be turned away at the stage door. Instead of leaving with their tails between their legs, they stuck around for months, doing package tours of the U.S., recording follow-up singles for Sceptor, and backing famous groups such as The Shirelles and The Crystals. But the records flopped, the tours paid nothing, and soon the group was back in Winnipeg. Bob Ashley had had enough and quit, and Chad Allan himself was becoming unreliable. He was missing shows, wanted to finish his education, and years of untrained singing and shouting had harmed his voice. The Guess Who, still stars in Winnipeg but fading quickly elsewhere, were on the verge of collapse.

At least the group's success had inspired many others. The city had absolutely exploded with music. After the British Invasion, dozens more bands had been formed almost overnight. They all looked up to The Guess Who as the kingpins, as they had to The Expressions and The Reflections before that. By 1964 the number two band in the city was The Deverons, sixteen- and seventeen-year-olds already playing the better gigs such as the Town n' Country club, or the Hudson's Bay Company's Saturday morning Touchdown Club for the Winnipeg Blue Bombers football team. The group featured a dynamic young lead singer and piano player named Burton Cummings, who had it all: looks, talent, a big voice, and a wild stage presence. He'd become known for his abuse of pianos at the community clubs, standing on top to roar out a number, scratching their finish. They got their own record deal on a Quality subsidiary, and on April 27, 1965, earned a slot on a major local show. They joined Chad Allan and The Expressions as the opening acts for Gerry and The Pacemakers, a show that drew four thousand fans to the Winnipeg Arena. There was a bit of a riot that night, as fans charged the security guards, leading to a lot of hair-pulling and a threat to call off the headliner's set. But before that, a more important event took place, at least in CanRock history. Cummings did his usual piano abuse, and Bachman took notice of the kid who was becoming the talk of the city's rock.

By December, something had to change in The Guess Who. With Ashley gone, and Allan becoming a liability, new blood was needed. Randy Bachman, Garry Peterson, and Jim Kale decided to shake things up, and invite Cummings into the band. This gave them a keyboard player, and co-lead vocalist, one who could handle all the harder rock 'n' roll they now wanted to play. It also spelled the end for Chad Allan. No longer the name on the marquee, and now losing out much of his frontman status, Allan lasted only a few months longer, before heading back to school. With a hotshot lead singer a few years their junior, the band felt ready for another kick at the can. And really, still basking in the glory of "Shakin' All Over" back home, they were confident they could head back up the charts. There would be a brief delay.

Neil Young's move to Winnipeg was less than happy. His parents' separation was bad, and he was fourteen years old, a tough age in the best of circumstances. He was arriving in Winnipeg without friends, into a tough city with old values and a somewhat hostile environment in more than one way. The experience was turned into another of his biographical songs, "Don't Be Denied." It tells of a schoolyard beating, but also of meeting a friend who played guitar, sitting on the steps at school and dreaming of being a star.

Neil Young's first band, The Jades, made their debut in 1961 at the Earl Grey Community Centre. They were mostly an instrumental band, and Young was the rhythm guitar player, with the usual Fireballs and Ventures songs in the set. It was the group's only gig. But Young had the rock 'n' roll bug bad, and hung around the clubs watching all the groups, and waiting for another chance. A succession of short-lived groups followed, ones that had a lot of rehearsals but hardly any gigs. But Young kept looking, kept finding better players to work with, and by 1963, he had finally put a sturdy group together, called The Squires.

Although not in the same league as The Reflections, The Squires did get their fair share of gigs, and a small following. Young was watching Randy Bachman closely, his main guitar inspiration in the city. He loved his Gretsch guitar, his gear and effects, and his sound, especially the British influence. Thanks to The Expressions, The Squires were now playing Shadows numbers in their set. Young's own instrumentals were part of the show too. When the group's popularity had grown strong enough to attract local company V Records, two of Young's instrumentals, "The Sultan" and "Aurora," made up the group's debut single. His next move was to add the occasional vocal numbers to the set. At first, that didn't go over well with the high school fans, or his friends for that matter. It would not be the last time Young would take heat for his unique vocal skills, and it started a pattern where he would simply ignore criticism and do what he wanted. He still does that, playing whatever he wants on every album and every tour, with whatever band the muse tells him will work at that moment. And he still sings exactly the same way.

Eventually, the kids got used to his singing, and Young's future was mapped out. He quit Grade Twelve in the fall of 1964, and he and the rest of The Squires became full-time musicians. Although they had a bit of a reputation, and some regular gigs, money was very tight, and the band was struggling compared to Chad Allan and The Reflections and several others. Young's solution was to hit the road. He'd recently picked up a secondhand hearse he named Mort to haul the band's gear, and off they went to Fort William, Ontario, over four hundred miles away. Now part of Thunder Bay, it was the first city of any significant size east of Winnipeg, with about a hundred thousand people in the area. Young figured The Squires would go over great there, because of the novelty of being from out of town. Despite arriving with no gig, he was able to land the band five nights at one venue, which turned into a return engagement a month later. Back in Winnipeg, the community club circuit was far less appealing, and Young's days there were numbered. By April of 1965, he'd made the decision to take the band back to Fort William, leaving Winnipeg for good.

The gigs and money weren't much better in Ontario, but what happened in Fort William was far more crucial. Young had set up a deal at the 4-D coffeehouse, part of a chain of 4-Ds in the area, including one in Winnipeg. The Squires were the regular opening act for the various folk groups that came through, and being a little nearer to the U.S., there were some interesting ones. Almost as soon as they started at the 4-D, The Squires opened for The Company, out of New York. That group featured a young Stephen Stills, who was itching to get out of folk and into the more electric sounds of folk rock. He saw the future of his rock 'n' roll that night onstage, in Neil Young. The Squires were a band in transition, as Young was introducing new elements into the set. Rhythm and blues was a stronger part of it, and wilder rock 'n' roll such as a cover of The Premiers' "Farmer John." Then there were Young's oddball treatments of folk standards, including "Tom Dooley" and "Oh Susannah," where The Squires would take the originals and add a rock 'n' roll beat. Young, never one to rush a concept, finally recorded an album of those folk song treatments in 2012 with Crazy Horse, called *Americana*. But in 1965 in Fort William, Stills was riveted each night, and Young liked what he heard as well. They struck up a friendship, and even planned to work together down the road. Stills gave Young his contacts in New York, and Young had a new goal, heading to the U.S. to work with his new friend.

In June of 1965, the next important move of Young's career came, completely by accident. A musician friend asked him to drive him from Fort William to Sudbury, Ontario, for a gig, around one Great Lake and halfway around another. Young and a group of other friends piled into Mort the Hearse, but nearing their goal, the transmission dropped out of the hearse. Mort was towed to Blind River, and the tragic trip gave Young one of his most-loved songs, "Long May You Run" (although he dates the events as 1962 instead of '65). Young had to figure out a way to get some money to fix it. By this point, he was a lot closer to his father than he was to Fort William, and given the fact he was living in the YMCA and barely scraping by, it seemed a better choice to make his way to Scott Young. Neil was about to hit Toronto.

Across Canada, scenes similar to Winnipeg played out in the early to mid-'60s. Instead of community clubs, they might be in high school gyms or church basements or radio station–sponsored dances. The best players in each area would gradually move from one teen band to a better one, finally becoming the top act. Then there were the folk performers, still filling coffeehouses, with Dylan dreams in their heads. Some of them would try to carve out a career at home, but at some point, most of the best would head to a bigger scene, usually Toronto or Montreal, maybe Vancouver.

Neil Young wasn't the first rock star with a connection to Port Arthur. Bobby Curtola was born there and made his first record there in 1960 at seventeen years old for the Tartan label. His youth and good looks quickly got him lots of exposure, and Curtola became Canada's first homegrown national rock 'n' roll star, hitting the road west and east, pioneering a touring circuit. He was a teen idol with a string of hits, and lots of TV appearances as well. Curtola was smoother than other rock 'n' rollers, but had a bright, solid pop sound thanks to top studio production in Nashville. After a couple of years of national hits, Curtola released his biggest to date, "Fortune Teller." A smash in Canada, influential Vancouver DJ Red Robinson was convinced it could be bigger, and sent the 45 to friendly stations in Seattle and Hawaii. While it wasn't a radio hit, stalling at forty-one, it sold a very impressive 2.5 million copies and put him on the road with Dick Clark in the U.S., and across in England. Curtola continued to rack up pop hits right up until 1970 in Canada, hosted two national TV shows, and worked Vegas and club shows for years.

Montreal's The Beau-Marks also made their mark in 1960 with "Clap Your Hands." The piano-driven number was an old-school rocker, not sophisticated but raw and danceable. The infectious tune made it to number one in Montreal and Toronto, and has the distinction of being the first major Canadian rock 'n' roll hit recorded inside the country. It was also a smash in Australia and New Zealand, and managed to get to forty-five in the U.S. There's one other interesting first as well; the group was bilingual, with English and French members, and also recorded the song *en français* as "Frappe tes mains." While chansonniers were climbing to fame in Quebec, rock 'n' roll would become just as strong, if perhaps not as culturally significant. As it was in France, rock 'n' roll was called *yé-yé* in the province, after the refrain to "She Loves

You," with hundreds of groups in business after The Beatles shook up the pop world. Major acts included Les Mégatones, Les Classels, and Les Baronets, which included one René Angélil, who would go on to manage and marry Celine Dion.

A child star, Montreal's Ginette Reno had her first hit at the age of fifteen in 1961, "Non Papa." It was the beginning of an illustrious career that has seen her enjoy decade after decade of hits, including the 2011 Felix Award for Francophone album of the year. She's had an impressive TV and movie career, and great success in English Canada as well, with the 1970 hit "Beautiful Second Hand Man" earning her a Juno Award. Long before Dion's breakthrough via U.S. talk shows, Reno had appeared on the *Tonight Show* and several others in the 1970s, the enchanting voice of French Canada both inside and out of Quebec.

Sometimes the scene was just too small and far away to hold on to local talent. Halifax, Nova Scotia's Denny Doherty wanted to sing, so in 1960 he went to Montreal and helped form the folk group The Colonials. They worked in Montreal and Toronto, and like Ian & Sylvia, headed down to New York to join in the folk boom. Impressively, the group got signed to Columbia Records, and changed their name to The Halifax Three.

Out of Ottawa came The Esquires, not to be confused with Neil Young's Winnipeg Squires. That certainly wouldn't have happened in 1963, as The Esquires became the first band signed to Capitol Records in Canada, which had become a dynamic label in the country. Thanks to forward-thinking A&R head Paul White, the company had already released the first Beatles 45s and albums in North America, a year ahead of the U.S. branch, which turned down the chance. White actively pushed all the British Invasion bands in advance, even creating Canada-only compilations and album covers for many artists, including The Beatles. The first record to be released in North America under The Beatles' name was "Love Me Do" on 45, in February of 1963. It sold a grand total of seventy-eight copies, but White was not deterred. By September of 1963, things were heating up for The Beatles as word was coming over from England about them, and "She Loves You" was gaining Canadian airplay and sales. In December White made up his own Beatles single, "Roll Over Beethoven" backed with "Please Mister Postman." It proved so successful at the height of Beatlemania the next year, that copies were imported and sold in the U.S. by the thousands, putting it on the charts there as well at number sixty-eight. In November of 1963, White and Capitol released the first Beatles album in North America, called *Beatlemania! with the Beatles*, containing a unique track listing. "She Loves You" was number one in Vancouver in December of 1963, and topped the charts at Toronto's top radio station CHUM a full two weeks before the band appeared on *The Ed Sullivan Show*, joined by "Roll Over Beethoven" and "I Want to Hold Your Hand" in the Top 10. White had managed to break The Beatles in Canada without the help of the U.S. media frenzy.

Meanwhile, The Esquires reaped the benefits. Heavily influenced by Cliff Richard and The Shadows, they won the inaugural RPM Award in 1964 for Top Vocal Instrumental Group, the precursor to the Juno Awards, and opened for all the major Capitol bands when they came to Canada, including The Beatles, Dave Clark 5, and Gerry and The Pacemakers. The group's lineup went through many changes, and eventually ground to a halt in 1967, with the final membership including a young Bruce Cockburn.

Vancouver's rock 'n' roll scene developed in a fiercely independent way, thanks to the great distance from Toronto, and closer connection to the Pacific Northwest and even Los Angeles. Local bands were plentiful, with rich histories, such as The Prowlers, Vancouver's first rock 'n' roll band, who opened for Bill Haley & The Comets in 1956, at the first major rock 'n' roll concert ever held in the city. The band was led by Les Vogt, who went solo later, and had a huge local hit with a song called

"The Blamers" in 1960, which knocked Elvis's "It's Now Or Never" off the top of the charts. A local band called The Chessmen enjoyed their first chart success in 1964, with the local Top 20 hit "Meadowlands." Their ranks included Terry Jacks, who would later have international hits both with The Poppy Family and solo.

It was Terry Black who nabbed the first major national hit for a Vancouver artist, with "Unless You Care." A fifteen-year-old sensation in his hometown, Black was paired up with hipster L.A. writer/producers P. F. Sloan and Steve Barri, and recorded the song with members of the famed studio players The Wrecking Crew, including Leon Russell and Glen Campbell. The handsome kid got on *American Bandstand,* and the song was a decent hit on the U.S. West Coast, and number two across Canada. The only bigger Canadian hits that year were Lorne Greene's "Ringo," and actress-singer Gale Garnett's "We'll Sing in the Sunshine," which won her a Grammy Award for Best Folk Recording. She'd only lived in Canada a short time, having been born in New Zealand, lived in England, emigrated to Canada, moved to New York, and then to Los Angeles where the song was recorded. After a modest singing career, she eventually did settle back in Toronto, a respected stage and film actress.

Joni Mitchell was born Roberta Joan Anderson in Fort McLeod, Alberta, and later moved with her family to Saskatchewan, eventually settling in Saskatoon. She was an artist, a dancer, a singer, and a free spirit. She first started playing a ukulele, and would join others singing folk songs at parties around the campfires at one of the nearby lakes. At graduation in 1963, she moved to Calgary to go to art college, and it seemed painting was her priority. But singing also came naturally; she had a golden voice, and found that she could make extra money in the folk clubs. In 1964, now with a guitar, she traveled to Toronto, with the stated goal of going to Mariposa and making it as a folk singer. But there was more than music behind the trip. Mitchell was pregnant, and it was still a time when a single young woman had few options, especially if her parents weren't supportive. Mitchell was alone in the city. There was, however, an even bigger folk scene there now, and Yorkville Village was calling musicians from all over Canada.

UGLY DUCKLINGS

Yorkville Village Booms, and Canada's Future
Rock Stars Congregate

I t's an old cliché about Canada, that everybody knows everybody. We smile politely when Americans find out we're Canadian, and then ask us if we know Bill in Regina even though we're from Kingston, Ontario, about three thousand kilometers away. Of course, inevitably, once it turns into a conversation, it turns out we do know some relation of Bill's, or went to school with his boss, and we all make plans to meet up next summer. In Canada, it's usually only three degrees of separation.

So, it should come as no surprise to find out that if you asked Joni Mitchell from Saskatchewan if she knew Neil Young from Winnipeg in 1965, before either of them came to Toronto, the answer would be yes. Young started hanging around the 4-D coffeehouse in Winnipeg in 1964, and The Squires were the first rock 'n' roll band to break the folk/poetry/beatnik barrier of the place. It was part of the same 4-D chain he'd later play in Fort William, and it was where he first picked up on acoustic and folk music, soon to become an important part of his career. While his guitar playing got him recognized in the rock 'n' roll scene, it was his reflective, folk-based songwriting that set him further apart. At some point Mitchell, still Joni Anderson, came through the 4-D circuit during the months when Young was soaking up every act coming through the doors. It was a friendship that would play out over the next decade, two of the world's most idiosyncratic songwriters darting in and out of each other's lives, sharing a goal of rising to the top of their art.

The Toronto scene Anderson encountered was blossoming. In the fall of 1964, she was able to get gigs at clubs such as The Bohemian Embassy on the Yonge Strip, and The New Gate of Cleve in Yorkville Village. She stood out, playing the baritone ukulele or the slightly larger tipple, with eight strings. She quickly captivated the Toronto scene, and earned enough accolades to grab a major spot at 1965's Mariposa Festival, given equal billing to such recording acts as Ian & Sylvia, Gordon Lightfoot, Son House, and Phil Ochs. She was still playing classic folk music, and covers of others, including songs Judy Collins played on her records, but had also just begun to write her own. By now her baby had been born, a girl, but she was in no position to raise her on her own. She was placed in foster care, and shortly after, Anderson met and married Detroit folk singer Chuck Mitchell. He was more established, with good connections in the folk club scene, and there was some hope that with his support, the now–Joni Mitchell could get her baby back. But that didn't happen, and instead, that summer, the couple headed to Detroit. Joni Mitchell's stay in Toronto had been barely a year, but it was full of life-changing events, including the loss of her child and her hasty marriage. This period would inform her lyrics for the next several years, culminating in songs on 1971's *Blue*.

Neil Young arrived in Toronto about the same time Mitchell was leaving, in June of 1965. Fort William was now over. Young had his gear and belongings shipped to his father's house, and began checking out the music possibilities. The other Squires were summoned, and Scott Young loaned Neil money for a rehearsal space and living expenses.

Young was hoping to play the new style the band had been developing, combining folk and rock. The Byrds' *Mr. Tambourine Man* had just been released that month, the birth of folk-rock, but Young was a little ahead of the curve for Toronto. Folk was in Yorkville; rock was on the Yonge Strip. The Squires were renamed, becoming 4 To Go, rehearsed daily, and a manager tried everything to drum up some interest. Nothing worked, and the band finally gave up months later without ever playing a gig. Young was forced to take a job at a Coles Bookstore, which was the only nonmusic job he ever held in his life. All five weeks of it. He was fired for being constantly late or not showing up at all.

Needing work, Young was convinced by former Squire Ken Koblun, who had stayed with him from Winnipeg to Fort William to Toronto, to join him at a ski resort gig in Vermont. It was dire, and Young and Koblun moved on, deciding to visit New York City. For Young, it was a chance to meet up with Stephen Stills again. But when he went to the address Stills have given him, he found another musician instead. Stills had left for California months before, but his roommate Richie Furay had stayed in the apartment. He saw the same promise in Young that Stills had, and during the encounter, Young taught him his new song, "Nowadays Clancy Can't Even Sing." The significance of yet another classic Canadian coincidence would come to light in the months ahead.

Back in Toronto, Young now saw the solo folk scene as his best option. He sold his electric Gretsch guitar, and bought a twelve-string acoustic. He fared a bit better, getting a few Yorkville gigs, performing some of his own like the new "Sugar Mountain," and others from Bob Dylan and Phil Ochs. Once again, it was a period Young would return to much later in his career. His 2014 covers album *A Letter Home* featured acoustic numbers by Dylan, Ochs, Gordon Lightfoot, Tim Hardin, and a letter addressed to his late mother, Rassy. But Young was not a popular performer, at least among patrons and club owners. He was better liked by his peers. He ran into Joni Mitchell again, and even visited her in Detroit, playing her his coming of age song "Sugar Mountain." She responded by writing "The Circle Game," to give hope to Young and herself. Finally, Young seemed to get the break he'd been in need of in Toronto, through another musician on the scene. In January of 1966, bass player Bruce Palmer ran into him walking in Yorkville, and found they had lots in common. Most importantly, Young was looking for people to play with, and Palmer had a group that needed a new guitar player. They were The Mynah Birds, managed by the owner of Yorkville's Mynah Bird club. Solo Young was back to being in a band, a flip-flop pattern he has continued through his career. But Young wouldn't be the frontman this time; that job belonged to Ricky Matthews, later to be famous as raunchy funkster Rick James. Doing R&B, Young added some folk flavors, and the group was among the first wave of rock 'n' roll bands changing the Yorkville scene.

This time, Young was seemingly onto something. The band had the financial backing of John Eaton, of the wealthy family behind the national Eaton's department store chain. They had expensive gear, lots of gigs, and a dynamic lead singer. Young and James even started collaborating on songs. Interest was so high that Motown Records, the premiere black record label in North America, signed the mostly white band, and brought them to Detroit to record. A single was chosen, a James-Young cowrite called "It's My Time," and album sessions were underway when bad luck struck again. Somebody had informed Motown that their new act's singer was actually named James Johnson, and he was AWOL from the U.S. services. James was arrested, The Mynah Birds project was shelved by Motown, and Neil Young was once again adrift, back in Toronto. "It's My Time" was finally released by Motown in 2006.

Neil Young's Toronto experience had been a failure, and he was about to give up on the city. Others were having a lot more success. Mid-'60s Toronto still had no real recording industry, but it did have lots of performers, and its own hit makers as well. Richie Knight and Mid-Knights were one of the bands playing the clubs on the Yonge Strip in 1962–63, and were spotted by local record label ARC. "Charlena" was unleashed on the city in mid-1963, and eventually became a number one hit for the group, the first-ever Toronto band to top the pop charts. The door was now open. A Bell Telephone employee by day, Shirley Matthews was one of the featured singers at the Club Bluenote, the top R&B and soul bar in the city. Her debut, "Big Town Boy," was a happy dance number with a girl-group sound, and was a major Toronto hit. Released in December of 1963, the song reached number four on the CHUM chart, and grabbed Matthews the first-ever RPM Award for Female Vocalist of the Year. David Clayton-Thomas and The Shays scored several hits including "Walk That Walk" and "Take Me Back." His massive voice was perfect for Toronto-style rhythm and blues. "I still had my regular bar job with Ronnie Hawkins," explains Clayton-Thomas,

and The Shays and I played more of the teen hops, the plaza dances, and high school dances, we played mostly one-nighters. If The Shays didn't have a gig some months, Ronnie would say, come on, you're in my band this month, so it was an off-and-on thing, over a period of a couple of years. One of the characteristics of those gigs is that you played matinees on Saturdays. And at the afternoon matinees, there would be no liquor served. So all the young musicians could get in, and everybody used to come down on Saturday afternoon and jam with The Hawks. And they were glad to have you because they were glad to get the afternoon off and take a break. So on Saturday afternoons, we all would turn the club over to everybody sitting in. We were all basically exhausted, because we did five shows a night, forty on, twenty off, all night long. By Saturday, we just wanted a break, so the fact that all the young musicians could get in, it turned into a free-for-all, a jam session every week.

On Yonge Street, you played Top 40, we would play until one o'clock in the morning when the bars closed, we'd all go out for breakfast, and all the bands would meet up at Fran's, the restaurant up on Dundas, because we had to be back at the club to rehearse. And we would rehearse from three a.m. until the sun came up, because we had to constantly keep the material new, we had to play what was on the charts. One of the things that is missed in the history is that those were tough bars. They were full of steel workers from Hamilton and lumberjacks from Sudbury, and everybody's in town with a week's paycheck and just looking to party, and if they didn't get laid, they would get in a fight. Ronnie was such a genial, lovable kind of guy, but he was a tough son of a bitch. Nobody messed with him. And you pretty much had to be that way in those days.

The RPM Awards came thanks to a new magazine for the music industry. Walt Grealis, a former Toronto police officer and record company employee, had started *RPM* in 1964. He was passionate about Canadian music, and the possibilities he saw around him. He recognized a huge need in the country, an industry trade paper that could share information from coast to coast. The U.S. had long had *Billboard* and *Cashbox*; now there was finally a national chart, and radio stations in one city could see what was becoming a hit elsewhere. That quickly led to the awards as well, chosen from a poll of the magazine's readers. The RPM Awards would eventually become the Juno Awards, still Canada's top annual awards for the recording industry.

Events were happening at a rapid pace on Yonge and in Yorkville. Denny Doherty's Halifax Three came back from the U.S. to play a gig, but lost their guitar player in the process. A replacement was needed, and Doherty was led to a Yorkville character named Zal Yanovsky. A prototypical hippie, Yanovsky was disheveled, zany, somewhat dirty, but a stunning guitar player. The Halifax Three took him back to New York, a future Papa and a future Lovin' Spoonful member. Some other future famous folks were also on the move. Late 1963 saw The Hawks bristling under the dictatorial leadership of Ronnie Hawkins. They were tired of all the rules, all the rehearsing, and the low pay. Hawkins was by then commanding a big price at the Le Coq D'Or, but it was not trickling down to the band. Meanwhile they recognized how good they had become. All the other musicians came to check them out. Early weeknights Hawkins often didn't even appear with them, letting Richard Manual, Rick Danko, and Levon Helm handle the vocals. Finally, after one too many fines, the group had it out with Hawkins, and threatened to leave en masse. Hawkins wouldn't give in. The next day, agent Harold Kudlets went to his office in Hamilton, and found the entire group there waiting, wondering if he would represent them on their own.

Levon and The Hawks had been chaffing to play their own music anyway. Night after night of "Bo Diddley" and "Who Do You Love" had sharpened their skills, but they wanted to branch out with more rhythm and blues, and use the fantastic chops they had developed. They had all become experts on their instruments, and quickly picked up plenty of gigs on Yonge Street, just down from Hawkins's shows. They hit the road as well, back in London and Hamilton, up to Montreal, and down to New York City, including the famed Peppermint Lounge. Two singles in 1965, one as The Canadian Squires (no relation to the Neil Young band, or Ottawa's Esquires), and the other as Levon and The Hawks, were released but neither did anything of note, but the group's fame as a live act would continue to grow, and some very influential people were checking them out.

Originally formed in Toronto in 1956, The Consuls had played teen dances at the start of the rock 'n' roll era. One original member was guitarist and singer Gene MacLellan, who would later move to Prince Edward Island, and meet up with singer Anne Murray on the TV show *Singalong Jubilee*, giving her the hit song "Snowbird." But back then the future folk singer was playing doo-wop such as "In the Still of the Night" to "Roll Out the Barrel" and "She'll Be Comin' 'Round the Mountain" if the crowd needed a sing-along. The band ranks expanded in 1958 with the addition of fifteen-year-old Robbie Robertson on guitar. The original Consuls splintered soon after, but regrouped without Robertson and MacLellan, and were rechristened Little Caesar & The Consuls. One of the most popular bands for dances, the group had lots of teenage fans, who in turn demanded their records be heard on Toronto radio. The first big success was a cover of the tune "Hang On Sloopy," which made the Toronto Top 10 in July of 1965. That was three months before The McCoys had a number one hit with the same song, which had been a soul hit the year before called "My Girl Sloopy" by The Vibrations. Then Little Caesar broke through again, this time with a cover of Smokey Robinson's "You Really Got a Hold on Me." While local Toronto powerhouse CHUM passed on it, with it just reaching number nineteen, *RPM* magazine saw it hit number one nationwide, just the third Canadian number one on its year-old chart.

By 1965, bands playing the Yonge Strip and Yorkville clubs had a lot better chance at these radio successes. Ronnie Hawkins, still reigning on the Strip, took his cover of "Bluebirds Over the Mountain" into the Top 10 in March. Gordon Lightfoot had a couple of hits that year: "I'm Not Sayin'," and interestingly, a cover of Bob Dylan's "Just Like Tom Thumb's Blues." Even a visiting Terry Black, in from Vancouver, found his new disc jockey friends happy to shake his hand for photos, and push his cover of "Only 16" up to number two that summer. The relationship between radio and the artists was mutually beneficial, and more bands continued to find local and sometimes national success out of Yorkville and Yonge.

The British Invasion was still dominating Canadian music, and Jack London and The Sparrows had the accent down perfectly. They got signed to Capitol Canada and put out a string of Merseybeat-inspired singles in 1964 and 1965. London was really Dave Marden, and the group also featured the brothers Jerry and Dennis McCrohan, who would change their name to Edmonton, because they felt it sounded more British. Their debut, "If You Don't Want My Love," was a national hit, but London's insistence on the group pretending to be British was wearing thin on the other members. Bruce Palmer had joined on bass, but quickly soured on the British affectations, so The Sparrows swapped bass players with The Mynah Birds, picking up Nick St. Nicholas for Palmer and a player to be named later, who turned out to be Neil Young. Or something like that. It got more confusing when the entire band quit London, sick of the charade, and the fact that he'd cut himself a better royalty share with Capitol. They took the band name with them, and played a tougher brand of British-flavored rock in the Yorkville clubs, now leaning toward The Rolling Stones' sound.

The Sparrows needed a new lead singer, and found one named John Kay, except that was made up too. He was actually the German-born Joachim Krauledat, who had already lived through tremendous upheaval to get to Canada. His father was a German soldier, killed by Soviet Union troops before he was born. His mother had to flee the advancing Russians a year later, but still ended up in Communist-controlled East Germany. Then, they made a daring escape to the West four years later. When Kay was thirteen, they emigrated to Canada. In Toronto, he stayed glued to the radio, learning English from the DJs and from the lyrics to his beloved music. The family moved to the U.S., and eventually settled in Santa Monica, California, in 1963, with Kay by then proficient enough to start a career as a folk singer. After traveling the continent, he wound up in Toronto again and quickly became a popular performer in Yorkville. That's where the rest of The Sparrows found him, playing blues and folk at the Half Beat on Avenue Road. With their new singer, they became the toast of Yorkville for 1965, regulars at clubs such as Chez Monique, and even landed a record deal for a couple of singles. They picked up bookings in New York, and changed their name to the hipper-sounding The Sparrow. They would not be long for Yorkville, and it was a pattern that would be repeated; there wasn't a big enough music industry to keep the best bands around, as the major players would swoop in and offer deals, if they would move to the U.S.

Yorkville was attracting plenty of musicians, and plenty of new onlookers, some of whom hung out in the area, even lived there, and some who just showed up to watch what was going on. A youth culture developed, bohemian in nature, the people who would soon be called hippies. There was a rowdier side too, greasers and bikers. The streets were becoming packed at peak hours, with cars of tourists driving through to see the long-hairs, the motorcycle gangs looking for action, the greasers looking for a fight, and police keeping a watch on all of them. There were also lots and lots of kids from all over the city, looking for something to do on a Friday night. Mostly Yorkville attracted attention, good and bad. There was so much publicity about the area, it became a national issue of sorts, with negatives or stereotypes blown out of proportion, rowdiness being called a riot, each arrest a social problem. It did make for good stories on TV and in newspapers; there was sex, drugs, and rock 'n' roll.

Folk was still popular as well. Even with lots of competition, the Riverboat was always the top club in Yorkville. Bernie Fiedler opened it in late 1964, and over the years it attracted almost every major player on the folk circuit. Every Canadian of note played there, and the main U.S. touring artists as well, including blues greats Sonny Terry and

Brownie McGhee, and John Lee Hooker, as well as folk stars Tim Buckley, Phil Ochs, and Tom Rush. Joni Mitchell went from waitressing there to headlining by 1966, and the best Neil Young could do during his stay was appear at Hoot Night, the '60s equivalent of the open-mic show. The club held just under 120 patrons, so it was often jam-packed, especially for hot acts such as Simon and Garfunkel or grand veteran Howlin' Wolf. But the top act was a local. With Ian & Sylvia in New York, Gordon Lightfoot was the city's leading folk artist. He liked his long-standing gig at Steele's Tavern on Yonge, and he loved palling around with Rompin' Ronnie Hawkins, but he wasn't getting star pay even though his songs were being covered by major U.S. performers. Fiedler stole him away with more money, and Lightfoot kept packing the place. Eventually he was doing four separate shows a night for four different paying audiences.

Even David Clayton-Thomas was lured away from Yonge:

> After The Shays had had a couple of hit records, and I started to get bigger gigs, opening for The Rolling Stones at Maple Leaf Gardens, that kind of thing, I started hanging out in Yorkville. We started going up and seeing people like Oscar Peterson, Lonnie Johnson, Lenny Breau. And a lot of the acts from Greenwich Village in New York started to come up and play the little clubs on Yorkville. So you could see folk acts like Tim Hardin. And we were all playing the little clubs on Yorkville, little one-nighters, there was no money there, most of us couldn't afford a band with the money they paid in the coffeehouses. So I kind of juggled both for a while, the gigs downtown which actually paid not much, but they at least paid a living, and Yorkville, which paid zero. I just got all tangled up in the scene in Yorkville, and started to play less and less on Yonge Street.

Yorkville was even able to draw back one Canadian-born performer. Buffy Sainte-Marie had been born on the Piapot Cree First Nation in the Qu'Appelle Valley, Saskatchewan, in 1941. "Oh, did she know Joni Mitchell?" you ask. "She's from Saskatchewan too." Look, just because they are both folk singers born in Saskatchewan in the 1940s, doesn't mean they knew each other. But, being as this is Canada, of course they did. It didn't happen until Yorkville in the '60s though, an important event for both women. Sainte-Marie had actually grown up in Massachusetts, having been adopted by relatives. In the brutal poverty of Canadian First Nations, many of the children ended up removed from their homes. Discovering and understanding more about her heritage would become a driving factor in Sainte-Marie's life, music, art, and social activism.

Already a folk performer in college, when she graduated in 1962, she hit the road solo, touring campuses, coffeehouses, and clubs. She was a striking, individual talent. Her vibrato made her stand out, bringing an intensity to her serious material, and a power edge to her romantic numbers. She joined Dylan and the Tysons in the small group of folk performers writing their own material, much of it influenced by her growing interests in a wide range of political and social topics, especially the treatment of Native Americans, as heard in her song "Now That the Buffalo's Gone." She also stood on her own as a talented performer, with a set that included old Appalachian folk songs and blues numbers from the likes of Blind Willie Johnson. She did well in Greenwich Village, got a deal with Vanguard Records along with Ian & Sylvia, and quickly became a favorite at the Purple Onion. The feeling was mutual, Sainte-Marie loving the vibe of the Village, the constant exchange of ideas, and the desire for change.

She wrote her most famous song in the Purple Onion. Waiting for her flight from San Francisco to Toronto for a date at the club, she saw a group of U.S. Army soldiers just returning from Vietnam. There were wounded men among the ranks, in wheelchairs and on stretchers. Sainte-Marie was taken by the sight, at a time before the U.S. was even acknowledging they were involved in a war in Southeast Asia. Once she got to Yorkville, she started writing a new song at the Onion. It became "Universal Soldier," one of the most popular of the era's protest songs. Its lyrics reflect Sainte-Marie's realization that we are all responsible for war, thanks to old thinking and voting that puts us into countries, and pits us against neighbors. The song was featured on her first album, 1964's *It's My Way!*, and became controversial almost immediately. Her passionate delivery barely concealed the anger behind the words. *Billboard* magazine named her Best New Artist of 1964, but the song was still just an album cut on the folk scene. The next year, Scottish folk singer Donovan did a cover version that was a huge hit in England, and a significant one in North America, where he was fast becoming a major star.

This all helped turn Sainte-Marie into a leading folk performer, including a star billing at Mariposa (that's who Joni Anderson was keen on hearing when she made her trip east). She continued to be a fearless songwriter, including the song "Cod'ine," a harrowing number about a 1963 addiction after she got a throat infection. There was "My Country 'Tis of Thy People You're Dying," a bitter diatribe against some of the crimes of the U.S. government. But there was a sensitive and beautiful side as well, as found in "Until It's Time for You to Go," a song about two lovers torn apart by their different backgrounds. The tender number, with a sublime melody and haunting chord changes, could have come from Edith Piaf or perhaps one of Quebec's grand chansonniers. The song became a British hit for the band The Four Pennies in 1965, but is best known as one of Elvis Presley's favorite concert numbers. Joni Anderson had made a good choice when she moved from Calgary to Toronto to see Sainte-Marie perform, and they did eventually meet. Their bond would become even stronger after Yorkville.

Some clubs held on stubbornly to folk—you could still even find Dixieland trad jazz in Yorkville—but it was the rock bands that were bringing the most energy into the Village. In 1965, the first exclusively rock 'n' roll clubs had opened, and bands such as The Sparrow(s), The Paupers, The Ugly Ducklings, and Luke and The Apostles became regulars. Even former Yonge Street staples Levon and The Hawks and Robbie Lane and The Disciples made the move. Luke and The Apostles was a play on the name of Lane and The Disciples, hugely popular in Toronto at the time they formed in 1964. Luke was singer Luke Gibson, a bluesy belter, with a distinctive growl and great front-man looks. They played a fast-paced, guitar-and-keyboard-driven blues, with a touch of early psychedelia, and some British frenzy added in. They soon became the house band at the Purple Onion at a time when the U.S. record companies were starting to check out the scene for potential stars. They caught the attention of Paul Rothchild of Elektra Records, who was so thrilled with them, he had Gibson sing over the phone for his boss, Jac Holzman. In New York, Luke & The Apostles recorded their original number "Been Burnt" for a single for Elektra, but before it could come out, Rothchild was busted for marijuana and spent a year in jail. It finally was released in 1967, but got no notice, and the band was quickly dropped. In the meantime, Holzman had seen and signed The Doors in Los Angeles, another band with a charismatic frontman, heavy guitar and keyboards, and a bluesy sound. The similarities didn't end there, as "Been Burnt" had much the same sound as The Doors' first single, "Break on Through." But Luke & The Apostles were back in Yorkville, confused about a next move. The talented group split that year, and the players scattered like seeds to other bands, Gibson joining the emerging Kensington Market, guitarist Mike McKenna switching to The Ugly Ducklings, and later forming the much-loved blues outfit McKenna-Mendelson Mainline, and drummer Pat Little hooked up with David Clayton-Thomas, who was still searching for success.

Clayton-Thomas had left The Shays a proven hit maker, with his "Walk That Walk" making number three on the national *RPM* charts. For all that was worth; as he moved from Yonge Street to Yorkville, Clayton-Thomas had to scramble for gigs, even playing pass-the-hat sets for small change. He put together another outfit called The Bossmen, with the goal to develop more of a jazz-rock sound. The result was "Brainwashed," a fascinating slice of protest song-meets-head music, with a heavy bass, crazy piano breaks, and the usual huge vocals from Clayton-Thomas. It fit in well with the heavier sounds on the CHUM charts in the summer of '66, joining "Wild Thing" by The Troggs and "Mother's Little Helper" from The Rolling Stones, ending up at number six. That was the lone highlight for the short-lived Bossmen, but Clayton-Thomas had laid down the jazz-rock theme for his future.

The Ugly Ducklings were Rolling Stones fans and a classic garage band. They were also the loudest of the Yorkville bands, and like The Stones to The Beatles, they got the reputation as the dangerous ones on the scene. They liked their music loose, with no muss and no fuss. They made one of the great Canadian debut singles ever, the wonderfully conceived "Nothin'." "It was the first real song we ever wrote," remembered singer Dave Bingham. "As soon as Roger (Mayne, guitarist) played the chords for me, I knew it was special. I wrote all the lyrics, it took maybe two hours." For a topic, the pair decided it needed to be some kind of protest. "I was one of those guys that was always rebelling against something," Bingham reflects. "So Roger and I thought, what are we gonna write about? Because we really hadn't lived a life yet that we could write about, so I said 'Why don't we write about nothin'?' The idea of writing a song called 'Nothin'' was just perfect and anti to me." The Ugly Ducklings caused enough of a national stir to warrant a tour to the East Coast provinces. As part of the promotion, radio stations were offering listeners a chance to "Win a Date with an Ugly Duckling." The band eventually fulfilled their dream, getting to open for The Rolling Stones at Maple Leaf Gardens. Famously, Mick Jagger named them as his favorite Canadian band.

The Paupers were a tight group that started playing Village clubs in 1965. They also boasted some terrific players, including drummer Skip Prokop, also a natural leader. He was a driven musician, having learned drums in the Sea Cadets in Hamilton, Ontario, eventually chosen to serve in the Royal Canadian Naval Band. He learned and diligently practiced every paradiddle and ratamacue in the forty drumming rudiments, already a technically superb player at sixteen. The group's first single, "Never Send You Flowers," was folk-flavored with a little mystery, and some exceptional playing. Prokop's drums and Denny Gerrard's bass solos were big highlights and the band became one of the top draws of 1966, right at the height of the rock band explosion in the Village. "We were playing at the El Patio," remembers Skip Prokop,

> That was the very first place that The Paupers got hired into, and we started to build a really big fan base. Kind of like, on a Friday-Saturday night, lined-up-around-the-block type of thing. Along with that, you had Jon and Lee & The Checkmates over on the Avenue Road club, which was about a block and a half away. You had Johnny Kay and The Sparrow, and you had Neil with The Mynah Birds and Ricky James. We were all playing clubs together. There was a restaurant over on the Colonnade building on Bloor, and that's where everybody hung out after we were through playing. The place was packed. I'm not really sure that this exists today with young musicians, but at that time, man, everybody kinda rooted everybody else on. There just didn't seem to be any animosity. We were all playing, we were all around the same age, and we were all looking to do the same thing, which was get a break, and get a U.S. record deal. We figured

if one of us gets it, they'll come looking to see who else was there. At that point, Canada didn't mean more than a spit in the bucket, music-industry speaking, compared to the States and England.

The line-ups to get in to see The Paupers were ridiculous. We played over at Boris's Red Gas Room, after we had a bit of a falling out with Tony at the El Patio, so we were playing over there, just down the street from Jon and Lee & The Checkmates, and there was always this huge rivalry between our fans. On Yorkville Avenue for about two blocks, you've got The Paupers' fans. And for about three blocks north on Avenue Road, you've got the Jon and Lee & The Checkmates' fans, and they're ready to beat the crap out of each other. They're in their blue colors and their suspenders, and winkle-picker shoes, and our guys are all with long hair, belts, they just looked stoned, flower kids, right? It's funny, because the bands were really good friends.

Word was flying fast about the group, and they had a feisty new manager, Bernie Finkelstein. "Bernie had great ideas, and we tried them, and it was just a good marriage," says Prokop. "And typical of me, that band was so tight, it was scary. It was a military operation in that band, it was just absolutely, flawlessly tight. Denny (Gerrard), to this day is still one of the highest-rated, monster bass players. At that time, nobody had every seen anything like it before, what he did with live distortion, and speed on both hands, like a flamenco guitarist, it was just dazzling." Finkelstein had presented them with another of his great ideas. He was going to take The Paupers where none of the Toronto rock bands had been yet, where they all wanted to go, across the border to the U.S.

In terms of airplay, exposure and even record sales, 1965 had been a good year for Canadian groups. The *RPM* charts had fifty-three Canadian songs enter the Top 40 that year, including two number one hits and twenty-one in the Top 10. There were The Great Scots from Halifax, Wes Dakus from Edmonton, Terry Black from Vancouver, The Guess Who from Winnipeg, and Michel Louvain from Quebec. Every nation has a capital, and for Canada's music nation it was Yorkville Village. Almost as good was 1966, with forty-five Canadian singles in the Top 40. But as David Clayton-Thomas and the guys in The Guess Who could attest, there wasn't a windfall with each hit in Canada, far from it. The big sellers were still The Beatles, The Beach Boys, and The Supremes. The best musicians, or the most driven, were getting tired of scuffling. The pattern was soon to be set: if you wanted to be a successful musician in Canada, you had to go to Yorkville, make a name for yourself, or make some good connections, and then go to the States. For some of the stars of Yorkville, that worked very well; there were also some spectacular flameouts.

URGE FOR GOING

Canadian Talent Makes an Exodus to the U.S.

Neil Young was running out of options in Toronto. His latest rock band, The Mynah Birds, had disintegrated, and he was doing worse as a solo folk performer. He still knew what he wanted to do: play that hybrid of folk and rock he'd conceived back in Fort William. He'd missed out on being a founding father of the sound, when The Byrds beat him to it with their jingle-jangle take on Dylan's tunes. But now that the world was mad for it, there had to be a place for him as well. The guy who had gotten it in the first place, Stephen Stills, was still on his mind. After missing him in New York, Young decided to give up on Toronto, and search for Stills in Los Angeles. Despite the musical magic of Yorkville, a man needs a paycheck after all.

It didn't take much to convince Bruce Palmer either. He wanted to keep making music with Young, and had nothing to keep him in Toronto. To finance the trip, they pawned all The Mynah Birds' equipment. And once again, Young turned to his road-trip vehicle of choice, buying a 1953 hearse. Some like-minded Yorkville friends decided to join in the fun, and a troop of three guys and three girls headed to the U.S. It was a long and arduous trip, which included a rest stop of several days in Albuquerque where two of the woman and the other guy decided to abandon the L.A. dream. On April 1, 1966, they arrived in Los Angeles, and headed straight for the intersection of fate and coincidence.

Actually, it was Sunset Boulevard, and it took a few days. Young and Palmer had no idea where Stills was, and searched all the clubs and cafes, any place a singer might be. After a week, they gave up and decided to try San Francisco, by then a well-known musicians' destination. About to head north on Sunset, they hit a traffic jam. Just behind them was none other than Stephen Stills. Seeing a hearse with Ontario plates, he correctly figured it must be Young. With Stills was Richie Furay, the same guy Young had met in New York months earlier. By then, Stills had convinced him to move to Los Angeles, and join his nonexistent band. They were, however, singing Neil Young's song "Nowadays Clancy Can't Even Sing," which Young had taught to Furay, and Furay to Stills. With Palmer on board as well, four-fifths of the future Buffalo Springfield made plans to jam, in the traffic jam.

Casting about for a drummer, they were hooked up with Dewey Martin, who had come west from Nashville where he was a touring pro, having played with Roy Orbison, The Everly Brothers, and others. Fittingly, he was also Canadian, from the Ottawa area originally. The crushing collapse of The Mynah Birds had only been weeks before, and now Young had joined with the band of his dreams; two great singers in Stills and Furay, two exploding songwriters in himself and Stills, and another lead guitar player with whom he could do battle. Such was the spirit of the times, and the level of confidence they shared, that they fully believed success would be immediate. All they needed was a name, which they took from a passing steamroller.

How fast did it all happen? Two weeks after the Sunset Boulevard meeting, Buffalo Springfield opened a short tour for The Byrds. Word spread, and by June the band was booked into the Whiskey A Go Go club on the Sunset Strip for six weeks, a prime gig in front of every mover, shaker, and scene-maker in L.A. This was when the Sunset Strip clubs were at their zenith, with thousands of teens going back and forth to see the likes of The Doors, Love, The Byrds, The Lovin' Spoonful, and even Captain Beefheart. Buffalo Springfield stood out, playing a harder-edged folk rock with all original material, including the trippy imagery of the early Neil Young songs. Young wasn't singing at that point, leaving the sweeter voices of Stills and Furay to handle that. He was at the back with his long fringe coat, an image he adopted called the Hollywood Indian. Among the packed crowds each night were all the industry heavyweights, would-be managers, publishers, and record labels. Buffalo Springfield were duly signed, and seemingly headed to rock stardom.

The first Buffalo Springfield album reflected a hot group on the rise. Stills wrote seven songs, Young five, and Neil even overcame his initial reluctance, singing a couple of numbers. The group put "Nowadays Clancy Can't Even Sing" on the self-titled album, keeping the vocal by Richie Furay and harmonies from Stills, a winning arrangement. Unfortunately, as a lead single, it didn't fare well enough to chart in the Top 100, the song a little too abstract for pop audiences. A second Young tune, "Burned," was chosen as a second single, this time with the writer's own vocal. Despite the excitement around L.A. for the group, it fared even worse nationally, failing to chart at all. Stills finally saved the day, after quickly writing and recording a song about the teen riots on the Sunset Strip, protesting strict ten p.m. curfews just imposed. "For What It's Worth" leaped into the Top 10 in early 1967, finally making Buffalo Springfield an international concern. The group was considered one of the top bands from L.A., but hardly a mention was made that the majority of them were Canadian.

Despite the quick fulfillment of his goals, Neil Young was not a happy camper. It turned out he was not a good team player. Used to leading his bands, other than his short-lived time in The Mynah Birds, Young was having issues with Stills, the other natural leader in the band. In a move that would be repeated over and over again through five decades, Young left the group, only to return a short time later. Then he quit again, and a couple of other times, including just before the band's appearance at the Monterey Pop Festival, where David Crosby took his place. Meanwhile, recording for the group's second album, *Buffalo Springfield Again*, was a mess, with Stills and Young insisting on producing the tracks they wrote. Things weren't going any better for Bruce Palmer, who was busted for marijuana and deported back to Canada. The group would never have a solid lineup again. The soap opera played out for another few months, until a final show in May of 1968. Buffalo Springfield has become more famous for being the first group featuring Stills and Young than for the music it produced, and it never lived up to the potential each felt in that fateful meeting on the Sunset Strip. It did, however, get Neil Young into the spotlight, and he was determined to continue on his terms.

Neil Young was just one of a large group of Canadian musicians who moved to the U.S. in the mid-'60s, convinced that success lay just across the border. They had to move; there just weren't many good managers or well-equipped studios; there were few agents, hardly any pop music media, and seemingly no chance of moving up in the rock world. Most of them had been slogging it out in clubs for a few years by then, and had little to show for it, aside from their reputation. The touring musicians from the States, landing gigs in Yorkville clubs for a few nights, would rave about how great these Canadians were, and if they would head to Greenwich Village or San Francisco or even Nashville, they'd be stars. Certainly a ridiculous amount of talent had flowed into Toronto from all over the country, and sure enough, a lot of those players were soon to become stars.

Levon and The Hawks were one of the groups with ridiculous talent.

Playing rip-roaring sets across southern Ontario, down to New Jersey and New York, and as far west as Texas, the band did night after night of killer early rock 'n' roll, favorites such as "Lucille," "Not Fade Away," and "Twist and Shout." They were tight, mature, and had their own special arrangements; few live groups of the day could compare. Helm handled the rockers, and when it was time for a waltz for the dancers, Richard Manuel took the soulful leads, such as on the weeper "You Don't Know Me." Garth Hudson was a keyboard wizard, his swirling organ spreading colors all over the songs. Robbie Robertson would spray chicken-scratch guitar all over the stage, chugging through chestnuts like "Bo Diddley," left over from their time with Ronnie Hawkins. Their arrangement of that song, heard on a famous bootleg from July 12, 1964, in Port Dover, Ontario, is one of the most powerful performances ever recorded, despite the very poor surviving audio. Robertson and Helm in particular push each other with unmatched intensity. Shows like that one are what Hudson was referring to when he dismissed The Band's legendary Last Waltz concert, saying, "I think the cookin' live stuff is The Hawks, Levon & The Hawks. Some of the tempos are impressive. That's when the band was real tight, I was impressed with some of that stuff."

Sometimes you just have to know the one right person at the right time. For The Hawks, that was Mary Martin, not the Broadway actress and *South Pacific* star, but instead a woman from Toronto who was a big fan of the band. She used to love to hear Richard Manuel sing Ray Charles, saying it made her swoon. Martin had landed a job in New York, as an executive assistant to none other than Albert Grossman, the manager for Ian & Sylvia, Gordon Lightfoot, and of course, Bob Dylan. Martin knew that Dylan was going to put a band together, after his first, famous electric gig at the Newport Folk Festival in July of 1965. She boldly suggested to Dylan he should check out these Canadian guys. The group had been in residency in the summer of 1965 at

Somers Point, New Jersey, at the thousand-seater club Tony Mart's, where they were advertised as "Canada's Greatest." Grossman's people found Helm, and first talked to him on the phone. Helm always said at that point, he'd barely heard of Dylan. The result was that Robertson first was asked to a rehearsal with Dylan, and Robbie, not liking the drummer, suggested he bring Helm along next. That worked, and on August 28, 1965, Dylan performed at the Forest Hills Tennis Stadium in New York, with Robertson, Helm, keyboardist Al Kooper (remember that name for later reference), and bass player Harvey Brooks. The same group took the stage six days later at the Hollywood Bowl.

Dylan then proposed the group go on tour with him, but Kooper wasn't keen, after the rough ride the audience had given them. Helm didn't want to break up his band, so it was decided Dylan would come check them out. The Hawks were booked into Friars Tavern on Yonge in mid-September, and Dylan arrived on the fifteenth, and waited for the set to end. He rehearsed with them all that night, and the next, and the deal was done; The Hawks had just gone from being a bar band to playing the most important stages in North America and Europe. The second gig they did together was at Carnegie Hall. Two months after leaving Friars Tavern in Toronto, they were back, this time playing Massey Hall.

The shows would follow the same format each night, and usually the same set list. Dylan would play an acoustic set, and all would go well. When the curtain opened for the second set, The Hawks would be revealed, and on many nights, the booing would begin. Old fans and folk purists were appalled at the idea of electric rock music being played on top of supposed folk songs. Not just that, it was a noisy, explosive sound, with the group under orders to not back down. At the time, in the rarefied air of some of those halls, Robertson's guitar attack alone would have filled the room with electricity and a little danger. Dylan was going to prove his point, and didn't waver, playing the same show from September until the next May, from the East Coast to the West, from Hawaii to Australia, to the U.K., over to the Continent and into Scandinavia, and ending at the Royal Albert Hall in London. With ten days left to go on the tour, in Manchester, someone in the crowd taunted him with the cry of "Judas." Dylan responded by turning to The Hawks and ordering them to "Play fucking loud." He had the right band for it. With four Canadians on the stage with him, it is widely considered the greatest single moment in rock 'n' roll history, as The Hawks tore into "Like a Rolling Stone."

Levon Helm missed that show, and most of the tour. He'd become sick of the booing in the fall of '65, and left his band in Dylan's hands. He drifted down to the Gulf of Mexico and went to work on an oil rig. Meantime, with the world tour over, Dylan went home to Woodstock, New York, to plan his next move. In July of 1966, he had a motorcycle accident, and all of a sudden, those four Canadians were at a loss again. Without their old (Helm) or new leader (Dylan), the best band in the world didn't have a gig.

The Paupers were considered by many the best band in Yorkville Village. The group's manager, Bernie Finkelstein, had come to the conclusion that what was happening in Toronto was just as hot as what was going on in the U.S., and that all they needed was a high-profile gig, in New York. "Bernie went down to the States," explains Paupers leader and drummer Skip Prokop,

> And talked to Howard Solomon at the Cafe au Go Go, and said, "We've got this great band up there, blah-de-blah-blah, we'd love to come down and open for one of your groups." Howard said yes, so they picked some dates, it was locked in [February to March 1967], and there was this band that was coming from California, and they were on this huge wave of buzz. They were coming to the East Coast for first time,

and that band was Jefferson Airplane. So we went in the first day and did the sound check. At that point, we were using the three kits of drums, against Chuck's [Beal, lead guitar] Echolette, which is like a multi-delay pedal now, it was a little machine with a tape and you could get four or five different settings of echo, and he would play against three drummers. You had Adam playing the two high toms, you had Denny, and we flipped the bass drum up and a floor tom, and me, on a full kit. I taught them parts and all that, they were very, very good. At the sound check, the place just exploded. The staff was putting their trays down, going "Who are these guys?" They'd never seen anything like it.

We played that night, and the place goes berserk, packed and berserk. They won't let us off the stage. Here's the Airplane standing backstage, going, "What the hell's going on?" We had to play three or four encores and we ran out of material. By the next night, everybody who was anybody in the music industry, in the upper echelon of management, recording, booking agents, were at the Cafe au Go Go. The word went out that this band was not to be believed, you've got to see it, and that place was jammed. That included Brian Epstein, Albert Grossman, all the people from William Morris, it was crazy. Albert tracked Bernie down in the crowd and said, "Why don't you come over to the office and have a chat?" So Bernie went there the next day, and meanwhile we got wined and dined all over New York by agencies, this guy and that guy, it was really crazy. And the end of that story is, we got the first U.S. record deal, through Albert Grossman, with Verve-Forecast. That was really celebrated up here by all the Canadian bands, going, wow, great! Guys were calling Bernie, going "Can you go down and get us a deal?"

Historically, it really opened the door for Canadian bands, they looked and went, wow, there's actually talent up there, they're not all chasing raccoons or something.

Finkelstein joined Grossman's management team, bringing the band with him, and Grossman went to work. He was truly impressed, as was the entire music industry and press. Veteran critic Ralph J. Gleason, one of the founders of *Rolling Stone* magazine that year, was one of the biggest cheerleaders. Grossman wasn't usually one given to hype, and he really didn't have to do much with artists such as Bob Dylan, Janis Joplin, and Peter, Paul & Mary. With The Paupers, he couldn't help himself, and declared they would be the biggest band since The Beatles. He even got them a prime spot on the biggest show of the Summer of Love, the Monterey International Pop Music Festival, in June in Monterey, California. The three-day event, featuring such big names as The Mamas & The Papas, Simon & Garfunkel, The Byrds, and The Who, made instant stars out of many of the groups who played that weekend, including The Jimi Hendrix Experience, and Big Brother & The Holding Company. What is forgotten is that the biggest pre-festival buzz was for the Canadians. "The big downer was Monterey," admits Prokop.

Everybody was there, everybody wanted to see The Paupers. We were being predicted as the band that would walk away with that festival, we would be one of the biggest acts in the world. Long story short, we got on stage, Denny (Gerrard) is stoned on acid, he tunes his bass about a quarter-note sharp or flat, it sounded awful. We start to play, and just before, I'm counting in the first song, and he's tuning his bass! I'm going, "Oh . . . my . . . God." So we started to play, the big, big drum thing and all that. We hit the first song, and all of a sudden there was cackling and weird crap going on with the amps. By the second song, the tape had broken on the Echolette. So instead of it sounding like thunder from God coming down upon everybody, it was "wee-waw, wee-waw." There was no echo at all. Then Denny's amp blows up. Then Chuck's amp blows up. That left me on acoustic drums, Adam with a rhythm guitar and vocals, that was it. It was hugely disappointing. And that was it.

It was a complete and utter disaster, such a dismal set that nobody wanted to talk about The Paupers anymore. The band struggled through a few more months of the underground club circuit in the U.S., made a second album, but still only had any sizeable support back in Toronto. So Prokop went to Albert Grossman, to deliver the bad news. "It just got too crazy," says Prokop of the band, post-Monterey. "We couldn't deal with Denny anymore, because you just didn't know what the heck he was going to do. There was no dependability and no consistency there. You just didn't know if he was going to walk out in the first song and shove his bass through his amp. So we had to get rid of Denny. Then it just got weirder and weirder, and I went and talked to Albert, and said, 'I'm outta here, man. I can't deal with this anymore, I don't see any future, and I don't see why we're doing this.'" Luckily, Grossman had already come up with an exit strategy for Prokop that would lead to the creation of a brand-new sound in rock music.

The Sparrow had loved Yorkville, but New York offered big money, hot clubs, and a new record deal for them with Columbia. Guitarist Dennis Edmonton was writing folky-psychedelic numbers like "Tomorrow's Ship," the group's first single for the label. Another, "Green Bottle Lover," written by Dennis and his brother Jerry, was more bluesy and tight, but still with acid swirls. With nothing to show for these efforts, the group decided California was the place they oughtta be, and headed out to L.A. They started working Sunset Boulevard clubs, but then the Strip riots hit, the same ones Stephen Stills had written "For What It's Worth" about. Clubs were closing in the wake, and gigs drying up, so The Sparrow flew north to San Francisco. The Summer of Love was about to explode, and The Sparrow weren't really part of the scene there. They did get some gigs, including at the soon-to-be-famous Fillmore, but the group was crumbling. Dennis Edmonton quit, as did Nick St. Nicholas, and John Kay was left struggling to pick up the pieces.

Kay still had Jerry Edmonton and Goldy McJohn onboard and decided to fold the old Sparrow name. He landed a new record deal and recruited two L.A. musicians to fill out the ranks. Renamed Steppenwolf, the band dropped the psychedelic touches, and harder rock became their sound, plus some of the old Toronto R&B. The group was tough and exciting, and as the Summer of Love drifted away, and hard rock replaced much of the mellow folk, Steppenwolf started taking off in California.

Still living in Los Angeles was Dennis Edmonton. He also had a new name (his third in life), Mars Bonfire. "Being in The Sparrow gave me a chance to observe and participate in many aspects of the music business," Bonfire said in 2010, "such as being a musician, producing, creating songs, arranging, running a studio, and more. What ended up appealing to me the most was songwriting, so much so that I decided to concentrate entirely on that and let go of being a musician." He hadn't severed his ties with Kay and company, and was offering them first crack at his latest works, just as he'd done in The Sparrow. That included a new one that roared with power, and came to symbolize the ties between the open road, big motorcycles, and heavy rock: "Born to Be Wild." The ultimate driving song, it was written by Bonfire about his first car. Was it something awesome and powerful? No, it was a used Ford Falcon. Well, at least it did change his life. "The Sparrow had a vehicle for getting ourselves and our gear to clubs, but I had no transportation of my own and saw nothing of California except motel rooms, nightclubs, and Hollywood. When I got the Falcon I drove to the ocean, to the mountains, and to the high desert, and I was amazed and thrilled with the beauty and diversity of southern California." Generations of motorcycle and car enthusiasts will be forgiven if they don't imagine a humble Ford Falcon when they sing "Born to Be Wild."

There's no clear understanding of how the term *heavy metal* came to be used to describe the hardest of rock music, but its first usage in song seems to be this one. "I first heard the term as a category of the periodic table when I was studying science," Bonfire explains. "During my Falcon ramblings I experienced some thunderstorms in the mountains. The darkening of the sky, the flash of lightning, and the crack of thunder prompted the phrase, 'I like smoke and lightning, heavy metal thunder.'" The song hit number one in Canada, number two in the U.S., and hit the charts in Europe as well. Then, it was chosen for the iconic film *Easy Rider*, where it really picked up its lasting connection to motorcycles. It also became a hit once more, and sealed its classic status. Bonfire thought it was perfect: "I was thrilled. It gave a captivating imagery to the words of the song that is similar to what was going on in my head when I wrote it." Steppenwolf was now a star band and landed a string of Top 40 albums into the '70s, as well as another huge hit, "Magic Carpet Ride."

Joni Mitchell chose to leave Yorkville for a different reason than the others. She headed to Detroit in late 1965 with new husband, Chuck Mitchell, where he was an established performer. They were by then performing as a duo, mostly in the coffeehouses of Detroit, as well as small tours and trips back to Toronto. With lots of friends and folk connections, the Mitchells made their apartment the crash pad for touring musicians, including Eric Anderson and Tom Rush. Mitchell, by now writing up a storm, was on the lookout for chords and guitar tricks, especially since an episode of childhood polio (another trait she shared with Neil Young) had left her left hand weak. She found the alternative tunings that Anderson and Rush taught her could help, as she wouldn't have to stretch her hand as much. An equal benefit to that was the wide array of different chords she could use in her writing. New melodic possibilities opened up, immediately putting her on a different perch from all the other singer-songwriters using standard tuning. Early songs such as "Urge for Going" and "The Circle Game" have haunting and heart-touching melodies that move from note to note in beautiful combinations, with so many options and combinations at her grasp.

By 1966, Mitchell had become a bit of a star back in Canada, performing on folk singer Oscar Brand's national TV show *Let's Sing Out*, with such guests as The Chapin Family (with Harry) and Dave Van Ronk, and she was certainly one of Yorkville's favorites. "Oh, Joni Mitchell just blew me away," says David Clayton-Thomas, "She still does to this day, I think she's one of the greatest songwriters we've ever produced." She was still performing with Chuck Mitchell, but increasingly she was the captivating one of the duo, and their bookings were by then including clubs in Philadelphia and New York. On radio in Philadelphia, she even performed a version of her friend Neil Young's "Sugar Mountain," saying she hoped he would someday record it. As well, her songs were now attracting attention from her peers. Tom Rush started performing "Urge for Going" and "The Circle Game." After veteran performer George Hamilton IV heard Rush one night, he recorded a country version of "Urge For Going" that made the Top 10. Buffy Sainte-Marie was a big fan and supporter, and also recorded two Mitchell compositions, "The Circle Game" and "Song to a Seagull." Sainte-Marie even went as far as traveling around with a tape of Mitchell's songs, playing the songs for anyone she could interest.

Things soured with Chuck Mitchell, and Joni left their Detroit home abruptly. She moved to New York, and there was a receptive audience waiting. Sainte-Marie's encouragement paid off, when she introduced Elliot Roberts to Mitchell. He saw her perform at the Cafe au Go Go, and soon agreed to manage her. Roberts was partners with David Geffen, who became Mitchell's booking agent. It would prove to be a powerful organization. Another new fan in New York was Al Kooper, the former Dylan keyboardist whom we have already met once regarding The Hawks, and will become entangled with two more Canadian bands before this chapter is over. In Mitchell's case, Kooper heard her perform and woke up Judy Collins in the middle of the night to listen to Joni sing. Soon Collins would record "Michael from Mountains" and more significantly, was the first to record "Both Sides, Now." It was a major hit, reaching number eight on the pop charts, and winning the Grammy Award for Best Folk Performance. Mitchell was now a star ascending in the U.S. as well as Canada.

Mitchell was able to command prestigious folk gigs such as the Newport Folk Festival, and clubs up and down the East Coast, as far as Florida. That was important, because she found another big fan in the Sunshine State. David Crosby had recently been kicked out of The Byrds for various sins, and was in Coconut Grove, buying a sailboat, as you do when fired from one of pop's biggest groups. Joni Mitchell was playing at the Gaslight South club when Crosby stopped in, and fell in love, in a couple of ways. The two had a short relationship, but Crosby's love of the music was the stronger crush, and he offered to produce her. Mitchell had been considering a move to Los Angeles, and decided to follow Crosby back. At this point, she had her pick of record companies. With Crosby's sponsorship and name attached to a new album, and the growing list of stars recording her songs, Joni Mitchell was in great demand. Gaining complete artistic control, she signed with Reprise Records, and settled into a Los Angeles community that also included her old friend Neil Young.

Leonard Cohen did visit Yorkville a couple of times, but he was hardly a singer in those days. He was a well-known poet instead, with four collections as well as two novels, and had been the subject of a National Film Board documentary in 1965, *Ladies and Gentlemen . . . Mr. Leonard Cohen*. But if there was one job that paid worse than pop singer in Canada in the mid-'60s, it was poetry. Even stars weren't making a living. "No, I wasn't," Cohen admitted, "Not as a writer, not at all. I published my first book of poetry, *Let Us Compare Mythologies* [1956] and it sold a few hundred copies. Then I published *The Spice-Box of Earth*, and that didn't sell at all. *Beautiful Losers* [1966], it was panned. It sold maybe three thousand copies worldwide."

Cohen had tried working in the family clothing business in Montreal before, but it wasn't for him. He preferred an isolated life on the Greek island of Hydra, quite a cheap spot in the early '60s, but eventually he went through what money he had. That meant moving back from Greece, and finding an alternative source of income. The only other position of note he had held was as a member of a country and western band in the '50s, The Buckskin Boys. "When I discovered I couldn't make a living as a writer, I naturally returned to the other thing I could do." He did have some experience performing his words to music, from dabbling in a little coffeehouse material back in the day, reading over accompaniment. And there were some songwriters who were being called poets, such as Dylan. But Cohen claimed to have not really been familiar with the whole folk music scene. "I didn't know too much about it," he explained. "I was living in Greece and listening to Armed Forces radio, which was mostly country music, which I always loved. So when I came back to Canada, I figured I'd try to go down to Nashville. I was going through New York, and that's where I came across the so-called folk song renaissance."

First, he made contact with singers, hoping to sell his material.

> I bumped into Judy Collins and I found out what was going
> on. So I thought I'd try my hand at it. I played her a couple of

songs that I had. She didn't like them very much. She said, "If you have any other songs, give me a call." So I went back to Montreal and started writing, and I wrote "Suzanne." I played it for a couple of friends, and they said it sounds like everything else. I phoned Judy Collins up, and I played it for her over the phone, and she liked it and eventually recorded it.

He was late to the game, but had the number one currency in his pocket, new songs. Cohen got himself into Albert Grossman's office, looking for representation. Grossman didn't bite, but another Canadian came to the rescue, and again, one who had already played a major role in rock history. Mary Martin, after having set up Dylan with The Hawks, and mentored with Grossman, decided to start her own management company. Cohen became her first major client, and she was able to set up a meeting with Columbia Records. It was with the illustrious John Hammond, the Columbia legend who had signed Billie Holliday, Count Basie, Aretha Franklin, Bob Dylan, and would later bring in Bruce Springsteen and Stevie Ray Vaughan. But the ill-prepared Cohen, unfamiliar with the music biz, didn't even have a portfolio to take to the meeting. "Before we did that," remembered Mary Martin at a forum at the Country Music Hall of Fame in Nashville in 2009, "I had to have some kind of a tape to show Leonard's work. So I put him in the bathtub (for better acoustics). And a friend of mine had a Uher tape recorder, and Leonard in the bathtub strumming his guitar, and the Uher outside the bathroom, and all these songs got recorded." Cohen, like Springsteen and Dylan, continues to record for Columbia.

Back in Yorkville, David Clayton-Thomas was soaking up the scene, and loving the new emphasis on songwriting. "People there were writing their own music," he remembers, "And you had brilliant songwriters like Neil Young, Joni Mitchell and Gordie Lightfoot playing the clubs. I was already bitten with the writing bug, I wanted to write my own music,

I just didn't want to play recycled Top 40 stuff. It was a very creative community." But much of the talent was leaving, and despite liking the community that had developed in Yorkville, soon Clayton-Thomas saw the writing on the wall. "Along about 1967," he says, "The fathers of the city of Toronto decided Yorkville was full of junkies, was full of sex, drugs, and rock n' roll, and they'd better close it down. And they did, it was amazing. They closed it down in about a week. They would come in, set up a paddy wagon at each end of Yorkville, and then about fifty cops would just sweep the streets and pick up anybody who wasn't moving along fast enough. And after about a week of that harassment, the Yorkville era ended." Or, at least the heyday of it was over. But more and more the bad side of the Village got the headlines, and the attraction wore off. Some clubs lasted into the '70s, new performers such as Bruce Cockburn and Murray McLauchlan made their way to the scene, but by the end of the '60s, Yorkville Village had lost its luster. Developers had long spied opportunity in the area, and eventually turned it into one of the most expensive retail districts in the world.

That didn't help Clayton-Thomas. He was a bona fide star in Canada, barely surviving. "I had three number one records in a row, and I was still working for two hundred dollars a week, because there was no music industry in Canada. It was obvious that Yorkville was no longer an option. My only option was to go back to the bars on Yonge Street where there were beer fights every other night, or strike out and do something different." Another Yorkville player was about to be lured to New York.

> I was a big fan of the Delta blues style, and whenever Sonny Terry and Brownie McGhee or John Lee Hooker or Lonnie Johnson would come and play, they usually played at The Riverboat, and I was playing one of the other little clubs. So between sets, I used to take my guitar and run over, and go

sit in with them. One of those gigs was with John Lee Hooker, and he told me he was opening in the Cafe au Go Go in New York City the following week, and I said, "Take me with you, I'll go with you." And he did.

He actually had an ulterior motive, because John was functionally illiterate, he grew up uneducated, a very wise man, very smart, but he couldn't get a driver's license. His driver had been busted at the border on the way up and he left his Cadillac in Niagara Falls, New York. So I made a deal with him. He said, "You go down to Niagara Falls and drive my Cadillac back down to New York, and I'll have a gig for you when you get there." I said okay, and two weeks later, I did that. I went down to do the gig with John, and apparently he had been booked to do something called the American Blues Tour of Europe, and wasn't going to do the gig that week. So there I was in New York with forty dollars in my pocket and my Telecaster, and no gig. Howie Solomon, who was the owner of the Cafe au Go Go, said, "Well I'm in a bind too, I was supposed to open John Lee Hooker tonight and he's not going to make it, do you have a band?' Now, I'd been in town maybe forty minutes, but I said, "Sure, no problem. I'll be back at five for rehearsal." I went out looking for anybody with a guitar or who looked like a musician, and we put together a little blues band and opened at the Cafe au Go Go, and that was my first gig in New York. It led to me meeting the guys in Blood, Sweat & Tears.

Like Ronnie Hawkins before them, the New York players were in awe of Clayton-Thomas's mighty pipes. He also believes that anyone coming out of the Yonge-Yorkville school had an advantage in New York. "We were that great, absolutely, maybe even better than the Greenwich or

L.A. scenes because we had struggled for so long up here without a real music industry. We spent the time, seven years or more, on Yonge Street and Yorkville, learning the trade. So when the artists did go to New York they were very well-seasoned."

Once again, and not for the last time, keyboardist Al Kooper enters our story. A visionary of sorts, Kooper had foreseen that jazz and rock were going to meet soon, something that Clayton-Thomas had been thinking as well. Kooper had joined with some of New York's finest young jazz players to form the new Blood, Sweat & Tears, who had released a respected first album. Clayton-Thomas thought they were great.

> I had seen them several times. There were guys like Randy Brecker and Bobby Columby in that band, so they were really something to go and see. They put out their first album, and then the whole band dissolved from infighting, between [Steve] Katz and [Al] Kooper and Columby. And Kooper was out, they pushed him out I guess. They wanted to get a real singer, they didn't feel his vocal chops were up to the musicality of the band. So I was playing a little club on Forty-sixth Street called Steve Paul's Scene, and that was the happening place in New York. When Clapton and Cream came to town, when Jimi Hendrix came to town, when The Who came to town, that's where they hung out after the gigs. We got a chance to meet all these guys. There was a big interplay between the Village and Uptown anyways. So I already knew Bobby Columby, Jim Fielder, Lew Soloff, Randy Brecker, so they asked me if I wanted to join the band. That caused a lot of problems with Kooper. I said, "Well this isn't going to happen," and I had to go back to Toronto, I like to say my visa ran out, but I didn't really have a visa. A few weeks after I got back to Toronto, Bobby Columby phoned

me up and said, "Kooper's gone, do you want to join the band?" At that point they had put out their first album, it had got wonderful critical acclaim but it didn't sell, so the record company was a little disillusioned with them, but Clive Davis [Columbia executive] hung with them. Bobby was very tight with Clive. Bobby said, "We still got a recording contract, wanna come down to New York?" I said okay, they sent me an airline ticket this time, and I flew down, rehearsed with the band one afternoon, a sort of audition, and within ten minutes everybody was looking at each other, saying, "Yup, this is it, this is what we're looking for."

All that songwriting Clayton-Thomas had been trying out in Yorkville was an added bonus. He brought the group his song "Spinning Wheel," which became a huge hit off the first album he recorded with them, simply called *Blood, Sweat & Tears*. The 1968 album topped the charts in both Canada and the U.S., a seven-week run in the States, with "Spinning Wheel" hitting number two on the pop charts. Two other singles from the album, "And When I Die" and "You've Made Me So Very Happy" also reached number two. Ultimately, the album was awarded the Grammy for Album of the Year. There was no doubt the new lead singer had made the difference.

Denny Doherty and Zal Yanovsky had played together until the end of The Halifax Three, and ended up back in New York City. They knew several others in the folk circle there, including Cass Elliot in The Big Three, and John and Michelle Phillips, John being part of The Journeymen. Elliot got the pair a gig with her group, which was in the process of changing. Elliot introduced Yanovsky to another local player, John Sebastian, at a party at her house to watch The Beatles on *Ed Sullivan*. That group became The Mugwumps. Doherty claimed years later that he named the group, after a saying from his grandmother

Doherty, and the original heavy metal thunder of Steppenwolf. Quietly, Canadians had helped define the '60s. But it had come at a drastic price for their homeland, as many of the best musical minds of a generation had been lost to Canada. The scene back home was suffering, and drastic action was needed to reverse the flow across the border.

HELPLESS

Canadian Musicians Feel Unloved at Home in the Late '60s

C anadian music should have had a great year in 1967. It was the Summer of Love after all, and the country had a scene in Yorkville Village to rival Haight-Ashbury in San Francisco and Swinging London. Plus, it was Canada's Centennial, and a yearlong celebration was planned, centered in Montreal at Expo '67. Canadian musicians were making breakthroughs in the U.S., and for every one that left, another two bands seemingly formed to take their place. Toronto now had Kensington Market, Mandala, Three's a Crowd, Murray McLauchlan, The Lords of London, and The Stitch in Tyme, originally out of Nova Scotia. Montreal's The Haunted had a great garage band sound, and a big hit, "1-2-5," that got played right across the country, reaching number twenty-three on the national chart. As well, some brash new singers were on the scene in Quebec, including Robert Charlebois and Michel Pagliaro, who were ready to shake up the chansonnier tradition. Ottawa was home to The Staccatos, a group that had been building since 1963, but would score their biggest hit, "Half Past Midnight," that year. Vancouver's Terry Black was still just eighteen and racking up pop hits such as "Baby's Gone," a gorgeous piece of sunshine pop. He also made the unfortunately titled album *The Black Plague*. The Collectors were taking the city by storm as well, and had two national hits, "Fisherwoman" and "Looking at a Baby." Winnipeg was still in thrall to The Guess Who, and they were also still enjoying national airplay, although not to the same level "Shakin' All Over" had brought.

However, all was not well, despite the talent around and the hoped-for good vibrations of the year. Yorkville's problems were coming to the surface, and instead of music, it was about to be known for drugs, bike gangs, and even a hepatitis scare. Young entrepreneurs such as Bernie Finkelstein who were willing to invest in Canadian musicians were few and far between. The artists earning the real money needed to build an industry were staying in the U.S. The worst blow of the year, though, came from a group of people the artists had once considered friends and partners. Radio station DJs, music directors, and program directors started to lose interest in playing Canadian music, focusing more and more on the hit artists from the U.S. and England. It was baffling, especially at a time when Canadian nationalism was at an all-time high. The radio executives, however, thought Canadian music wasn't up to par with the exciting sounds coming out of London, Los Angeles, and New York.

The year did start off well though, and on an all-Canadian theme. The man responsible was Gordon Lightfoot, who had built himself a pretty successful career by then. He'd toured the U.K. with Ian & Sylvia, played the Newport Folk Festival, and sold 3,500 tickets to a single show at Toronto's Varsity Stadium. His first album, *Lightfoot!*, had done quite well in the U.S. and Canada, too, where it went Gold. Still, this being Canada, you could just pick up the phone, and ask him to write a song; at least, if you had a TV show that was paying for the privilege. "Bob Jarvis called me up from CBC one day," Lightfoot explained, "And said they were doing a New Year's Day special. There's a railroad segment, could you write a song about it? And I said, about how long? As long as you want to make it. I said it should be fairly long. Then he sent me a book to read about Sir William Cornelius Van Horne, who was in charge of building the railway. Three days later I had the song, and I was singing it for him at his desk."

It was called "Canadian Railroad Trilogy," and was aired on the CBC-TV special *One Hundred Years Young*, which aired New Year's Day of 1967 to celebrate the Centennial year. It was a variety show featuring current stars such as comedians Wayne & Shuster and impersonator Rich Little. The broadcast was a huge hit, and Lightfoot appeared singing with a forty-piece orchestra, and a crew of railroad workers swinging sledgehammers in the background. The song was the highlight of the broadcast, and a lot more palatable way for Canadians to be taught one of the nation's most important history lessons. It was about the completion of the Canadian Pacific Railway in 1885, the country's original transcontinental railway. It truly built the nation, coming out of a political promise to British Columbia, connecting the West Coast to central Canada.

Lightfoot read about the Navvies, the thousands of manual laborers, mostly European or Chinese immigrants who were paid starvation wages during the construction. The obstacles were almost impossible to defeat, including a rebellion on the Prairies, and dynamiting a pass through the Rocky Mountains. The Chinese workers suffered the most, commonly dying in rockslides and collapsed tunnels, from disease or exhaustion. It's estimated two men died for every mile of track laid. As late as 2006, the Canadian government issued an apology to the Chinese-Canadian community for the treatment those workers received. Yet the country was opened up for good, and new immigrants could now take the train to the Prairies and beyond, to settle the farms and sow the wheat fields that fed the country.

Somehow, Lightfoot wrapped up the epic, national experience in six minutes and ten seconds. It's called a trilogy, because it was written in three distinct parts, a mid-tempo opening, a slower middle where he tells the Navvies' story, and an exciting finish, much like a train at full speed crossing the land. He borrowed that form from one of his early idols, folk singer Bob Gibson, and his similar "Civil War Trilogy." But Lightfoot's tune went further than folk music. Although never a single, coming in at six minutes and impossible to edit, it was a popular hit, as released on his *The Way I Feel* album, played constantly on CBC, and even in the classroom, with teachers using it for history lessons. Superlatives have been piled around it since, some going as far as referring to it as Canada's second national anthem. It was certainly a remarkable achievement, a pop song that doubled as a piece of national pride, without any jingoistic language or really any amount of flag-waving, typically Canadian, of course.

There was a quite a bit of flag-waving going on in other quarters, as Centennial year celebrations grew. Canada even gained a theme song for the year, one that was soon on the lips of every citizen. It was performed in both French and English versions, connected with young and old, and even the rock crowd couldn't resist its catchy chorus. It was officially called "Canada," but everybody knew it as "Ca-Na-Da," thanks to its stretched-out syllables in the opening line. It was sung by two children's choirs, called The Young Canada Singers in English, and Les Jeunes Chanteurs du Canada in French. Plus, each version was actually bilingual, as the alternate language was used by half the choir, sung as a round. Even though it was commissioned by the federal government, Canadians embraced it, and made it the number one song on the pop charts. Most people born in the county before '67 can still sing it, word for word, start to finish.

The song itself was written by Bobby Gimby. He was a radio and TV bandleader, originally from Saskatchewan, very much a showman, as well as a jingle writer and happy spirit. In addition to a songwriter, Ottawa had found its Centennial pitchman, as Gimby took to the road and the airwaves to promote the song. With his trumpet, he'd lead groups of kids, earning him the title Pied Piper of Confederation. Gimby dashed back and forth across the country the entire year, leading the locals in every town where a Centennial celebration was planned. The record, with the French version on one side and the English on the other, flew off the shelves. It was the top-selling single of the year, and eventually sold a half million copies.

Another shared experience in 1967 was the vacation to Montreal. Expo '67 was held that year from April to October, and with sixty-two nations involved, the most successful World's Fair of the century. The international exposition was a huge success, drawing visitors from across Canada and around the world. Originally it was expected to bring thirty-five million tourists to the city, but that number finally topped fifty million. It seemed like every Canadian family made the journey that summer, whether it was in the station wagon towing the tent trailer, or on a Boy Scout or Girl Guide trip. After all, it was not only patriotic, it was incredibly fun, with ninety different pavilions from many nations around the world, and its exciting theme park, La Ronde. It featured the incredible Gyrotron, a roller-coaster ride that took travellers into deepest space, and then plunged them into a volcano.

All that, and music: countries sent their best, and their hottest names, including Duke Ellington and Sarah Vaughan from the U.S., along with The Grateful Dead and Jefferson Airplane, and even Tiny Tim. Luciano Pavarotti, Marlene Dietrich, and Maurice Chevalier appeared. Of course, Canadian performers from coast to coast to coast were there every day. Quebec stars such as Diane Dufresne and Gilles Vigneault could be found at the Youth Pavilion's Café Dansant, as well as Leonard Cohen, just beginning his performing career, and still trying to record his debut album. Bobby Curtola, Gordon Lightfoot, The Ugly Ducklings, The Guess Who, and The Travellers played the band shell. Every type of amateur group who could make it played free shows, and with crowds of up to a half million a day through the gates, there was always a full house for the bagpipes, marching bands, and pop groups that had come in, including the Woodstock High School Band from New Brunswick, The Corner Brook Choral Club from Newfoundland, or rockers The Raving Mad from Quebec.

All things Canadian were being celebrated, and music was certainly a big part of it, everywhere. Everywhere except radio, that is. Stations did play "Canada," and it did go to the top of their charts, they couldn't ignore that one. They did, however, ignore almost everything else from the country. Only two songs that year had made the *RPM* Top 10: "Canada," and The Staccatos' "Half Past Midnight." In the year-end Top 100, only "Canada" made the list. During the entire year, only twenty-eight Canadian songs had managed to reach the Top 40 charts, barely half the number from the year before. More and more, radio stations were losing interest in local bands, and paying attention to *Billboard* or *Cashbox* magazines. Consultants were also starting to appear, industry experts who would dictate playlists, almost always American-based companies. Plus, radio stations were making fortunes for owners, with licenses limited to a few per area, and teenagers now huge consumers of music. Program directors were hardly likely to go out on a limb for a local group, let alone one from across the Prairies, when they were unproven. It was a lot easier to program the new hit from The Beatles, or something like "Somebody to Love" by The Jefferson Airplane, because *Billboard* had already said it was a hit. That's even though The Paupers had just blown them off the stage. But it was the day of the *Beaver Bin*, a term DJs coined and used for decades, the name of the round, metallic receptacle where unknown records made by Canadians were thrown, without even a listen.

It wasn't all radio's fault. The record labels in Canada were almost entirely owned by American companies, who had already invested in artists, studios, and promotion machines. The bulk of the work was already done, with publicity about their artists flying across the border on television shows or in teen magazines, and Canadian radio following all the hard work the labels had done getting their acts broken on the *Billboard* charts. The Canadian subsidiaries really just had to fill the orders for Rolling Stones or Herb Alpert or Jimi Hendrix albums and singles. It was much, much harder work creating an interest in Canadian performers, but there were a few that tried, to limited success. The other major issue of the day was the technology. Recording studios in major centers were quickly moving from two to four to eight tracks, the rooms themselves were better designed, and the elite engineers and producers were becoming artists. The most advanced of them, including George Martin and The Beatles, Brian Wilson, and Phil Spector, were using the studio as an overall instrument, experimenting with sound combinations and releasing grand achievements, such as *Sgt. Pepper's Lonely Hearts Club Band* and "Good Vibrations." Canada had nothing like that. Hallmark Studios in Toronto, where "Canada" was recorded, had been considered the best in the city, but it had been built for classical, band, and jazz recordings, and would close in 1968. The famous RCA Victor studio in Montreal had closed in 1958, secretly becoming the plant where Canada's first satellite was built. It was reopened in the 1980s.

It was a vicious circle. Radio wouldn't play Canadian records because, they argued, they didn't sound as good as those made in the U.S. or England. Modern studios weren't being built, because record companies weren't interested in recording Canadian bands. Canadian bands were leaving because record companies and radio weren't interested in them. And things went from bad to worse in 1968, as that year saw only seven Canadian songs reach the national Top 40 the entire year, including Steppenwolf's two U.S.-fueled number ones, "Born to Be Wild" and "Magic Carpet Ride," and a pair by the popular TV folk act, The Irish Rovers, "Whiskey on a Sunday" and "The Unicorn Song." Clearly somebody had to have a little faith in Canadian talent.

Bernie Finkelstein did, at least. After pulling off the coup of getting The Paupers signed in the U.S., he quickly soured on being part of the Albert Grossman team. Another deal was reached, and he sold his interest in the band to Grossman. Finkelstein and his money returned to Toronto. Then he did something so few had been willing to do. He invested the cash back into music. This time, he decided to put together a killer band that would bring something new to the scene, like the new psychedelic sounds that were changing pop. He had in mind a songwriter from Sault Ste. Marie, Keith McKie, and the two of them brought in the right players to create a different sound, including hot guitar player Gene Martynec. The idea was to be inventive and experimental, but not sound British or American. The new group was called Kensington Market, after the Toronto landmark. McKie's lyrics were smart and sophisticated, and musically the group was ready to try surprising sounds. The group's first single, "Mr. John," had a folk-rock feel, an old street sweeper for a lead character, and a mystical, musical breakdown for a bridge, with a recorder, some shimmering, tinkling sound effects, and echoed oohs and ahhs. The next release, "Bobby's Birthday," was even further out, a hard rocker with slashing chords and a wild lead from Martynec. There was lots of distortion, but only some of that was intended. The 45s had been recorded at a local studio and the sound quality was horrendous. You couldn't always blame radio for not getting behind new Canadian bands.

Finkelstein knew the band was good though. They had quickly become Yorkville favorites, thanks to their modern sound that had taken them past the classic Toronto R&B, and the impressive players in the group. But Toronto just couldn't offer the gear and talent to record them properly. Finkelstein pulled a rabbit out of his hat again, landing Kensington Market a major record deal, just as he'd done with The

Paupers. This time the band had some outside help too. Word had gotten to Greenwich Village producer Felix Pappalardi that he had to check the band out. Pappalardi was known as a strong arranger, and had worked on albums by Buffy Sainte-Marie and Ian & Sylvia. Plus, he'd just produced the huge album *Disraeli Gears* by Cream, cowriting "Strange Brew" with Eric Clapton. With Pappalardi's pull and a two-album deal, Kensington Market was signed to Warner Brothers. One more major move was adding Luke Gibson, the former frontman for Luke & The Apostles, to the lineup, giving the group a strong double-guitar front and solid backing vocals.

Pappalardi could play half the orchestra, and his ideas for extra instruments and little touches fit in with the band perfectly. The first album was called *Avenue Road*, after the Yorkville street where the band had debuted, at the Night Owl. The cover was classic Canadiana, the group outside in a snowstorm, in winter coats and scarves, their long hair full of snow. The single "I Would Be the One" sounded great, with rich brass throughout, a mournful trumpet solo following a lead guitar break, and a mysterious, hypnotic backing. It was trippy like the '60s, and this time, you could easily argue that Canadian DJs missed the boat. Kensington Market was never able to find favor outside of Toronto, despite trips to San Francisco and Detroit. The group went further into new sounds by bringing on Moog synthesizer player John Mills-Cockell for their second album, *Aardvark*. It was all to no avail, and with a lot of late-'60s drug issues, the band dissolved shortly after *Aardvark*'s release.

The Mandala (later just Mandala) was another fantastic group that deserved far more attention and success. Originally the house band at the Club Bluenote, the members became The Rogues and then The Five Rogues, stepping out on their own. Featuring the soul singer George Olliver and flashy and fine guitar player Domenic Troiano, they were cut from the same cloth as The Hawks and The Disciples, with a mighty soul sound and supremely talented performers who had learned how to wow a crowd working night after night on the Strip. Olliver did the whole act, including preaching in the instrumental breaks between songs, trumpeting the Five Steps of Soul. They were also one of the very first bands anywhere with strobe lights, and a Mandala show could be a mind-blowing experience. The Mandala were regulars at the Hawk's Nest, played all around Southern Ontario, and then decided to go big instead of staying home, with a trip to Hollywood.

The group got gigs in November of 1966 at the Whiskey a Go Go and then the Hullabaloo. With their gangster pinstripe suits and Soul Crusade act, they soon were packing houses. On their next trip the following spring, they hit the other coast, playing several days in New York at Steve Paul's The Scene, plus guesting at a big Murray the K concert featuring Cream and Wilson Pickett. A spectacular single, "Opportunity," had been recorded at the famous Chess Studios in Chicago, telling the trip of their visit to Hollywood. It has some marvelous Olliver falsetto moments and a sizzling Troiano fuzz-drenched solo. Plans and recordings for a first album, *Soul Crusade*, began, but Olliver wasn't happy, and quit the group to go solo. Somehow they survived the loss of such a tremendous singer, thanks to drafting Toronto's Roy Kenner, not as powerful, but a bit smoother and more tuneful. Atlantic Records had taken note of the band, and one of the label's best producers, Arif Mardin, took over the album sessions. The band made the single "Love-Itis" under his direction, not as raw as "Opportunity," but still exciting. It was a Top 10 hit in Toronto, but only managed to crack the Top 50 nationally, and got nowhere in the U.S. The *Soul Crusade* album was a gem, but a follow-up single, "You Got Me," stalled, and everyone in the group lost heart. Troiano and Kenner found more success, first forming the band Bush, and then joining The James Gang after Joe Walsh quit. Troiano then joined the last strong lineup of The Guess Who in the mid-'70s.

With radio stations showing such little interest in Canadian artists, it was once again a territorial market. If it was hard to get your hometown stations to support you, it was ten times worse getting a station in another part of the country onboard. One of the rare triumphs came from Vancouver group The Collectors. They came together in 1966 as a house band in an R&B club, including Howie Vickers singing, Bill Henderson on guitar, and Clare Lawrence on keyboards, sax, flute, and such. Vancouver's proximity to Los Angeles helped the band very early on, as they were noticed and signed right away to Valiant Records, then loaded with dollars made from The Association's hits. The group hadn't even chosen a name then, but they were in Los Angeles recording with Dave Hassinger, famed engineer for The Rolling Stones, and founder of the Sound Factory studio. Right away they had a hit with "Looking at a Baby," with its psychedelic touches, a bit of flute, and groovy L.A. sound. While it went Top 10 in Vancouver, it did even better at CHUM in Toronto, making it to number four, and to twenty-three on the national charts. A follow-up, "Fisherwoman," did even better nationally, peaking at eighteen.

The group's first and only album came out in 1968, and went even further into jazz and classical sounds, with strings accompanying Lawrence's flute, and large, almost-choral vocals. The album contained the ambitious "What Love (Suite)," which took up the entire second half, a nineteen-minute piece that including everything from jazzy instrumental bits to psychedelic explosions. By now Valiant Records had been bought up by Warner Brothers, and a lot of effort was spent trying to find a hip audience for The Collectors in the rock ballroom circuit. All for naught, but not all for nothing; singer Howie Vickers quit after the band did a film soundtrack back in Vancouver, and the rest reformed under the name Chilliwack, becoming one of B.C.'s most loved and successful groups.

Montreal's The Haunted was another group getting big airplay away from home. After winning a battle of the bands, they took the prize of a recording session and made a killer single, "1-2-5," in 1966. A garage band classic, it features a nasty guitar solo, pulsing Farfisa organ, and bluesy harmonica, and immediately shot up the Canadian charts, ending up at number twenty-three, while of course a huge local hit in Montreal. The original version was very raw as well, covered in fuzz and one step below "Louie Louie" in clarity. That led to an album deal for Trans-World, but lead singer Bob Burgess had jumped ship, replaced by Johnny Monk. A new version of "1-2-5" was recorded, much cleaner and with far better sound, with Monk certainly a better singer (or at least he could be heard on this record). Collectors, of course, prefer the rawer original. Either way, it's now incredibly rare, and The Haunted's 1967 self-titled album is considered the Holy Grail of garage rock in Canada, usually selling for four figures when it shows up, and all of their records are highly collectible. Wonderfully, the group's final single in 1968 was a French-language version of Jimi Hendrix's "Purple Haze," "Vapeur Mauve," just as violent and a little scary as well. The Haunted remained a terrifically popular club band until breaking up in 1971.

Francophone Montreal's music scene had a different problem with radio stations, and all media. The province was bombarded by English culture, both from the rest of Canada, and the U.S. Many feared their language was being eroded thanks to the steady stream of pop culture, in movies, TV, magazines, as well as radio. The biggest stations played the same diet of Beatles, Motown, and California groups that the rest of Canada was hearing, at a time when much of Montreal was still working primarily in the English language as well, despite the majority of French speakers. Because Francophones supported their artists so well, there was still lots of interest in the chansonnier and French-language pop singers, but it was hard to compete against the big rock 'n' roll stars. Especially when they seemed so glamorous on TV shows such as *Ed Sullivan*, which made a special trip to Expo '67 to broadcast live, featuring Petula Clark, The Seekers, and The Supremes singing their new hit, "The Happening."

French Canadians loved rock 'n' roll, but it took until the mid-'60s to develop their own twist. It came from the ranks of the chansonniers. Robert Charlebois had started out as a folk singer, using the poetic and intellectual style that had become popular in the province for his 1965 debut, as well as a touch of theatrics. Everything went head over heels when he visited California in the middle of the Summer of Love. After soaking up the psychedelic ideas, he came back a changed performer, and became the single-most important figure in modern Quebec rock. In came an electric guitar, lots of theater, costumes, humor, and, most radically, he often sang in *joual*, the more common language of working-class Montreal rather than the Parisienne French of the chansonniers. He was backed by a jazz-rock group, and performed with a banshee of a vocalist named Louise Forestier. Their 1968 album, *Robert Charlebois/Louise Forestier*, was the game-changer. It included the landmark hit "Lindberg," which perfectly summed up what was happening to Quebec music: it started out slowly with gentle guitar chords, and built into a dramatic, theatrical rocker, Forestier even imitating a siren with her voice. French radio stations abandoned the local groups who were still doing covers of American pop hits, and instead seized upon "Lindberg," and more original Quebec pop that followed in its wake.

Michel Pagliaro started his career in the mid-'60s as a pop balladeer. As lead singer of the group Les Chanceliers, he also scored a Quebec hit in 1966 with "Le p'tit popy," a sweet little French-language cover of James and Bobby Purify's "I'm Your Puppet." He even had a hit with that song from France with the melody that had so intrigued Paul Anka, "Comme d'habitude," in a big orchestral arrangement that predated Sinatra's "My Way." But Charlebois's dramatic intervention in Quebec rock changed Pagliaro's direction, and soon he was writing his own songs in French, and with a full, hard-rock sound. "J'ai marche pour une nation," a 1969 release, had a heavy organ, some talk about a revolution, and showed that he was going to be a great rock vocalist. The '70s would see him become a star not only in Quebec, but across English Canada as well.

Charlebois had changed Quebec, but English Canada still needed stars to break through, and not just the ones who had moved to the U.S. The problem with that kind of star is that the money didn't flow north. Even if Neil Young had mailed everything he had back to his mother in Winnipeg, that wasn't the real money. The publishers, record labels, studios, managers, venues, roadies, ticket printers, instrument rental companies, truck drivers, all of the many people making money off the growing success of Young and Buffalo Springfield, Joni Mitchell, Paul Anka, Ian & Sylvia, Steppenwolf, and the rest were all in the U.S. What Canada's almost nonexistent music industry needed was more people like Bernie Finkelstein, willing to invest money in some Canadians, in Canada. And so it was that the major break came not from local business, but rather an American company, and actually the quintessential American company. Canadian musicians found out that things go better with Coke.

Jack Richardson was a former bass player for a '50s radio and dance band who had become an ad executive in Toronto. He did a lot of jingle work, and one of his major clients for TV and radio was Coca-Cola. Richardson had ideas for connecting Coke with the youth market, and went to Coke with the idea of having rock 'n' roll bands do commercials for the company. He created the youth radio advertising campaign, and soon Canadian acts were supplementing their meager paydays with plugs for every teen's favorite soda, including Bobby Curtola, David Clayton-Thomas, Robbie Lane, Jack London, The Collectors, and most significantly, The Guess Who.

Then Richardson had a bolder idea. He approached Coca-Cola with a plan to make an album. Coke could offer it up to their customers, if

Ottawa's teen idol Paul Anka had the biggest rock 'n' roll hit of the '50s, with "Diana." (Michael Ochs Archives/Getty Images)

TOP: Good friends Conway Twitty (left) and Ronnie Hawkins (right), with Tony Guilbert, who, in the late 1950s, managed The Brass Rail Tavern in London, Ontario, one of the very first places both stars played in Canada. (© John Rowlands)

LEFT: David Clayton-Thomas started as Ronnie Hawkins's protégé and became the voice of Blood, Sweat & Tears. (© John Rowlands)

Gordon Lightfoot's songs helped establish Canada as a hotbed for singer-songwriters. (© John Rowlands)

TOP: Aw shucks! Leonard Cohen gets some corn from his backyard garden in Montreal. (© John Rowlands)

LEFT: Yorkville Village buddies Bruce Cockburn and Murray McLauchlan, classic Canadian folkies. (© John Rowlands)

Anne Murray had radio's most-played song of the year with 1970's "Snowbird." (© John Rowlands)

Hey, who's that with Gino Vanelli? Captain Fantastic gets pithy as he meets the golden-voiced singer backstage. (© John Rowlands)

Neil Young got his start in the teen clubs of Winnipeg, his schooling
in Toronto's Yorkville, and took a hearse to L.A. to find Stephen Stills.
(Photo by Rob Verhorst/Redferns/Getty Images)

Geddy Lee of Rush. The prog titans' album-sized epics have inspired three generations of air drummers and guitarists. (Photo by Timothy Hiatt/ Getty Images)

they collected ten bottle-cap liners and sent in a dollar. Coke went for it, and Richardson set up his deal. He approached two of the country's more popular groups from outside Toronto. Ottawa's The Staccatos had a recent big hit with "Half Past Midnight," and agreed to do one half of the record. The Guess Who was still considered a top Canadian group, even though none of their later singles had matched the 1965 success of "Shakin' All Over." They jumped at the chance to record the other album side.

Richardson took care of the rest himself. He'd gained lots of experience as a music producer doing jingles, and he was a well-trained musician. He had also worked quite a bit with Phil Ramone, who was a good friend, and one of the top engineers in New York, where he co-owned the highly respected A&R Studios. Richardson ended up producing both sides of the record for The Guess Who and The Staccatos, and called it *A Wild Pair*. Richardson had also recently formed a company outside of the ad agency with some other partners, called Nimbus 9, and *A Wild Pair* became its first record, and a major hit. Kids went crazy for it, saving up their ten bottle caps, and mailing them in by the thousands. In the end, over eighty thousand copies were sent out, well over the number needed for Gold record status in Canada, although it didn't count since it was a promotional offering. Obviously something was going on with Canadian music and young people, something that record companies and radio were missing.

Life after "Shakin' All Over" had brought only disappointment to The Guess Who. Returning from the U.S. with nothing to show for the chart success there, they knew that at least Winnipeg still thought them stars. But the follow-up singles failed to match the group's number one hit, and more and more radio stations were ignoring the latest 45s, consigning them to the Beaver Bin. They made an ill-fated trip to London, convinced there were concerts booked and a record deal ready. They got there only to find out it was a scam, and a trip ended up putting them in serious debt. Only a weekly gig as the house band on the national CBC-TV pop show *Let's Go* got them back on financial track. It also gave them a wonderful opportunity. Initially they were asked to play cover versions of the big hits of the week, songs from The Doors to The Beatles to The Association. But they convinced the producer to let them play some of the new songs Randy Bachman and Burton Cummings had been writing. Soon Canadians were hearing rockers such as "No Time," and the new ballad, "These Eyes." One of those Canadians who caught "These Eyes" was Jack Richardson, very much interested in the group's fortunes.

Richardson was so taken by the Canadian pop scene, he decided his future was with Nimbus 9 instead of in advertising. "There was such a tremendous pool of talent and nobody knew who they were," said Richardson. "We decided that we would take a flyer and see if we couldn't do something about that. So I left (ad agency McCann-Erickson) and talked to The Guess Who, who decided that they would come with us. We bought The Guess Who's contract out from Quality Records for a thousand dollars." This is the Canadian equivalent of Sun Records owner Sam Phillips selling Elvis's contract to RCA for $35,000. Phillips might have even gotten a better deal than Quality.

The next step was to make a full album, with Richardson producing the band, using Toronto's "best" studio. "We did the first session at Hallmark," explained Richardson,

> And when I brought it back to the office and listened to it I was not happy with it at all. I told my partners I wanted to redo it, and they said, gee we spent this much money for it, you know. The group had decided pretty much the same thing, they were unhappy. They flew into Toronto, and I said, guys, I want to scrap the first session and do it again. They said, that's why we came down, wonderful. We finally

decided we would go for broke. I called Phil (Ramone), and Phil said sure, come on down. We decided we would take them to New York and do an album.

Richardson actually mortgaged his own home to finance the New York sessions, an unbelievable act of faith that still amazes Burton Cummings. "It's kind of a Cinderella story," he said. "We'd had a lot of back-to-back heartbreak before. I joined the band in January of 1966, and over the next three years we had about fifteen singles, all of which really kind of bombed." But now Richardson had gotten them a U.S. record deal with RCA, and a new album made in one of the very best studios. Plus, there was "These Eyes," which a lot of people thought would be a big single. Except the band. "Oh no, absolutely not," Cummings confirmed. "We fought tooth and nail against it as a single, because in '68, '69, everybody wanted to be Led Zeppelin. We absolutely didn't want a ballad." Wiser heads prevailed. The song was sent to Canadian radio in December of 1968, making the Top 10 on the national chart, including number one in Toronto. When it came out in the U.S. in April of 1969, it followed the same path, settling at number six on *Billboard*, and earning a Gold single.

Then The Guess Who and Jack Richardson did something revolutionary: they went home, to Canada, even with a big hit in the U.S., and the world opening up for them. The band kept its base of operations in Winnipeg, and Richardson and Nimbus 9 set up shop in Yorkville, eventually building a world-class studio in downtown Toronto. Richardson produced every Guess Who album until the band broke up in the mid-'70s, and produced Poco, Alice Cooper, Bob Seger's "Night Moves," and more. Ringo, Neil Young, and Dr. John used the facilities. A new young producer, Bob Ezrin, came on board, and brought Peter Gabriel to Toronto to make his first solo album there, and became Pink Floyd's producer for *The Wall*. The Guess Who and Jack

Richardson had changed the game for Canadian music, reversing the money flow.

Canadian radio now had to take The Guess Who seriously, but a bigger battle was brewing. After the near-disappearance of Canadian artists on radio in 1967 and 1968, complaints had started to build. There had been calls all through the 1960s for some sort of quota to be placed on radio stations, that a certain percentage of the music they played should be Canadian. Radio howled with disaster scenarios, predicting their listeners would leave them overnight. The Board of Broadcast Governors, which oversaw radio in the country at the time, nixed the idea as unworkable. But *RPM* magazine, with Walt Grealis and Stan Klees, loudly championed the idea of a Canadian quota. In 1968, the BBG was replaced by the Canadian Radio and Television Commission, and that board was much more interested in the idea. The new commission was headed by Pierre Juneau, formerly with the National Film Board, a successful funding program that saw tax dollars used to help producers of Canadian movies. Juneau listened closely to Grealis's ideas, looked at studies of legislated radio, and heard the horror stories from musicians trying to get their music played. Meanwhile, radio at first ignored such talk, or scoffed. When it became stronger, stations and disc jockeys reacted with disdain, saying few Canadian records were up to American standards, and that it wasn't their job to spoon-feed Canadian artists.

When the talk became serious in 1969, radio acted with too little too late, offering a plan to develop and encourage Canadian talent, but it collapsed after a few months of little action. In 1970, Juneau shocked them all with proposed legislation that would require every station in the country to play a minimum of 30 percent Canadian Content, or CanCon for short. After angry and desperate hearings, the CRTC announced that the new regulations would go ahead in January of 1971. Radio predicted a disaster. Supporters predicted a new dawn for the Canadian music industry, which is exactly what happened.

Where there was a void, Canadian talent stepped up to fill the need. Record companies were formed, signing all those groups and singers across the country that had previously been missing out. The big American companies got in on the act quickly, realizing the potential. Once audiences heard all the Canadian records on the radio, they reacted as some had predicted they would: they not only liked it, they bought it. Record stores in Winnipeg started putting Canadians on display in the windows. Ben Goldstein, the owner of Goldstein's Music Centre in Saint John, N.B., said his Canadian sales had jumped 20 percent. The Treble Clef in Ottawa thought it might be 30 percent. And when Sam Sniderman, owner of the most famous record store in the country, Sam's on Yonge Street in Toronto, declared that sales of Canadian product had gone up 25 percent, it was official, Canada's music scene had a bright future. Now records made in local centers such as Montreal, Vancouver, or Toronto would be available everywhere. "If it's selling well in Toronto, we'll have it here," declared Woolco in St. John's, Newfoundland.

Canada now had its own roster of stars, some of them with hits in the U.S. and overseas, many others without. Much like the CPR's national railroad in 1885, CanCon legislation had opened up the country, only this time it was music flying across the many miles. World-class studios were built, booking agencies started, and national touring opportunities were developed, as bands such as April Wine and The Stampeders started coming to play the hockey rink in your hometown. The radio stations continued to make fortunes, so their continued complaints about having to play Canadian music were really just sour grapes at that point, as they cued up the latest from Edward Bear, Anne Murray, or The Poppy Family. The listeners loved it all, and a golden age of Canadian pop music began.

SIGNS

Canada's Hit-Making Machine Revs Up in the Early '70s

The Guess Who had become Canada's favorite band by 1969. The smash hit "These Eyes" sold a million copies worldwide, and the band was chafing at the bit to showcase its rock side. The members had been happy with the success of the song, but were wary of being considered a pop band. The trouble was, that's exactly what the record company wanted. "We had 'These Eyes' and it was a monster hit, and it was a ballad," explained Burton Cummings. "Don Burkheimer, the guy who signed us to RCA, took us to the Carnegie Deli in New York, just Randy (Bachman) and me, not the other two. He said, 'Please give us one more ballad, something in the vein of "These Eyes."' Of course, we rebelled; we said, 'We're a rock 'n' roll band, we don't want to have ballads, come on!' Well, he convinced us. Randy and I wrote 'Laughing' specifically as a follow-up to 'These Eyes.'" The suits were right this time, and "Laughing" gave them another Top 10 hit in the States, plus the band's first Canadian number one since "Shakin' All Over" back in '65. Only this time there was no question mark after the band's name, and no questioning its star status.

Even the song's B-side was a hit on both sides of the border. "Un-dun," an easy-going jazzy number written by Bachman, had disc jock-eys flipping the record over to satisfy the growing demand for Guess Who songs. Again, it wasn't a rock song. The group did have one they thought would be a big hit, but there was a problem: it sounded ter-rible. The song was "No Time," which had been the lead-off track on the recent *Canned Wheat* album. The band and Jack Richardson were in the middle of a fight with RCA over where they could record. Now that they were full-fledged signees with the U.S. company, they had to abide by the RCA rules. "We were forced to do it in the old, ancient RCA Studios where Bing Crosby had recorded," says Cummings about the *Canned Wheat* album, "and it was just antiquated. It was one of those corporate things contractually we had to do." But they didn't want to give up on the song. "We all agreed," says Bachman, "and Jack Richard-son thought 'No Time' had the potential of a hit song: guitar riffs, good melody, sing-along chorus, harmonies."

The band went into a new RCA studio in Chicago, and this time shortened the song for radio, toughened it up, and got a much better vocal sound. Plus, it had a killer lead guitar solo at the top. "I consciously make every song have a recognizable intro," states Bachman, an ardent student of hit records. "I did study the best: Elvis, Chuck Berry, The Beatles. Every one of their hits, bam! You know what it is before they even get to the chorus, which is what the title is usually, or where it's sung for the first time." Professor Bachman was proven correct by the vote of the people, who pushed "No Time" to number one again in Canada, and number five in the U.S.

With its rock band credentials now solidly in place, The Guess Who could have the say over the next single. For Canadian rock music history, what came next was the equivalent of The Shot Heard 'Round the World. Only it was more of a twang. Randy Bachman had just broken a string.

SIGNS

It happened at a gig at the Bingeman Park Roller Rink, in Kitchener, Ontario, in August of 1969. The band had been doing lots of shows in the U.S. thanks to the recent hits, but that usually meant half a dozen tunes in a show featuring two or three other groups. Back in Canada, they had the full night to themselves, and the crowd ready to dance. They were enjoying jamming a bit, when "I broke a string, and Burton Cummings announced that the band would be taking a break while I changed my string," Bachman remembered. "I had no guitar tech, spare guitar, or even a tuner, so I put on the low E string, went over to Burton's electric piano, kneeled down in the dark, and started tuning my guitar to his piano." With the tuning almost done, Bachman started playing something off the top of his head, just a little riff like all guitar players do. Only this time, the muse gave him the ultimate gift, the riff of riffs, something Bachman swore he'd never dreamed of before. "No, no, no," he said in 2010, "I had not written the riff before. I started to play the riff, and heads in the audience jerked around. I stood up and kept playing the riff. The band, sensing something going on from my head motions, came onstage and we started to jam that riff. Burton came up and played a flute solo, a harmonica solo, and then started singing the opening line."

Cummings had spent a lot of time in the U.S. since "These Eyes," and had grown tired of all the negative situations he was seeing in the country. There were continuing race problems, the Vietnam War, riots, protests, and poverty. It was kids versus their parents in the Generation Gap, and Cummings basically had been picking up bad vibrations when traveling in the U.S. of late. Whether there was a woman involved, Cummings has never divulged that part of the story, but that night in Kitchener, when it was his turn to sing something into the microphone during the lengthy jam, he came up with "American woman, stay away from me." Someone in the audience was taping that night, and the band got ahold of the bootleg. They presented it to Jack Richardson,

Cummings came up with the American-themed lyrics, and the band's next single got recorded along with the entire *American Woman* album in just two weeks.

Released in the spring of 1970, "American Woman" stormed on to North American radio, during one of the most fertile periods of pop music. Simon and Garfunkel had just released the monumental "Bridge Over Troubled Water." The Beatles answered with "Let It Be." Fresh off their Woodstock success, Sly & The Family Stone topped the charts with "Thank U (Falettinme Be Mice Elf Agin)," and a new group had exploded over at Motown, The Jackson 5. The band's second straight number one single, "ABC," had just topped the charts for two weeks in late April–early May of 1970, when "American Woman" knocked it off, and stayed at number one for three weeks itself. The song would sell two million copies, and be the third-biggest hit of the entire year. The *American Woman* album hit number nine on the *Billboard* chart and eventually sold two million copies as well. Home and abroad, The Guess Who were now in the top echelon, one of the highest-selling groups of the year. Once again, DJs flipped the single over, and "No Sugar Tonight" made the record a rare two-sided number one.

It's easy to be impressed by the success of The Guess Who outside of Canada. After all, it had been six years since a Canadian had topped the *Billboard* charts, and that was Lorne Greene's "Ringo." Far more impressive, though, is the uphill battle the band had fought. Since 1961, Bachman, Gary Peterson, and then Jim Kale had been playing together out of Winnipeg. On the one hand, they had always been told they were good; the best band in Winnipeg, or in Canada. On the other, they'd received no support from radio much of the time, even hostility, and been told they just couldn't match up to the groups from England and the U.S. Now, The Guess Who were pushing them all off the charts. Thanks to a lack of top professional management early on, they'd been suckered and swindled by fast talkers in New York and London. Now, the White House called and asked them to come and play, as they were Tricia Nixon's favorite band. Most importantly, The Guess Who had broken an invisible barrier, a perception that Canadian-based bands would never match up. Once that had been proven false, Canadian hits went from a trickle to a deluge overnight.

Randy Bachman had reached his goal, too, to be at number one. Since he'd been an early teen, he had wanted nothing else, and had worked harder than anyone else for a decade. He'd faithfully studied guitar under Lenny Breau. He'd learned all the tricks of the songwriters and guitar players from England he admired. He'd spent two years doing a TV show mimicking U.S and British bands, to pay off debts and get yet another chance at the top. He'd driven countless thousands of miles across the Prairies and east, to play and pay dues. He'd stayed clean and sober, and even played the game with the record company, writing a ballad when they wanted a ballad. Now, it had all happened for him, bigger than he'd probably ever hoped. So what did he do? He quit. But, he'd be back.

Rock 'n' roll and pop music were gaining much of the headlines in 1969, but it could be argued it wasn't the favorite music in Canada. Pop's audience was still mostly under thirty. Adults, and a good number of the youngsters, liked their folk music, and country, too. On TV, folk was a big draw. You could join the Carleton Show Band each week for Irish tunes on the long-running *The Pig and Whistle* show. Or, you could head to the Maritimes, and watch *Singalong Jubilee*, the Halifax-based show that presented a more modern folk, with newly written songs by the large cast, or covers of popular numbers from the likes of John Denver or Kris Kristofferson.

Over the '60s, *Singalong Jubilee* had assembled a top-notch group of musicians and singers, some of whom were featured on cast albums or had even gotten their own singles and LPs. There was bandleader and producer Brian Ahern, songwriter Ken Tobias, and sisters Catherine and Patrician Anne McKinnon, and several featured performers each season. The cast evolved over the years, especially the large group of singers. One who joined in 1966 after failing to impress on an earlier audition was a fresh-faced singer from Springhill, Nova Scotia, who had just started working as a schoolteacher. Anne Murray had a golden voice, sang with a smile, and had a great image. Her style was folk songs, with some country, and an equal amount of pop. She sang barefoot, wore casual clothes, and appealed to all sorts of fans. She had become a breakout artist on the program, the biggest star each week, and had started a recording career. A 1968 album *What About Me* included the hit title song written by Scott McKenzie, Joni Mitchell's "Both Sides Now," Tobias's "Some Birds," and a couple from producer Ahern. It was successful enough for Capitol Records to sign her the next year, as the label's Paul White was expanding the Canadian roster.

When *Singalong Jubilee* was in TV production in Halifax, several of the crew also did double-duty on the highly successful *Don Messer's Jubilee*, which featured old-time fiddling, step dancing, and Irish songs. It was often the top-rated TV show in the country that didn't involve a puck. On one of the shows, an unknown songwriter appeared from Prince Edward Island. Messer had liked his music, but was a little leery of his appearance. He had some scarring around one eye from polio as a child, something that had afflicted Neil Young and Joni Mitchell as well. The solution was to give him an eye patch, even though he could see perfectly fine from that eye. It was hastily cut from a bolt of black velvet by the makeup department, and the singer was made to wear it.

Gene MacLellan's TV debut was a huge hit, at least in the studio. Messer's star singer, Marg Osburne, turned and said, "a star is born." Producers and stage crew had the same idea, and it was quickly suggested that MacLellan join the *Singalong* bunch the next day, as they were headed for a remote broadcast at a nearby army base. He was soon invited to join the show as a featured performer. He had several of his own songs that knocked everybody out, but the one that they all loved was called "Snowbird." It was, according to MacLellan, only the second song he had ever written. A shy and incredibly humble man, MacLellan had been working as an orderly in a mental hospital in P.E.I. before, until he decided to get back into music full time. He didn't bother to tell anybody about it then, but it was his second go-around in the business, as he'd been one of the founders of the Toronto group The Consuls back in 1956, and even used to play with Robbie Robertson just before he joined up with The Hawks. It's a small country, Canada.

It didn't take long for Anne Murray to hear MacLellan's song and decide she needed to record it. Brian Ahern thought so, too, and for Murray's next album, the first for Capitol, she did "Snowbird," and another of MacLellan's, "Bidin' My Time." When it came time to pick the all-important first single, they turned to the man who had broken The Beatles in North America, Paul White. "At the end of the session, there was Brian, her producer, Anne, and myself," White remembers,

> at three o'clock in the morning sitting in the studio, and they said, okay you're the wizard here, pick a single. We'd got it down to "Snowbird," "Bidin' My Time," and (folk singer Eric Anderson's) "Thirsty Boots." And I was still into the folk thing at the time, and I said, oh it's obviously "Thirsty Boots." We released "Thirsty Boots" and sold about thirty copies, and then we came out with a second single, and the A side was "Bidin' My Time," which was by Gene, and we put "Snowbird" on the B-side. A guy named Happy Wilson, working for our publishing company in the States, was the guy who fell in love with "Snowbird," and pushed it like crazy. He got it on the country charts first, and then it went pop, and very, very big.

Very, very, very big: "Snowbird" made Murray Canada's biggest solo star, and that was just the beginning. It was number one everywhere in Canada, and in the U.S. it was close to perfect as a crossover hit. It made the Top 10 in both country and pop, and number one on the Adult Contemporary chart. It did well in England, and immediately started to attract cover versions. Lynn Anderson, sailing high herself with the hit "Rose Garden," was one of the first, followed soon by Loretta Lynn. It became Elvis's favorite song, and he recorded it the next year. So did Bing Crosby and Count Basie and that old Nova Scotia country singer himself, Hank Snow. As the numbers started to add up, records and achievements came to both Murray and MacLellan. The single went Gold in the U.S., the first time a Canadian woman had achieved that. And with all that airplay on all the different radio formats, plus all the cover versions, "Snowbird" was everywhere. The head of BMI (Broadcast Music Inc., the organization that collects royalties for composers) made a special trip to Toronto to present an award to MacLellan as the first Canadian to write a song that received a million broadcast performances in the United States alone. He also announced that "Snowbird" had become the most widely played song in the world for that year. In his typically humble way, MacLellan chose not to go to the ceremony, staying home in the Maritimes while his parents accepted the honors.

Murray had more plans for MacLellan's songs. He had another one called "Put Your Hand in the Hand" that seemed like another surefire hit. Murray recorded it, and fully intended it to be a follow-up single. "Oh absolutely, and Brian (Ahern) did, too," confirms Murray. But Capitol Records in the U.S. was now running things, and nixed the idea. "Ya, they said it wasn't representative of me, it didn't sound enough like 'Snowbird,' or, I don't know, it was stupid, whatever they said was dumb, in my opinion. It didn't sound like an Anne Murray song . . . well, what the hell was an Anne Murray song? I'd just barely got started. It seemed to me at the time to be so stupid. And it does today, too." Instead, Capitol released the lovely "Sing High, Sing Low," which made it to number one on the Canadian country charts, and number four in pop. But in the U.S., it was a flop, only fifty-three in country and eighty-three in pop.

Meanwhile, word got around the still very-small music industry in Canada about Capitol's blunder. One of the people who heard about it was Toronto booking agent and artist manager Tom Wilson. In another classic, everybody-knows-everybody moment in Canadian music, Wilson had grown up with MacLellan, had even been in his very first band in the 1950s, had been around for all the jams in Gene's parents' garage as The Consuls were formed, and eventually joined up with Little Caesar and The Consuls after MacLellan had left. Wilson knew what almost everyone else knew, that "Put Your Hand in the Hand" had something magical. He also was managing a new band that could use a hit, Toronto's Ocean. "We just thought it was a great song," says Wilson, who was hearing everything Canadian writers had to offer around then. "I'm seeing two bands every day, getting material in every day, I got to listen to a lot of stuff, and I remember Gene's stuff was good. The hits come from the craziest places." Like your old best friend.

Since Wilson was also an agent, he had some good connections, and used them at the perfect time for Ocean. "I phoned Three Dog Night's manager, another friend of mine," remembers Wilson. "I said I needed a date in the States, what do you have going on that I can get on? He set me up with this show with Steppenwolf and John Mayall, at the L.A. Forum. We were first on the bill, and did (Crosby, Stills & Nash's) "Helplessly Hoping" about three numbers in, a cappella, and it brought the house down. And of course, "Put Your Hand in the Hand" got roars, so it was a fabulous night." The gospel-themed song had come along at a perfect time, when Jesus had all of a sudden become hip. The rock opera *Jesus Christ Superstar* had just come out on album, the play *Godspell* would follow within months, and a new young Christian movement was growing, with acoustic guitars, jeans, and long hair starting to show up in the more liberal churches. There was a group spreading across North America called the Jesus People, and they adopted "Put Your Hand in the Hand" as an unofficial anthem. "We threw it out there, worked radio stations, and hooked it up in the States, and boom, away it went," recalls Wilson. "It broke pretty quickly, L.A. right away. It went up really quickly." It settled finally at number two on the pop charts, an even bigger hit than "Snowbird" for MacLellan.

But sadly, not for Anne Murray; don't feel too bad for her though. One misstep did nothing to stop her momentum, as she quickly became one of the most popular performers on television. Her years on *Singalong Jubilee* stood her well, as the U.S. cameras loved her too. She became a frequent performer on *The Glen Campbell Goodtime Hour*, appearing more times than any other guest on the program, and had a series of hit singles and albums with Campbell as well. She continued to cross back and forth across airplay lines; her version of Gordon Lightfoot's "Cotton Jenny" was a country hit, while her reading of the Kenny Loggins number "Danny's Song" was number one in adult contemporary, seven in pop, and ten in country. That was in the U.S.; in Canada it was number one on all three charts. She took The Beatles back to the Top 10 with "You Won't See Me," and The Everly Brothers, too, with "Walk Right Back." Her biggest-seller came in 1978, the number one pop hit in all of North America, "You Needed Me." Brian Ahern did fine as well. He produced Murray until the mid-'70s, until another singer took his attention. In another classic, everybody-knows-everybody moment in Canadian music (I've said that before), the same woman who introduced The Hawks to Bob Dylan, and managed Leonard Cohen, Mary Martin, was now working for Warner Brothers in the U.S. They had just signed Emmylou Harris as a solo artist, and Martin flew Ahern out to see her perform. He signed on as producer, and helped put together her group, The Hot Band. Ahern produced Harris's great run of '70s and '80s albums, and the couple were married from 1977 to 1984. Ahern also built the famous Enactron Truck, a mobile studio that has been responsible for some forty Gold and Platinum albums, for work with Bob Dylan, Bette Midler, Barbra Streisand, Black Sabbath, Roy Orbison, Willie Nelson, and many others. The Halifax-born Ahern started working with Harris again in the 2000s, and produced the Grammy-winning Harris/Rodney Crowell 2013 album *Old Yellow Moon*.

Another old associate of Ahern's was Ken Tobias, from Saint John, New Brunswick. Tobias had gone to Halifax in the mid-'60s and ended up playing with Ahern in the band The Badd Cedes. Ahern was also music director for *Singalong Jubilee*, and Tobias was selected for the show, eventually doing some of his own material and performing duets with Anne Murray. He was good friends with them all, including Gene MacLellan. His next career move took him to Montreal, and that's where Righteous Brother Bill Medley spotted him. Tobias was signed up to The Righteous Brothers' company, and moved to Los Angeles, where he continued to write and get his songs published, while preparing to record his first album. Unbeknownst to him, Canadian group The Bells, originally from Montreal, had heard one of his demos, and decided to follow up their 1970 Canadian hit "Fly Little White Dove, Fly" with his song.

"When I was in Hollywood, I got a call from (BMI, the royalties organization), and they said, 'Did you know your song "Stay Awhile" is climbing the Billboard charts?'" Tobias remembers.

> And I said, no I didn't, and they said, "Yes, it's up there with another Canadian, neck-and-neck, they're both going up together, it's called 'Put Your Hand in the Hand,'" and I said, that's Gene! Our songs were pounding at each other neck and neck, and finally his got to number one (in *Cashbox*

magazine, number two in *Billboard*) and mine got to number seven. They said to me, "Would you like some money?" And I said, sure, can I have three hundred bucks? And they said, "How about three thousand?" I went what? Then I realized everything I had been seeking out, this was it. I had a hit song on *Billboard*, they were going to give me money, it was amazing.

The Bells' version of "Stay Awhile" sold over four million copies around the world. Tobias would have a series of hit songs in Canada in the '70s and '80s, including 1973's "I Just Want to Make Music."

Ottawa's The Staccatos had to make a big decision in 1968. They had been part of a huge success with Jack Richardson's *Coke* album, *A Wild Pair*, and Richardson asked the group to join him on the new Nimbus 9 label, along with The Guess Who. But the band already had a deal with Capitol Records, where they had just had a big hit, "Half Past Midnight," plus it was the home of The Beatles, so it seemed like a safer bet. Yet they followed that conservative decision with a decidedly risky one. "It was a strange thing," remembered lead singer Les Emmerson. "We were voted the number one band in Canada as The Staccatos. Then we go and change our name. Not a great business move." The new name came from one of the group's songs, "Five Man Electrical Band." But an album of the same name failed to give them any more hits, and by the end of 1969, the Capitol deal was done.

Emmerson had a song he had been working on that he felt was a surefire hit. It came from a couple of true stories, which were mixed together to create the ultimate Generation Gap anthem. "There was a friend of mine, and his girlfriend," explained Emmerson. "Both were refused jobs even though they were quite capable, just because of the way they looked. I got mad at that, thinking that shouldn't have anything to do with it. It wasn't as if they were dealing with the public. They were very smart people." Their tale inspired "Signs," the 1971 hit that made it to number four in Canada, and even higher elsewhere, number three in the U.S., and number one in Australia. There were lots out there who identified with the "long-haired freaky people" who couldn't get a job interview. As for the other big line in the song, "You gotta have a membership card to get inside," it "came from this bar we were playing," said Emmerson. "It was a golf and country club. What you did was you paid a dollar or two at the door and you became a member for the night. That was the loophole of how people were let in." For Emmerson, it was a sign that the band was going to be successful after all. The U.S. band Tesla revived the song in 1990, and Emmerson still leads a version of the group in Ottawa, doing fun gigs and charity projects.

So many bands had been toiling away through the '60s in Canada, that when the good times finally arrived in 1970, it was like a dam bursting. Most were battle-hardened veterans, who could play, sing, and might even have a bunch of original songs ready for all the record labels now looking for talent. The Stampeders were certainly no rookies, having been together since 1965. They were formed in Calgary, and even though they had nothing to do with the world-famous rodeo of that name, or the football Stampeders for that matter, they took the name as a business move. "We had an investor that wanted us to use that name, but we weren't keen on it," is how original member Rich Dodson remembered it. "And he never came up with the cash." But the band stuck with it, even after moving to Toronto in 1966, for good. They were the oddest bunch in Yorkville, playing up to the Western image, with cowboy hats, boots, and a cool brand of yellow jeans from the Prairie company Monarch Wear, called Tee-Kays.

The group had a good Yorkville following and toured quite extensively, to Montreal and back west, but three singles in from 1967 to 1969 did little for them. Eventually half the six-piece group quit, leaving the trio of Dodson, Kim Berly, and Ronnie King. The first single under that lineup, 1971s "Carry Me," was an instant national smash, number two in pop, but it was another track from the group's first album, *Against the Grain*, that went over the top. Dodson had written a number that looked back on everything that had happened to them since '65. "It was just a summation of us coming down from out west," he said. "Doing our country-rock thing in the city of Toronto, a meld of all those things. I guess the lick came to me, a funky lick, and we put it together and started playing it at gigs, and got really good reaction to it."

Funky, but country, too; ready to record the song, Dodson came up with the missing ingredient. "On the way to the studio, I thought the lick might be really cool with a banjo, so I rented one at Long & McQuade and used it on the session." Those were the days when country was country and rock was rock, though, and there were concerns that "Sweet City Woman" would be rejected because of the banjo. "That was the reaction of the record company," confirmed Dodson. "No way is anybody going to play a banjo in top pop radio, but it just took off like a rocket." The song followed and bettered "Carry Me" nationally, making it to the top of the pop charts, and number one at country radio, too. It broke the no-banjo rule at American radio as well, becoming a number eight hit in the U.S. It was awarded a Gold record and sold a million copies, plus the group won four Juno Awards, including Best Single, Group, and Composer for Dodson. Oh yes, the awards were by then called the Junos, named after Pierre Juneau, the CRTC head who had ushered in the CanCon era.

The Stampeders were touring monsters. With the explosion of the music industry came opportunities to tour nationally, since bands now had hits from one end of the country to the other. P.A.s had become better, and groups could load up a bus, and hit every decent-sized town along the Trans-Canada Highway that had a hockey rink. The boards went down on the ice, the stage went up between the penalty boxes, and a couple of thousand kids would see their first big-name rock show.

SIGNS

There's an entire generation that came of age in the early '70s who saw either The Stampeders or April Wine at their first real rock concert, and just as likely caught James Leroy and Denim or Ian Thomas as the opening act. Thomas remembered playing in Moncton, N.B., on one of those tours, and after the show, the tour bus started to rock back and forth. Kids from the concert were outside, shaking the bus. "We yelled out, 'Why are doing that?'" said Thomas. "And they yelled back, 'Take us with you!'" The Stampeders rolled right along with a string of big hits that went from ballads to heavy rock, including "Wild Eyes," "Devil You," "Oh My Lady," and "Minstrel Gypsy."

Kensington Market hadn't survived the '60s to enjoy the boom of the '70s, but Bernie Finkelstein hadn't given up on Yorkville's music. He figured if record companies weren't going to work hard for his artists, he would just form his own record label. That became True North, launched in 1970 with his first artist, Bruce Cockburn. The Yorkville regular had bounced around a series of groups, but had decided to get back to folk music, songwriting, and acoustic guitar playing. His self-titled debut quickly made him a national favorite, with his "Going to the Country" an ecological and hippie lifestyle statement for many. Cockburn followed that up with an album a year through most of the '70s, the very picture of a modern folkie. Soon on board the True North label as well was another Yorkville regular, Murray McLauchlan. He'd spent time in the Village, time in rougher parts of the city, and time crossing Canada, and his songs reflected back the nation. McLauchlan's "Farmer's Song" was a tribute to rural living, a thank-you card from a generation willing to forget the gap. He was another artist who split the difference between country and pop, with the song going Top 10 on both charts, the start of a long career straddling the genre boundaries.

Edward Bear was another semi-successful Yorkville act, another Toronto blues-rock outfit that in the late '60s was tough enough to open for Led Zeppelin at that band's initial visit to the city. That caught the attention of Capitol Records, the label having just lost The Staccatos and not wanting to miss out on the growing blues-rock scene. The band even gave them a hit first single, "You, Me and Mexico," which went to number three in 1970. It wasn't blues or rock though, and the focus of the band was shifting to singer/drummer/songwriter Larry Evoy, with a sweet voice and a smooth approach with pop songs. Guitarist Danny Marks left the trio, sticking with blues and Toronto, with a long and strong career as a solo artist, broadcaster, and bon vivant. Evoy steered the Bear into the Top 40, with the early synthesizer-helped "Fly Across the Sea" in 1972, followed by the big production "Masquerade," with echoes of George Harrison and Derek & The Dominoes, with more synthesizer and real strings coming in as well. It brought the band back to the Top 10, and set the stage for their next single.

"Last Song" was sugary-sweet, a sentimental good-bye, and very commercial. That direction had by then driven keyboardist Paul Weldon from the ranks, and Evoy was barely keeping the group together. But a number one single certainly helped convince him to keep going, and then the song caught on in the U.S., making it to number three and selling two million copies. Another pretty ballad, "Close Your Eyes," followed in 1973, number three in Canada and thirty-seven in the U.S., but another lineup change soon followed, and the Bear went over the mountain the following year.

Vancouver group The Chessmen had come to an end in 1966, leaving Terry Jacks adrift. Later that year, local singer Susan Pesklevits got in touch. She was a regular on CBC-TV's *Music Hop*, the after-school show that aired from Vancouver on Mondays, followed by Montreal, Winnipeg, Toronto, and Halifax through the week. The original *Music Hop* host had been local announcer Alex Trebek; it was the show The Guess Who worked on as house band, and Brian Ahern and Ken Tobias were band members in Halifax. Pesklevits needed a guitar player for a gig at the Elks Club in Hope, B.C., and was told Jacks was available. They hit it off and developed the idea of a band, which became The Poppy Family, and she became Susan Jacks as well.

The group added Craig McCaw on guitar, and like some others in the '60s, he'd also developed an interest in the sitar. He brought in a friend named Satwant Singh, who gave the band a unique percussion sound, using tablas and bongos. Terry Jacks was becoming increasingly interested in writing and studio production, and was able to land a deal with London Records. After a couple of singles in 1968, Jacks produced the group's debut album, called *Which Way You Goin' Billy?* The title cut was immediately picked up by radio home and away. Even before the official CanCon rules were in place, Canadian radio programmers were feeling the recent heat and there was no denying the production and writing quality of that number. It grabbed the number one spot in Canada, and along with The Guess Who, helped start talk in the U.S. about Canada's new growth, landing at number two on *Billboard*'s Top 10. Plus, it had worldwide distribution through London, finding success in far-flung markets such as South Africa where it was number two, and Ireland, top of the charts there. Altogether, along with its U.S. Gold sale, it topped 3.5 million in sales worldwide. That international success would prove even more valuable for Terry Jacks down the line.

The Poppy Family continued to pop out the hits, including "That's Where I Went Wrong," "Where Evil Grows," and "Good Friends," all Top 10 in Canada. But Terry Jacks was becoming increasingly less interested in performing, and being in a band. McCaw and Singh were dropped, and Susan Jacks became the face of the group, doing lots of TV appearances but less and less touring. The Poppy Family name was gone by 1972, and the couple were now making solo records, Terry having a hit with "Concrete Sea," and Susan adding "I Thought of You Again."

Terry Jacks was looking around for production gigs and had met The Beach Boys through touring. The famous family band had one of the world's best writers and producers in Brian Wilson, but his mental health problems were worsening. "Carl Wilson and Al Jardine both asked if I would produce them," Jacks said. "They knew I liked The Beach Boys, and Brian was out of it then." He had a song he'd been working on, a sad one in French by Jacques Brel, "Le moribond." The poet Rod McKuen had translated the lyrics, about an old man saying good-bye to life and friends, with a bitter tone. Jacks had recently lost a friend to cancer, and, imagining what it would have been like for him to tell people he was dying, rewrote and softened the lyrics and came up with a new arrangement. He felt it could be the smash hit The Beach Boys were looking for to revamp their stalled career at the time. But this was not a happy family. "None of The Beach Boys were hanging together, you had to bring them in separately," explained Jacks. "It wasn't unified because Brian had gone crazy. It was an honor to produce them, but I couldn't get the group together. I was just turning into a nervous wreck. I said, 'I can't do this anymore.' I just left. The thing never got done."

Jacks had already done work on his own version of the song, "Seasons in the Sun." But he'd had some negative feedback on it from his friends, who felt it too sad. This time though, he sought out the teenage audience for a preview. "My paperboy was there. He said 'Holy cow, this is some song.' He didn't know my friend who had died. The next day, he came by with about eight friends, and they loved it. That's why it says on the album, 'To the kids from Copper Cove.'" The eight-kid fan club grew much bigger. Those world-wide Poppy Family ones joined in as well, with the song finding markets most artists never heard of: Brazil, for instance, where it became the country's top-seller of all time. Of course, Canada, England, and the U.S. did their parts as well, as it reached number one in each country. It's one of the biggest-selling singles of all time, with various estimates placing it somewhere between 11 and 14 million copies sold.

SIGNS

Michel Pagliaro was a star in French Canada by the start of the '70s, and had developed a solid, modern rock style, that was the equal of the Top 40 music Quebecers were hearing from English Canada and the U.S. "M'Lady" had been a big hit, with lots of Beatles-influenced moments. Pag, as he was known, had often drawn on current pop hits for inspiration, and had put out singles of "Hey Jude," and Steam's "Na Na Hey Hey Kiss Him Goodbye," as a duet with blues belter Nanette Workman. Taking notice was the CHUM radio network, which figured if it was going to be forced to play Canadian records, it might as well own them too. The network started its own label, Much Records, and signed Pagliaro as an English-language artist. He scored an immediate hit with "Give Us One More Chance," and a full album followed, called *Pagliaro*, that was crammed with hit singles. In quick succession, "Lovin' You Ain't Easy," "Rainshowers," and "Some Sing, Some Dance" conquered English Canada, and Pag became the first artist to receive Gold records in both official languages. He wasn't about to be lured away from Quebec though; his next single in 1972 was "J'entends frapper," a strutting old-school rock 'n' roll guitar song that became the top-selling 45 in Quebec's history at that point. The next year, he summed up the whole experience with his concert album, *Live*, recorded in Montreal and Toronto, which featured both French and English hits. It sold 200,000 copies, this time the biggest-selling album in Quebec's history.

Jean-Pierre Ferland was another chansonnier who changed with the times in the late '60s. Already an established star in Quebec, he'd also had lots of success in Paris, where he'd moved for part of the late '60s. After his return, he realized it was time to enter the new music that was swirling around Montreal. The result was the landmark album *Jeune* in 1970, in some ways as important as Robert Charlebois's breakthrough music. Instead of solo performance, *Jeune* was a large-scale spectacle, with a rock band, orchestra, choirs of singers, synthesizers, studio effects, spoken word, and sharp, insightful lyrics. Led by the single

"Le petit roi," the album was different than anything made in Quebec before, and it was a totally-Quebec production, from Studio André-Perry in Montreal. It has a remarkable sound quality that sounds fresh and clear to this day, earning it the reputation as the *Sgt. Pepper* of Quebec albums.

Apart from the chansonnier and rock 'n' roll of Montreal, there were also vibrant R&B and jazz scenes in the city, and the members of Mashmakhan had their feet in both camps. Language didn't mean as much in the bar scene, and the group got together because of mutual musical tastes. "When I met Pierre (Sénécal, the group's organ player and singer), he didn't speak any English, and my French was modest," said guitarist Rayburn Blake. "He wrote 'As the Years Go By' when he had only been speaking English six or seven years. Some of it's a little unusual in its phrasing, but that's the French you're sensing. We left it alone, because we knew it was working." Along with Sénécal's colorful carnival organ, and different vocal, the song stood out on radio, propelling it to number one in Canada in 1970, and a decent thirty-one in the U.S., selling a half-million copies in the process. The band recorded for Columbia Records, who knew what to do with a hit single: ship it around the world. It became an even bigger-seller in Japan, topping a million worldwide. Columbia sent the group to play Japan, and cue the sound of Rayburn Blake's mind being blown: "We had still been playing the same bars in Montreal we had always played, even after the hit," he remembered. "We landed late at night, and there were about four thousand people at the airport waiting to greet us. There were a dozen little twelve-year-old girls with bouquets of flowers. I look out the window and they're actually rolling a red carpet out. We played Tokyo for sixty-five thousand people, and we played Osaka for about forty thousand." The group, still a progressive jazz-blues band, saw their next single bomb, and Mashmakhan never bothered the Top 40 again, in any country.

SIGNS

Nobody was happier about CanCon regulations than the group Crowbar. The rowdy bunch came together in that time-honored tradition, as backing musicians for Ronnie Hawkins. "If Ronnie got stuck on something, he'd call us in," explained leader Kelly Jay. "We could go and play a dinner club as well as play a rock 'n' roll show. We played the Fillmore East with Ronnie for five days, opening up for (Joe Cocker's) Mad Dogs & Englishmen, with Robbie (Robertson), Levon (Helm), and all the boys sitting in the third row. And Dylan! They wanted to see how the new band would do." They did exactly what the first Hawks had done, got great and quit, fed up with Ronnie's rules. But they stayed friends, too, even hanging around when John and Yoko stayed at Hawkins's farm during their peace trip. Crowbar became the couple's favorite boogie band, and they even recorded radio messages saying as much, telling people to buy their albums.

With such support, it was a wonder the band couldn't get on radio. Jay was one of the musicians asked to meet with Pierre Juneau as he was drafting the CanCon regulations, to explain what his band needed from radio. It turned out Crowbar got exactly what it needed. "Oh What a Feeling" from 1971 is considered the first-ever CanCon-made hit. It's still a beloved number in the country, heard at hockey games, in beer commercials, anywhere a good-time anthem is needed. "Juneau thanked me onstage one night at the Junos," Jay said. "My mother and father saw it, and oh my God they were thrilled." Now, don't forget, hits don't equal money all the time in the music business. It was the only one Crowbar ever had. "I've been making music in Canada for decades, and I've made hundreds and hundreds of dollars," Jay deadpans.

Some of course were making more than hundreds and hundreds, including those other old Hawks. They had been hanging around Woodstock waiting for Dylan to recover from his motorcycle accident and make some music. Eventually the musicians started to get together for jam sessions, including some old-time tunes they had in common,

133

and keeping with the Canadian theme, Dylan even went back to the Ian & Sylvia numbers he had learned back in the Greenwich Village days when they all were friends. Eventually Garth Hudson set up a reel-to-reel tape recorder and positioned the microphones so that decent-quality tapes could be made to document the proceedings, not that anything was planned. At first, Dylan, Hudson, Robbie Roberston, Rick Danko, and Richard Manuel recorded at Dylan's, and then they switched to a house that Danko had rented nearby, which affectionately became known as Big Pink, after its paint job. Now the instruments and taping equipment could be left set up in the basement. Dylan could stop by whenever, and the rest could work on their own material.

During this time, the group had been working on songwriting, especially Robertson and Manuel. Impressed by what he was hearing, Albert Grossman was able to shop around the tapes and land them a deal with Capitol Records in the U.S., including a nice fat advance. In true brotherly form, the four called Levon Helm, and told him to get up to Woodstock and share in the wealth. Recording with Dylan continued, with Grossman using the Hudson tapes to pitch some of the new songs around to other performers. Soon, the new batch of Dylan material was providing hits for Manfred Mann ("Mighty Quinn"), The Byrds ("You Ain't Goin' Nowhere"), and Peter, Paul & Mary ("Too Much of Nothing"). But Dylan still had no plans for touring, so the rest went off to make their album. They had originally been signed as The Crackers, but thought better of it, and became simply The Band. Taking some of the material from the basement, the group recorded "Tears of Rage," which Manuel had written with Dylan, "This Wheel's on Fire," a Danko/ Dylan composition, and "I Shall Be Released," sung so beautifully by Manuel in falsetto, a gift from Dylan to The Band. Robertson matched Manuel's amount of songs on the new album with four, his best-known being "The Weight," although Helm complained later that Robertson grabbed credit for characters from his life, while they all spontaneously composed the song in a jam. It was a long-standing grievance between Robertson and the rest that soured the latter part of the relationships. "The Weight" has only grown in significance over time, becoming co-lead singer Helm's concert theme song up until his death in 2012, and a staple of jam bands and summer music festivals for new generations.

Garth Hudson described the songwriting at that point as a process of sharing and talking between a bunch of small-town Ontario guys (and one from Arkansas), what they had been doing together since backing Ronnie Hawkins. "Each person contributed to the vignettes," Hudson insisted. "Everyone was a storyteller, and from these stories and our feelings about family and the rural life where we were brought up, this kind of heart was carried on. And being closer to a small town and rural community [in the Woodstock area] only reinforced a lot of the thinking about the vignettes and scenarios that went into the poetry." The results of the album sessions became *Music from Big Pink*, released to great acclaim in 1968. It wasn't a huge-selling album, but it affected all of rock music. Instead of joining the psychedelic movement, The Band had purposely gone back in time, to folk and gospel roots music. Producer John Simon had joined them to make the album, quickly becoming the sixth musician and member of the team. Ignoring modern studio techniques, he set the group up much like they had recorded in Big Pink's basement. "All in one room, on four-track tape, mostly all live," he described the sessions. The only thing we overdubbed were, for instance, on "Tears of Rage," the horns and tambourine. I think "The Weight" could've been one hundred percent live. It was the last song we did, different from the others, sort of an afterthought maybe."

Music from Big Pink became one of the most influential albums ever in rock 'n' roll. Critics loved it, spreading the word, but musicians were absolutely astonished. Eric Clapton immediately asked to join The Band full-time. The five thought he was joking, so we'll never know what might have happened there. Al Kooper (him again) was asked to review the album in *Rolling Stone* magazine, and called it hands-down his album of the year, despite the fact it was just August. Journalists went out of their way to describe how the writers (especially Robertson) had picked up on what was happening in America and used the music to search for the old-time values of the rural U.S. Plus, they mentioned all the great old musical connections to R&B, folk, original rock 'n' roll, and anything old-timey. Hudson, almost a savant at composition and musical elements, acknowledged the influence of American radio that they all heard crossing the border into Canada, but pointed out the Canadian quota in the DNA as well. "If you listen to the introduction of 'Chest Fever,' do-do-diddle diddle-diddle-loo," he hummed in 2007, "And then you hear a skip, wa-da-digadigadiga-da-da, that's a bagpipe lick." Hudson went on to list a dozen old-time performers he and the others had heard growing up on CBC radio, including fiddler Don Messer and His Islanders, and said, "This all went into Big Pink. All this stuff is more important than how we sat around and mulled it out. I just want people to know that I'm Canadian. This all goes into the hopper, it's very important. This is what The Band is founded on."

All the excitement over the first album paid off the next year, as 1969's *The Band* did sell in droves, a Top 10 album in Canada and the U.S. It included "The Night They Drove Old Dixie Down," which Joan Baez turned into a Top 5 hit, easily the biggest of her career. The Band's singles weren't really that successful on AM radio, more so on FM stations, but producer Simon says hits were never the goal: "It was part of the atmosphere of the whole album. I wasn't thinking commercially, just artistically." While those first two albums are generally considered the best of The Band's studio work, each subsequent album would include fan favorites, now-beloved songs such as "Stage Fright," "It Makes No Difference," "The Shape I'm In," and "Acadian Driftwood."

Many of the other Canadians who had moved to the U.S. before CanCon were doing just as well or better. Of course, being Canadian, they kept running into each other. Joni Mitchell met Leonard Cohen at the Newport Folk Festival in 1967, and they immediately started dating. As neither of them was famous yet, it wasn't a star attraction, so let's assume it was brains; or beauty. It's about the most perfect couple ever, but there was probably too much talent for one relationship there, and it didn't last, but apparently it did give us a few songs and a few lines, including Mitchell's "Rainy Night House," and its reference to a holy man on the FM radio, about a trip to Cohen's Montreal home. Some feel he might be the preferred beverage in her "A Case of You," although it's also been associated with James Taylor. But such gossip swirled around Mitchell then, as it has ever since. Because she dropped so many hints and clues from her life into her songs, they were ripe for speculation, and Mitchell became the ultimate confessional writer in the newly celebrated world of the singer-songwriter movement of the early '70s. Associated mostly with Los Angeles, the ranks included that other old Mitchell pal, Neil Young, all the members of Crosby, Stills & Nash, Jackson Browne, Laura Nyro, James Taylor, Carole King, Tom Waits, and England's Cat Stevens.

Mitchell had first worked with Crosby, then met Stills and Nash, eventually hooking up with the latter (Nash's "Our House" is all about their place). She had so many songs when she had moved to Los Angeles that at first, she didn't even bother recording the ones that had been hits for other people, such as "Both Sides, Now" and "The Circle Game." Laurel Canyon inspired her even more, referencing it in the title to her 1970 hit album, *Ladies of the Canyon*. That included her version of the song she had given to CSNY, "Woodstock," her song for Nash, "Willie," and her environmental warning and worldwide hit "Big Yellow Taxi." The ultimate singer-songwriter album was next though, 1971's *Blue*. Cohen aside, there are other identifiable men from her life, including Nash again (by then out of the picture), who is the singer in the band in "My Old Man." "The Last Time I Saw Richard" is about her ex-husband, Chuck Mitchell. "Carey" was a colorful character she had met while traveling in Europe, and there were several references to James Taylor, with whom she had had a recent, brief relationship.

All these people and their stories made for great songs, but with everyone focused on the gossip, they missed the real story, the one that truly mattered to Mitchell. It came from a song that was four years old by that time, which she had performed in concert in 1967, sometimes in a medley with "The Circle Game." "Little Green" was the only song on the album that didn't include the word *I*, a song about a girl named Green. At some shows, at a time when every word wasn't spread on the Internet, she'd sing the last, telling line "Kelly Green, be a gypsy dancer." Kelly was the name of the daughter she had given up for adoption, a secret still, and one that remained so until she was reunited in 1997 with the woman now named Kilauren Gibb.

The lyrics did affect all who heard them, and *Blue* continues to ensnare new generations, for its beauty and rich imagery; the frozen river she wishes she could skate away on, the lover so potent she wants to drink a case of him. *Blue* rocks, despite being all-acoustic, on "Carey" and "This Flight Tonight." It sounds like no other record, with her dulcimer and obscure tunings, and her ability to sing with joy in her voice on some tunes, sadness in others, a most expressive vocalist. Well praised at its release, if anything, it's even more highly thought of over the years.

Leonard Cohen did all right as well, with his debut album *Songs of Leonard Cohen* containing the immortal "Suzanne," and the similarly praised "So Long, Marianne" and "Sisters of Mercy." Initially uncomfortable performing, he finally took to the stage enough to venture out with a group, and found he had a large and devoted audience in Europe, not surprising given his style. "Famous Blue Raincoat" from 1971's *Songs of Love and Hate* was a fascinating tale of a love triangle, with Cohen and his well-known coat a principal character. "The chord progressions are kind of nice," felt Cohen. "I remember singing it for my mother before it had words, at her house. She said, 'It has a kind of Spanish progression and I like it.' The story's good, it's an intriguing story. It's not quite clear what happened. It's a mystery."

The U.S. was not as keen on Cohen as Canada and Europe, and he remained more recognized in the States than purchased. Perhaps he felt his work had become too gloomy, as his critics suggested. "I wasn't really happy with [*Songs of Love and Hate*]," he admitted. "At that time I felt it wasn't quite what I was striving for. I felt I lost it, and I couldn't put my finger on it. I think I was looking for something a little more like my first album, something where the songs were a little more amiable, more feelings, more love songs, where the songs were not so dark. I think probably that I wanted it, but that's not what came. You can't quarrel with it. It's not as though one has the luxury to spend them, to choose in what form they'll arrive." This negative view was about an album that contained the masterpiece "Joan of Arc," the "perfect woman," according to Cohen. Critics started to focus on his darker material, and debatable vocal skills, delighting in giving him a witty nickname. Laughing Lenny was popular, as were variations on the Grand Master of Melancholia. The fan website 1heckofaguy.com has delightfully listed 270 nicknames found in newspapers, magazines, and books. So a pattern emerged; with each new album Cohen would be received with rapture in Europe, with respect in Canada, and with dwindling interest in the U.S. He had a couple of more acts left in him though.

Neil Young had been disappointed by the failure of Buffalo Springfield, but it had put him on the map as a talent to watch. He quickly turned that cache into a solo career, with a self-titled first album in 1968 that continued down the folk-influenced path, with his typically cryptic and sometimes out-there lyrics. It pointed to a potent future with "The Loner," but also included many gorgeous moments, aided by former Phil Spector arranger (and future Mr. Buffy Sainte-Marie),

Jack Nitzsche. It didn't set the rock world aflame, but did establish Young as a solo, acoustic artist. Which, of course, he promptly gave up, when he found a local band he really liked. The Rockets were a bar band that had started out as a doo-wop group in the early '60s. The band featured guitarist Danny Whitten, and Young was particularly thrilled with his playing. He offered Whitten, drummer Ralph Molina, and bass player Billy Talbot full-time jobs as his band, killing The Rockets (there were other, less fortunate band members). The group now became Crazy Horse (with Nitzsche joining later on piano), and together they made the full-on rock album *Everybody Knows This Is Nowhere*. Where his first solo album had been moody and melodic, this was all about three chords, crunch, and wobbly harmonies. Young had written three of his best-loved songs in the midst of a major fever; "Cinnamon Girl" featured co-vocals with Whitten and classic electric guitar, and "Down by the River" and "Cowgirl in the Sand" were epics of nine and ten minutes, concert favorites ever since. Young had finally found his songwriting groove, plus a band that he completely loved, where he was the leader, but with a co-conspirator who brought all the brotherly spirit and talent he'd hoped to get from Stephen Stills. And even better, the album was a hit, reaching the Top 40. Neil Young was now an electric guitar hero and hit rock 'n' roll solo artist, which of course, he promptly gave up.

Young had quit Buffalo Springfield several times, more than once because of disagreements with Stephen Stills. But there was enough mutual respect that Young was the first person Stills thought of when it was suggested his new band, Crosby, Stills & Nash, needed some more instrumental help onstage. The others were skeptical, given Young's reputation, but they were also thrilled with the idea of having access to his songwriting skills. Young liked the idea of playing guitar with Stills again, hoping to recapture the magic of the early Buffalo Springfield days. It also didn't hurt that the trio's first album had been a huge seller, bigger than either of Young's efforts. At first he joined for the group's heavy touring schedule, the second gig he ever played with them being Woodstock. Joni Mitchell was on the road with them as well, another reunion of the Canadian club. Then the group went into the studio, and CSN got what they wanted out of Y, a couple of great songs, including "Helpless." The album *Déjà Vu* went to number one, and established the band as superstars. Then just three months after its release in March of 1970, Young read about the recent Kent State University shootings of students by National Guard troops, and quickly brought the group in to record "Ohio," which was then rush-released as a single. The band toured to capacity audiences everywhere, equally loved for their acoustic segments as they were for the full-out rock treatments featuring the guitar duels of Young and Stills. They were by then referred to as "America's Beatles." Now, Neil Young was one-quarter of the biggest band in the U.S., the whole reason he had left Winnipeg, Fort William, and Toronto: top of the world, which, of course, he promptly gave up.

Young didn't actually quit this time, but infighting had made the situation unbearable, and a break was called. For Young, it was simply a matter of putting out his next solo album, which he'd already been working on for several months. Although it was started with Crazy Horse, several of those songs were set aside, and more acoustic material was added, the result becoming *After the Gold Rush*. Once again, Young was being pulled back and forth between guitar workouts and acoustic, folk material. Some of the songs, including the title track, had been written for a proposed film by actor Dean Stockwell, which was never made. There was a sci-fi element to it, which inspired the time-trip adventure in "After the Gold Rush," a haunting piano number. Young even takes an up-tempo country classic, Don Gibson's "Oh Lonesome Me," and turns it into a slow, mellow weeper. But elsewhere, the Horse is on the loose, with full electric attacks on "When You Dance I Can Really Love" and "Southern Man." The Top 10 album was Young's biggest success to date, his first solo Gold album.

The fever that had inspired Young's great trio of songs back in 1969 apparently had yet to abate. Even while he was touring the brand-new *After the Gold Rush* album at solo shows, he started introducing completely new songs. Some of them ("See the Sky About to Rain," "Bad Fog of Loneliness") would be shuffled off to the archives, while others quickly became favorites for his next project. Because of serious back pain that would require surgery, he was playing acoustic guitar, and most of his new songs had a country feel to them. Arriving in Nashville to do a guest appearance on the *Johnny Cash* TV show, he was offered the chance to go into a studio to lay down some of the songs. In the next couple of days he committed "Heart of Gold," "Old Man," and others to tape, with a group of local players, along with singers Linda Rondstadt and James Taylor, also guests on the *Cash* show. Taylor also grabbed Young's six-string banjo guitar and added a part to "Old Man." More sessions were done in London, where Young was a guest on BBC-TV, and Jack Nitzsche brought in the London Symphony Orchestra to guest on "There's a World" and "A Man Needs a Maid." Young also reconvened the Nashville gang, now called The Stray Gators, for sessions at his barn studio in California, where they nailed the rockers "Alabama," "Words," and "Are You Ready for the Country." Led by the ultimate campfire song, "Heart of Gold," a number one single in Canada and the U.S., *Harvest* became the favorite album for nearly everyone in 1972. It topped the *Billboard* charts in the U.S., and did the same in Canada, Australia, England, and sold over a million copies in France. Neil Young was now bigger than CSNY had ever been, all alone at the top as a global superstar, which, of course, he promptly gave up.

The Canadian singer-songwriters were certainly fitting in well around the world, but for some reasons, Gordon Lightfoot didn't get mentioned in the same company. Somehow, other countries didn't get

Lightfoot the way Canadians did, although he had no shortage of hits. Perhaps it's his ability to write about the national psyche, from nature to long highways to nostalgia, or his steadfast belief in the value of folk music. Ever since his emergence in the mid-'60s, he's been songwriting royalty in Canada, an equal to Young, Mitchell, and Cohen. Elsewhere, he's known for a few pop hits in the '70s. That's despite Bob Dylan's famous quote, "Gordon Lightfoot, every time I hear a song of his, it's like I wish it would last forever."

Lightfoot's career had hit a plateau after "Canadian Railroad Trilogy" in 1967. There hadn't been any big hits, or hit covers in the late '60s, and his major work, 1968's "Black Day in July," about the Detroit riots of 1967 that saw forty-three people die, had been passed over by frightened radio programmers. Lightfoot started afresh, signing a new contract with Reprise Records, releasing the album *Sit Down Young Stranger* in 1970. At first Lightfoot pinned his hopes on a cover version of all things, by the hot young writer Kris Kristofferson. He'd met him at a song pull (where songwriters would sit around and play each other their work), and liked his "Me and Bobby McGee." It was a resounding success in Canada, number one on the country charts and number thirteen on the Top 40, but mustered no interest in the U.S. Lightfoot considered the title track, "Sit Down Young Stranger," the important song on the album, but it got little attention as well, and the album stalled. "It sold about eighty thousand copies and it stopped," Lightfoot explained. "I certainly wasn't going to complain about it, that was my very first album with Reprise, and they were treating me as a folk artist. They didn't expect it, they hoped there might be a single there, but they certainly weren't pressuring me to do anything in that regard."

However, a song Lightfoot didn't even consider as special did become a single, thanks to a DJ's interest. "They (Reprise) called and said that they'd got a nibble on a single on the album. By this time, it was seven or eight months later. In Seattle, a station was going to program

'If You Could Read My Mind.'" For Lightfoot, it was a sorrowful song. "I remember writing it really well, the afternoon I wrote it," he said. "It was a one-day thing. I had many songs like that. I could see that my marriage was going downhill, which it did about a year later. All of a sudden the words came to me. I found out I was writing about an upcoming event, a life-changing event that was going to take place for me personally, and it did." The beautiful melody and sad vocal took Lightfoot to number one in Canada, and the Top 5 in the U.S., his first single to ever chart there. The album was quickly retitled after the hit, and Lightfoot the folk singer had become Lightfoot the hit songwriter.

The Top 40 is fickle though, and Lightfoot's music moved back and forth, sometimes country and sometimes folk, as well as his ballads. That included the lovely single "Beautiful," which made number thirteen in Canada in 1972 but couldn't reach the U.S. Top 40. This period includes some of Lightfoot's best songs, such as "You Are What I Am," "Summer Side of Life," and "Talking in Your Sleep," the first a banjo-fired hoot, the latter an acoustic tearjerker, just guitar and stand-up bass. All were big Canadian hits, but Reprise was looking for another U.S. hit, and truthfully, so was Lightfoot. "I wanted the follow-up. I wanted to keep this thing rolling. I wanted to get into doing bigger shows, perhaps add a couple of more musicians. Not necessarily go rock 'n' roll. I've got lots of toe-tappers in my repertoire anyway, just as it stands. I wanted to be able to do it on my own terms, keep the folk idea into it."

It all came down to a good beat. Lightfoot had used drums before, but not much. For his new single, producer Lenny Waronker heard a groove, and laid down a drum track without Lightfoot knowing about it. It turned out he didn't have a problem with that, and for good reason. "Sundown" took him right to number one in 1974 in Canada and the U.S., a hit on the country charts in both countries as well, and in England and Australia, too. It was a timely hit. "We really needed it, and that was the perfect place to get one," Lightfoot remarked. "It set me up to continue on for another five or six years after that." Those years included the follow-up hits "Rainy Day People," "Carefree Highway," and "The Wreck of the Edmund Fitzgerald," the last one showing Lightfoot would never be far away from the folk tradition, writing about a modern-day shipping disaster. As for five or six years, Lightfoot underestimated his staying power. As of 2014, he continues to tour relentlessly to adoring audiences, playing his kind of folk music, even with a drummer in the band.

Of all the Canadians in the U.S., Skip Prokop had had the lousiest luck by 1968. His band The Paupers was nearing collapse, and Prokop went to manager Albert Grossman to quit. Grossman was ready to let him walk away from the band, but he had other plans for Prokop, involving a well-known musician, oddly connected to half of Canada. "Al Kooper and I had met in New York, and were hanging around a lot," says Prokop.

> We would hang out, talk about music, all the things you do when you have a really close friend in music, and you're sharing your musical ideas. So [Albert)] said, "Okay, here's the deal. Al Kooper and Mike Bloomfield want you to go play on *Super Session*. And then, Cass Elliot's people, they want you to come and play with their big, historically first rock show at Caesars Palace in Vegas. In the meantime, there's a bunch of stuff going on and you gotta be very, very quiet about this, but Janis [Joplin] is leaving Big Brother. I want you to go out to California, hang out, play with her, whatever, start building this relationship. Because Skip, you put great bands together, and I know that you'll put a sensational band together for her, and all I ask is that there's no pressure on her. She comes in, picks up the microphone, and you guys are ready to go. Are you interested?" I said, yeah, sure. So

> I went out, I played *The Live Adventures of Mike Bloomfield and Al Kooper* [recorded in September of 1968 with guests Carlos Santana and Elvin Bishop] at the Fillmore West [in San Francisco]. While I was out there, man, we did a ton of jamming. My next-closest friend was Steve Miller, and we ended up playing with Carlos during that period, we had a great time together. I hung out, did a lot of playing, got to know Janis really well.

Not a bad way to quit a band, really. Prokop was working with three superstar combos.

The job with Mama Cass was a huge eye-opener for Prokop. Having played the last few years in small rock bands, he had forgotten what it was like when he was a kid in the military band, with lots of musicians. "I went and played with Cass, which was an amazing experience," he says.

> We had a nine- or ten-piece group with vocalists, backup musicians, and that. We rehearsed for about four weeks in L.A., and then headed in to Vegas. We had two or three days to rehearse on the big stage at Caesars Palace, and they had a drop screen behind me. And behind that screen, a foot away from my shoulder was Jimmy Haskell, who was at that time, one of the top directors and writers for movies, and a forty-fifty piece orchestra. And I remember rehearsing and going, holy cow, this is power. This is like drum corps again, this is huge power.

It fit what Prokop had been thinking about, wondering what it would be like to add strings and horns to a touring rock band, something no one had tried at that point.

SIGNS

From Vegas, he also had to take care of getting Joplin's band together, and it was expected by all that he would be the drummer.

> I started talking to Janis over the phone about the people I was looking at for the band, and fully intended to start looking for a house, start looking for schools for the kids in San Francisco, and all of a sudden, she said, "I want to keep Sammy (Andrew), my guitarist, from Big Brother." And I said, "What? In my opinion, I don't think he's the guy we want." "Well, I want him," she said. So her and I got into a real bone of contention over that, and I thought, Albert's paying me to put a band together, and now she's telling me I gotta have this guy. I'm not knocking him as a person or anything like that, he's a really neat guy. I just think, in my head, what Albert was looking for from me to put together as a band, I didn't think he fit. So her and I got into a big long thing, and she would not budge on that. So I finished out the week at Caesars Palace, got on a plane, and flew back to Toronto.

And just like that, Prokop once again had no gig, no band, and now, no manager. But he did have a plan.

He had actually talked it over with a friend from Toronto, a keyboard player named Paul Hoffert.

> I said, "Paul, I have this really, really great idea. I'm thinking of putting a really big band together, like a full brass quartet, a full string quartet, a full rock quartet, probably a lead singer." He said, "Are you serious?" I said, "It would be incredible, we could play whatever we wanted, we could play jazz, rock, classical, fuse them together, do whatever we wanted to do." We talked, and he said, "Gee Skip, if you ever decide to do

that, you'll probably do it in California. But if you decide to do it in Toronto, call me." I was home for less than twenty-four hours from Vegas, phone Paul, and the next day I was in his living room and we were starting to talk, with the plans to put Lighthouse together.

Janis Joplin struggled to put together a band without Prokop's help. Finally, she settled on a group led by guitarist John Till, called The Full Tilt Boogie Band, made up of ex-members of yet another of Ronnie Hawkins's versions of The Hawks. The Full Tilt Boogie Band stayed with Joplin until she died in 1970, and were featured on her album *Pearl* and hit "Me and Bobby McGee," the same song Gordon Lightfoot had recorded the year before.

Prokop and Hoffert put together their mega-band, Lighthouse, and were ready to launch the group at Toronto's Rock Pile club in May of 1969. They had a record deal with RCA already, and that was about to pay off with some unexpected support. "There was a guy named Stu Hertz who was a marketing/promotions guy in the States, and he was attached to RCA," explains Prokop.

He was up here [Toronto], he knew the guys and me, and knew the preparation and all the stuff we were doing, getting ready to do the album, and that this was our first gig. It just so happened that Duke Ellington was playing at the Royal York [hotel], and he had to go to the airport. So Stu, who is of the Hertz family, which paid off for us big-time a few times, said, "Look, why don't you let me take you to the airport, I got my limo right out there," and Duke says, "Oh! Okay!" So they get in the limo, and they're going up Yonge Street, right past the Rock Pile. And Stu says, "A few guys, some friends of mine, they got a really big band, you'll love it, it's like the

new Big Band. You gotta come in and meet them and then
we'll head out to the airport." So he said, okay, and he comes
in, he walks into the dressing room with Stu Hertz, he's got
a photographer, and he grabs Paul and I, puts Duke in the
middle, shoots the picture, and then Stu says, "Before we go,
they're going to go on, why don't you go on and introduce
them?" Duke says, "What do I say?" And Stu says, "You'll
think of something, the band's name is Lighthouse." So
he gets onstage, yadda-yadda-yadda, and then "I think I'm
beginning to see the light—HOUSE!" Then they put him in
the limo and take him to the airport.

With its unique lineup, Lighthouse quickly became a huge draw on the
burgeoning concert and festival scene across North America. Because
they could be jazz at one point, rock the next, and classical after that,
or any combination, they were getting invitations to play everywhere.
"When we went to the States, on tour, it was crazy," Prokop explains.

It was absolutely amazing. The banner headlines from Atlantic City Pop Festival—"Peace Band from Canada," all the
press, it was crazy everywhere we went, they just had never
seen anything like it, and of course, they never have since.
In Canada, we don't even get recognized for this. We were
the first rock band ever asked to perform at the Newport
Jazz Festival. First rock band ever asked to play at the Bos-
ton Globe Jazz Festival, which was really elite, maybe eight
acts, that's it, and we played with Sarah Vaughan. First band
ever asked to the Monterey Jazz Festival. It just went on and
on. First band to ever actually co-compose a rock ballet, with
the Royal Winnipeg Ballet, we did sixty-seven one-nighters
across Canada, completely sold out. This was top drawer.

The band's sales for the first three albums were looking more like a jazz band's than a rock band's. But there were those who believed the group was very close to a breakthrough in sales, too. It happened at the same time the group had introduced a new lead singer, Bob McBride. "This guy Jimmy Ienner shows up, wants to talk," Prokop says. "He says to me, 'Skip, I think you have the potential to be a great, great songwriter, but you just need to know how to craft the songs so that they'll become radio friendly, and I can teach you how to do that,' which he did. Hence, the big change in Lighthouse. One, he produced us, two, I had a whole brand-new way of writing an idea, and crafting it in such a way that didn't give up the soul of the song. That translates into a communication in a broad way, which translates into a hit record." Ienner has worked with everyone from Three Dog Night to Grand Funk Railroad to The Bay City Rollers, and produced the *Dirty Dancing* soundtrack, one of the biggest-selling albums of all-time. The results of his work with Prokop were immediate, with the 1971 song "Hats Off to the Stranger" the group's first hit single in Canada, which was then followed by "One Fine Morning," number two in Canada and twenty-four in the U.S. The next year, Prokop hit again with one of the most-played summer songs of all-time, "Sunny Days," number four in Canada and thirty-four in the States.

Prokop also knows the answer to that old show biz question, "How do you get to Carnegie Hall?" Jimmy Ienner invites you.

> Jimmy came to us and said, "Are you interested in doing a live album at Carnegie Hall?" We said, yes. It was really funny, I remember onstage, it's one of those memories that are indelible, I could never forget it. The place was packed. I remember, the second song we played, "1849," and Ralph [Cole, guitar] just started to play the opening chord, and the people stood up, a standing ovation, yelling and screaming

and clapping. I looked over at Ralph and said, "I guess this is what it means to make it." It was incredible. We got that released, and it went Platinum, the first Canadian album to go Platinum.

In 1969 there was still virtually no music industry in Canada. Three years later, Canadian acts were routinely equaling or surpassing U.S. and British bands' sales figures, at home and abroad. Major record labels now had rosters of Canadian talent, and Canadian-owned record companies were putting out highly popular music as well. Studios were popping up, including some that were attracting the best international talent, because the equipment was good and the producers and engineers were better. Around the world, the country had a reputation for turning out some of the very best songwriters of the times. Given the names involved, including Joni Mitchell, Neil Young, Leonard Cohen, Gordon Lightfoot, and The Guess Who, among many others, it could be argued that the early 1970s were the golden era of Canadian music. Except, the music industry really was getting started, and there were more and more talented Canadians now growing up knowing it was possible to make it in music. In particular, the next group (and some of the old folkies) now wanted to rock.

NOT FRAGILE

Canada's Rockers in the '70s

The Canadian music community's rapid growth through the late '60s and early '70s had been accomplished thanks to the talented musicians in several fields: singer-songwriters, coming through the folk tradition or the chansonnier; R&B players from the bar scenes; and pop hit makers with an ear to the Top 40 were the biggest success stories. Where there hadn't been a breakthrough was in the growing hard rock world. Ever since Led Zeppelin rewrote and rewired the blues, British and American bands had been getting louder and harder. FM radio was promoting albums, not singles, and bands had their own P.A.s and amp stacks to cart around, filling up the hockey rinks with power chords and volume. It ranged from serious artists such as The Who with their rock opera *Tommy*, to cartoon entertainers KISS and Alice Cooper, to the loud and proud heavy metal bands such as Black Sabbath. Aside from Steppenwolf back in 1968, Canadian groups weren't going to eleven.

It's not that Canadian kids didn't want to rock; heavier stuff was just as popular in Canada as anywhere else, it just hadn't become part of the tradition yet. They certainly liked their Zeppelin in the Toronto neighborhood of Willowdale, where a couple of teenagers, Alex Lifeson and Geddy Lee, started playing together in the late '60s. Eventually a solid band was formed, with drummer John Rutsey, called Rush. A couple of years on the local bar circuit toughened them up, and in 1973, the band felt ready for the recording scene. Lee and Lifeson wrote the songs, which were pretty basic power-trio numbers, including the bit of boogie that is "In the Mood," kind of half-Zep, half-Slade, along with a cowbell in the opening, so mid-'70s. The band had decided to release that first album, called just *Rush*, on their own independent label, with only a few thousand in sales. But then a Cleveland disc jockey started playing the song "Working Man," which got the group enough attention to have Mercury Records sign them up.

The rest of the group had no problem with drummer Rutsey, but he had diabetes and wasn't keen to tour, and in came the new guy, Neil Peart, found via an audition. A very different band emerged from that change. Neither Lee nor Lifeson wanted anything to do with lyrics, but Peart was that rare drummer who not only liked to write, he also happened to be a voracious reader and quite a literate fellow. He was keen on fantasy, sci-fi, and liked his Ayn Rand as well. He took over the word duties for the group's second release, *Fly by Night*, and in one year Rush had gone from basic rock lyrics to fantasy numbers such as "By-Tor and the Snow Dog." A little easier to follow was the single "Fly by Night," about a trip Peart had taken to England earlier in life. There was another big difference in the Peart version of the band, as heard on that song. There were some pretty impressive drumrolls on the chorus, and throughout the album, the playing by all three was interesting and progressive, although the songs still had some of the blues-rock of the early version of the band.

The new direction Peart offered was in full display on the following year's *Caress of Steel*, just five cuts in total, with side two of the album completely devoted to the epic "The Fountain of Lamneth," following one man's journey from cradle to grave in nineteen minutes. The flights of fancy in the lyrics now extended to the performing as well, and all three members were becoming known as leaders on their instruments. However, nineteen-minute numbers do not become hits, and *Caress of Steel* saw the band's sales take a big hit, and Neil Peart saw 1975 as "The darkest possible period of our career. We were touring small clubs and doing meager opening slots, and even at this time we called it among the band and crew the 'Down the Tubes' tour. That summer of seventy-five we were unable to pay the crew salaries and our salaries. That winter of seventy-five to seventy-six, I remember I didn't have a car running. I was sleeping on a friend's couch. . . . I was thinking about a return to the farm-equipment business with my dad to be a likely reality."

Mercury Records had laid it on the line. The band was told to be more commercial, and write some hit singles. Well, it turned out you couldn't say that to Neil Peart; he was a contrarian, who believed no business interests should interfere with art. So instead of writing singles, he came up with "a side-long opening piece and a couple of other weird songs." It was called *2112*, which Peart described as "a futuristic dystopia and the individual rediscovering music in the machine age." He also realized it was similar to Rand's novella *Anthem*, so inspirational credit was given. This time, those suburban kids loved it. It was part progressive rock, part heavy metal, told a story and you could play air guitar, air bass, or air drums all day long. Lee, Peart, and Lifeson were all being honored in the musician magazines as the best at their instruments, and now they were the headlining act on tour. In Canada, the album was an immediate Platinum success, and while initially Gold in the U.S., its reputation continued to grow, eventually selling over three million copies there.

Rush then embarked on a string of hit albums, and even the occasional single snuck onto the charts as well, such as 1977's "Closer to the Heart," from *A Farewell to Kings*. It was the rare Rush song under three minutes, although typically different from anything else on radio, with no verse or chorus structure. The band wanted to expand its sound, and toyed with adding a keyboard player, but in the end figured they could do it all themselves, and each member started adding in different instruments. Lee handled the keyboard synthesizers, Lifeson started adding more acoustic and twelve-string guitar, and Peart picked up all manner of percussion pieces, included tubular bells, wind chimes, and temple blocks. They became a band that wasn't afraid to change, or go down roads that might hurt their popularity. Fans still debate the synthesizer years. But somehow the band has survived every change and gathered new generations of fans along the way. Unlike most '70s rock bands, some of their biggest hits would come much further down the road.

April Wine had started out on Canada's East Coast, working out of Halifax in 1969. Montreal was the closest big city and the usual destination for Maritimers, so the band landed there a year later, trying to make it in a bigger market. It was good timing, as a new independent label was starting up, looking for CanCon talent. April Wine joined up with Aquarius Records, the beginning of a long and fruitful relationship, with Aquarius still a thriving company in its fifth decade. So is April Wine, for that matter. The group did have a harder edge, as heard on a first single, "Fast Train," with a pretty mean guitar solo. But it also had a Top 40 side, and that's where their initial success happened. Leader Myles Goodwin had written "Fast Train," but it had only scraped into the Top 40. For the next album, 1972's *On Record*, producer Ralph Murphy brought in a couple of cover songs he thought might work.

The first was from a new British group, Hot Chocolate, who would later have a big disco hit in 1975 with "You Sexy Thing." They had done all right in '71 with "You Could Have Been a Lady" in their homeland, but it hadn't charted in North America. The catchy number did the trick for April Wine, a Canadian smash at number two, and broke the band in the U.S. as well, at thirty-two. Despite a career that has seen them have another thirty-two chart hits in the country, it remains the group's most popular song in concert, played at every show, either at the end or in the encore. It's also stayed on half the radio playlists as well, one of the very favorite songs on every classic rock station. For a follow-up, Murphy picked another British tune. Elton John was just coming into his own at the time, with "Your Song" making him a star. Murphy grabbed a song that had been the B-side of his "Border Song" 45, "Bad Side of the Moon." The rocker did the trick again in Canada, hitting number sixteen. Most Canadians didn't even realize it was an Elton John song, so strongly was it identified with April Wine.

It was a promising start, but not quite what Myles Goodwin had wanted for the band. "We'd been making just a collection of two-and-a-half-minute pop songs for radio," Goodwin said. "We convinced the record company and the producer that we wanted to do a little more than that. We wanted to make it a little heavier, get away from the Top 40." What came next was a full-on hard rock album, called *Electric Jewels*. Released in 1973, it wasn't a success in the usual terms: none of its three singles ("Lady Run, Lady Hide," "Weeping Widow," and the title cut) made it higher than nineteen, none charted outside of Canada, and the album didn't sell as well as its predecessor. But it had a greater impact on the new, hard-rock teenage audience, particularly teenage boys. With its crunching metal guitars, "Weeping Widow" was another air-guitar classic, and the album was one that every group of kids knew. It had a huge effect on smaller Canadian cities, as April Wine was one of the first to really take advantage of the touring opportunities now open in the country. Not only were they often the first big-name band a teenager saw, they were the first real hard-rock group, too. "We realized that people wanted to hear the bands live that were out on the radio, but bands weren't coming," said Goodwin. "So we're gonna go down there, we're gonna see what happens, and it worked out well. The venues kept becoming bigger, playing hockey rinks and arenas, and it was great because it was just a whole other level. So it was a real concentrated effort."

Electric Jewels had served as the door-opener, the word-of-mouth album about the new, hard-rock direction for April Wine. Next, the group capitalized on that move by combining both of their paths; they put out some more Top 40 material with "I Wouldn't Want to Lose Your Love" and "Tonight Is a Wonderful Time to Fall in Love," and then snuck in the hard rock sound on the CanRock classic, "Oowatanite," famous for its fire bell at the start. Topping it all was 1976's number one album, *The Whole World's Goin' Crazy*. One thing about being a hard rock band, it never really goes out of fashion. April Wine continued to have decent-sized hits through the decade, and then at the end of the '70s, another door opened up, as the U.S. got interested in the band. The song "Roller" made the U.S Top 40 in 1979, the first time April Wine had been there since "You Could Have Been a Lady." The *Harder . . . Faster* album went Gold in the U.S. and Platinum in Canada, and *The Nature of the Beast* from 1981 was the group's biggest success yet, with more Gold and Platinum, a hit single in "Just Between You and Me," and a new audience in England as well. A big tour of England was planned, the home of the group's old stand-by, "You Could Have Been a Lady." "We weren't playing that tune when we played there," admits guitarist Brian Greenway. "It was during *The Nature of the Beast* days, and they had us billed as a heavy metal band." These days, April Wine is known as a lot of things to lot of different generations, still one of the favorite live groups in the land.

Montreal's Francophone community had a different take on rock, thanks to some European influences, just not the ones you might expect. In North America, Quebec was one of the very first areas to embrace the progressive rock coming out of England, and bands such as Genesis, Jethro Tull, and Pink Floyd had a stronger influence on musicians and fans in the early '70s. Jazz fusion had a stronger presence as well, and there was also folk in the air in the cafes. In 1973, three friends at the Université de Montréal, Serge Fiori, Louis Valois, and Michel Normandeau, got together just for some fun, to play together, and were far from professional. "Michel wasn't a musician," recalled Fiori, "so I taught him all the chords so he could play rhythm guitar and give support when I do solos. Day in, day out, we were literally living together. We cowrote some lyrics together in the same way we would play—we would sit around the table and improvise the lyrics until the sun was in our eyes in the morning. We started playing small clubs just for fun and to see if there was something to it. It caught on really fast."

Having combined all those influences, the group now known as Harmonium had brought something new to the table. The group really didn't have a connection to the chansonniers, nor was it the North American rock that Charlebois and Pagliaro did so well. When the group's self-titled debut came out in 1974, it wasn't just a success, it signaled a musical shift in the province. "It was a complete acknowledgement," described Fiori. "Everybody—critics, papers, television, fans—everybody was unanimous. Everybody played the total album on radio shows, which was amazing—they didn't play only cuts, they played the album. In about two months, we had a hundred and fifty thousand records sold."

As the audience got bigger, Harmonium grew as well, adding both a keyboard and a horn player, and moving into all sorts of exotic instruments, such as the zither, dulcimer, piccolo, and all manners of synthesizers and keyboards. The progressive side of the band's music actually did progress, and the audience moved right along with it, with the colorful and joyful "Dixie" the song of the summer. It had great long instrumental passages, a clarinet solo, and took prog rock down to Dixieland and back. It was the standout track from the group's second album, *Si on avait besoin d'une cinquième saison*, or as everyone called it, *Cinq saisons*. The group was even able to gain an audience in English-speaking areas, touring ambassadors for Quebec. "It was pretty nuts, it was really big," is how Fiori described that year. "We meant something for the people, the national thing, the French culture. It was fun to see the English audience respond as well. A lot of people knew the French lyrics."

Harmonium's second album, *Cinq saisons*, had been much different and a lot bigger than the group's debut. The third release, 1976's *L'heptade,* was just as different, and once again featured a bigger sound. This time, Fiori had expanded the band to seven full-time members, and the album featured more singers, plus orchestral sections performed by symphony members. Plus, it was a double album. Everyone, from the band to the record label, thought Fiori had gone too far this time. Even he couldn't really explain it. "Yes, it is big," Fiori conceded. "I wasn't thinking. If I would have thought, I would have died. Because of whatever was happening at the time, I just retreated for about nine months, and I got into something spiritual, blah blah blah. I got to thinking about this epic, Indian stuff, about the seven levels of consciousness. And I went for it." Despite all the fears, the ones who mattered the most understood the album, after the initial surprise wore off. "Oh, it was total shock, like, What the hell is that?" said Fiori of the public's reaction. "They put the record on and there's this string intro that's very bizarre. And then it did the same thing, it sold great." *L'heptade* eventually became the most-loved of the three Harmonium albums. But apart from a live album, that was it for Harmonium. "I got really sick, very, very sick, both mentally and physically," Fiori explained. "I was totally burned out. I just crashed, and I couldn't get up for about six months. By the time I did, it was gone for me. I didn't want to go back to that." Instead, Fiori built a studio, and worked on projects at his own, now much slower speed, including movie and television soundtracks, and some new age music in the '90s. After decades away from rock, Fiori returned in 2014 with a new, self-titled solo album.

Beau Dommage was the other big Quebec band of the day, joining in the joyful mix of folk, jazz, and progressive sounds, and really, anything could make the mix. The group's debut album from 1974 contained the beloved "La complainte du phoque en Alaska," about a seal on an ice flow whose love has left for the U.S. to perform. There's a wonderful French-language analogy in there about the danger of leaving your homeland for bright lights, if you're just going to be a trained seal. At first it's a lovely little acoustic guitar number, but eventually a kettledrum leads in the sounds of a sad circus. There was always a theatrical side to Beau Dommage, the music serving the story, and a feel-good energy. The sales figures were enormous, considering the French-language population in the country was only around five million. The group's debut sold 300,000 copies, besting almost every English-language album, and the follow-up, *Où est passée la noce?*, was the first Canadian album to sell 100,000 copies or Platinum status on the day it was released. Even though English Canada could now boast a successful industry, Quebec's was, and still is, a stronger one in the sales department.

The partnership of singer Diane Dufresne and writer Luc Plamondon was one of the longest-running and most successful in Quebec. The pair first met in Paris in the 1960s, where Dufresne was studying voice, and Plamondon was traveling and studying. Starting in 1972, over the next three decades Dufresne performed some six dozen Plamondon lyrics, featuring the music of several different collaborators, everything from theatrical numbers to rockers to disco. Dufresne was known for her wild costumes and dramatic, intense performances, and her hits included "Chanson pour Elvis," "Le Parc Belmont," and "J'ai douze ans maman." She was also one of the stars of Plamondon's 1978 rock opera,

Starmania, with music by France's Michel Berger. Originally a double album, and a year later a theatrical performance, the futuristic piece featured roles for Dufresne, the Parisienne pop star France Gall (Berger's wife), singer-songwriter Claude Dubois, who would dominate Quebec music in the '80s, and the Mississippi-raised singer Nanette Workman. Workman had a fascinating career before, including as a backup singer on The Rolling Stones' "You Can't Always Get What You Want," and after moving to Quebec became a star in a second language, often working and touring in France as well. *Starmania* lived up to its name, proving a huge hit as an album, with Workman's "Ce soir en danse à Naziland" and Dubois's "Le blues du businessman" usually included in lists of the favorite Quebec songs of all time. The rock opera has been presented several times in Quebec and Paris.

The Montreal songwriter Andy Kim came up with another way to rock in 1974. Kim had already had a huge hit in 1969, covering the old Ronettes classic, "Baby, I Love You," taking it to number one in Canada, and number nine in the U.S. a million-selling Gold single. He repeated the trick the next year, this time taking another Ronettes hit, "Be My Baby," into the Top 20. It was his own song that became his next success. Three years off the charts, and without a record deal, Kim self-financed a single, and caught the interest of Capitol Records. "Rock Me Gently" was a number one in the U.S. and Canada, and a number two in England. That's a huge hit by anyone's standards, but it actually wasn't the biggest one Kim had enjoyed. Somewhat secretly, he was one of the team responsible for one of the biggest songs of all time. Kim had been involved with well-known songwriter Jeff Barry in the late '60s, who just happened to cowrite "Be My Baby" and "Baby, I Love You." Barry had been signed to come up with songs for the new animated TV series, *The Archie Show*, based on the comic book characters. In the show, the Riverdale gang formed a pop band, much like The Monkees. The Barry and Kim songs became singles for the fictional group, and the original cut "Sugar, Sugar" sold a shocking 13 million copies, one of the very best-selling singles of all time. It was right up there with Terry Jacks's "Seasons in the Sun," or Paul Anka's "Diana." Fitting that, as Kim and Anka were cousins. See, everybody knows everybody in Canada.

Randy Bachman confused just about everyone by quitting The Guess Who in 1970 just as they had reached the peak with "American Woman." It wasn't even a desire to go out on top; Bachman felt he had to leave for his health, and his convictions. "I'd been with The Guess Who since the early '60s," he explained. "We grew together and then we grew apart. At the time I had a serious gall bladder problem, which was the most painful experience of my life. I needed medical attention and time off. We had hit number one and the band had to keep going." That left Burton Cummings as the main writer and lone front man. He was shocked, but knew what the problems were. "Things weren't going great, Randy was very religious at the time," remembered Cummings. "He had joined the Mormon church, and he had some kids, and he wasn't partying, you know, and [Jim] Kale and I were partying—we were into the rock 'n' roll pretty heavy. And [Garry] Peterson was somewhere in between. It worked for a while, but then Randy—he had health problems and issues with our lifestyle. It just came to an end in 1970. It was bizarre, of all the times, when we were on top of the world." But there was also a deep division in the band over Bachman's outside business dealings, with the other members believing he was trying to sign up bands and do publishing deals at the expense of The Guess Who. It all contributed, and whether Bachman jumped or was pushed has never quite been sorted out.

The Guess Who needed a new guitar player and songwriter, and right away. It was a tall order replacing Bachman, and in the end, the band decided to go with two new members. "We had to scramble to find other guys," Cummings said. "So we got Kurt [Winter] and Greg [Leskiw] from Winnipeg. We came back and picked guys from Winnipeg because we thought that was the right thing to do." It wasn't just a question of loyalty; the three remaining band members knew there was still a competitive and talented scene in the Winnipeg clubs. "We were all in rival bands," Cummings explained. "Kurt was in a trio called Brother, and they were phenomenal. I'd known him for years and he seemed to be the logical choice. It was sure big news in Winnipeg, I'll tell you that." It quickly became big news on radio and in the stores, too. Coming months after *American Woman*, the first album with the five-piece Guess Who, *Share the Land,* picked up right where the last one left off, with more hit songs. Winter was an accomplished songwriter who had brought some excellent material along from his old band. "We needed a follow-up to 'American Woman,'" said Cummings, with a sense of urgency still in his voice. "We were really scrambling not to lose the momentum we had. The lyrics to 'Hand Me Down World' were in the same vein as 'American Woman'—it was a 'Hey, wake up, world' song." It wasn't as big a hit, but it did the trick, getting to number ten in Canada and seventeen in the U.S. Winter also contributed the album favorite "Bus Rider" to the set. Cummings was able to supply the feel-good hippy ballad, "Share the Land," which confirmed the group's star status wouldn't disappear with Bachman, as it reached number two in Canada and ten in the States.

Now with a twin-guitar lineup, The Guess Who were moving into the rock side more and more. The next few singles and albums, with the Winter/Cummings partnership blooming, would see them almost abandon softer fair, for their all-out rock or Top 40 fun. "Hang On to Your Life," "Albert Flasher," "Rain Dance," "Heartbroken Bopper," and "Runnin' Back to Saskatoon" were all up-tempo hits for the group in Canada, although the U.S. wasn't responding as well anymore. Every so often, Cummings would write something softer, such as "Sour Suite," and show he had a terrific knack for piano material as well. But it was getting harder to keep the band together. Leskiw left in 1972, replaced by Donnie McDougall, and Jim Kale, who had joined back in the first Chad Allan era, went that year as well. Winter was gone by 1974, and this time the group turned to a proven pro, grabbing Domenic Troiano from The James Gang. It was just for a victory lap at the end though; The Guess Who was able to land a couple of more Top 40 hits in Canada and the U.S. with "Clap for the Wolfman" and "Dancin' Fool," but Cummings was losing interest in leading them further. After a final single, the nostalgic "When the Band Was Singin' 'Shakin' All Over'" couldn't even get them in the U.S. Top 100, it was time to call it a day, in Cummings's mind. He was ready to go solo.

Cummings was willing to embrace his ballad side again, using that rich and romantic tone that had made the band stars with "These Eyes" a decade earlier. It was a triumphant turnaround for him, as his 1976 debut single, "Stand Tall," put him right back in the Top 10 on both sides of the border. The dramatic number even took the top spot on Canada's Adult Contemporary chart. Some softer ones followed, "I'm Scared" and "Timeless Love," before Cummings got up from the piano for "My Own Way to Rock" and "Your Back Yard." But it was the ballads that kept bringing him the bigger hits, including 1978's "Break It to Them Gently" and the follow-up, "I Will Play a Rhapsody." Cummings would return to rock the country in the future.

Randy Bachman had no intention of going solo when he left The Guess Who, or quitting music either. He still wanted to do what he'd always done, play guitar in a band and write songs that would hopefully be hits. Returning to Winnipeg, it was time to take stock. "Yes, I felt I missed out on a lot of the glory and money from many years of hard work," he reflected. "But had I not left at that time, there would have been no chapter two of my rock story." Chapter two didn't start out that well. A chance meeting with his old singer and boss, Chad Allan, led the two of them to start working together. Initially Bachman was going to produce an album for Allan, but it turned into a band. Bachman was into the new country-influenced rock music out of California, including that by his old friend Neil Young, and still admired the late Buffalo Springfield. There was some fiddle, pedal steel, and Allan even played accordion. The band became Brave Belt, and after playing some tracks for Neil Young, the star helped him arrange a deal from his label, Reprise Records. Bachman brought in a bass player he knew from the old days in Winnipeg, Fred Turner. But the group didn't take off with the sound like Poco or The Eagles managed. Instead, it was pretty much a disaster. Allan's heart wasn't in touring, and he left. A second album was released, and there was even a minor hit with a leftover from Allan's time, "Dunrobin's Gone," but by that point, Bachman and Turner had begun to steer the group toward a harder sound.

Turner had become the main vocalist in the group after Allan left, and he had powerful, heavy pipes, totally unsuited for country rock. Reprise dropped the band, and they were scraping by playing small-town Canadian shows, trying to find someone interested in Brave Belt III, which by then also featured two of Bachman's brothers, Robbie and Tim. Bachman had been using his nest egg from The Guess Who royalties to finance the band, and had vowed to spend no more than $100,000 of his money. Between band salaries, recording costs, and money-losing shows, he was down to $3,000. After the band was refused by every label approached, finally Mercury Records took a gamble on them. The company wanted a couple of changes, though: add a harder guitar sound on some of the tracks, and a name change, something to capitalize on the Bachman name, still known from The Guess Who success. Brave Belt became Bachman-Turner Overdrive.

Bachman began to understand what was wanted from a band in 1973: basic rock 'n' roll, something the kids could dance to at home, and cheer on in concert. Like Rush, April Wine, and even his old bandmates in The Guess Who, BTO soon tapped into the hard rock market; not as hard as heavy metal, but still with lots of power chords, and enough hooks to get you on the radio as well. Then, the group set to work like no other; they toured relentlessly, back and forth, building a fan base one city at a time across North America. The first album got the ball rolling, but hot on its heels came *Bachman-Turner Overdrive II*, and its surprising 1974 hit, "Takin' Care of Business." Surprising, because it seemed to come out of nowhere and take over North American radio. It was perfect in its simplicity, with an instantly recognizable opening and a classic guitar riff, plus an oh-so-simple-it's-brilliant chorus, "Takin' care of business, and working overtime." Somehow, between all the touring, the band made it back into the studio before the year was out, and all of Bachman's hard work finally paid off. The first single off the new album, *Not Fragile*, shot straight to number one in Canada and the U.S., "You Ain't Seen Nothin' Yet," with its stuttered chorus.

It had taken Bachman four years and two bands, but he was back where he had been when he quit The Guess Who, at number one. "The success of BTO was due to many, many years of hard work," Bachman realized. "Knocking on doors that no one would answer and financing it myself with my earnings from The Guess Who. It was a tough couple of years of rejections, but in the end it all seemed worth it, as I was able to forge a completely new style of heavier, more guitar riff music. You better believe I was proud when we made it." BTO was significantly bigger than The Guess Who on the world stage, with a number one in countries such as Germany and New Zealand, and a major tour of Japan in 1976 that led to a live album from the gigs the following year. Now, it had all happened again for Randy Bachman, bigger than he'd probably ever hoped. So what did he do? Once again, he quit the band.

One of the side projects Bachman had going was as a producer. In 1975, he'd started working with a Vancouver group, Applejack, quite popular in the area. But they were a longtime bar band, so a name change was suggested for the group's first album, and Trooper was born. The first two Bachman-helmed albums did quite well, with a couple of Top

20 national hits with "General Hand Grenade" and "Two for the Show." For 1977's *Knock 'Em Dead Kid* album, leader Ra McGuire was worried that he hadn't come up with enough good songs for the sessions. After a rehearsal, a very good friend of his put his arm around his shoulder and said, "Hey Ra, don't worry, we're here for a good time, not a long time." Knowing a great line when he heard it, McGuire sat down the next day, and the song wrote itself, including the opening (true) line, "A very good friend of mine, told me something the other day." One of Canada's best-known and best-loved rock anthems was soon a huge hit, "We're Here for a Good Time (Not a Long Time)."

One year later, and it was the same story: a new album due, called *Thick as Thieves*, but not enough songs. This time it was producer Bachman who provided the impetus, pointing out the group only had nine songs, and ten was the norm for an album in those days. So the group reached back to the Applejack days, and a song they had been using as a set-closer for years. "We were so used to having it around, we'd forgotten all about it," explains McGuire. "It's funny, we played the song to close the set because people loved it, but we made three albums before it occurred to us to record it." That one was "Raise a Little Hell," the second of Trooper's one-two punch combination in The Great Canadian Rock Anthems list. While the band's albums always did well, with five of them either Gold or Platinum in Canada, the greatest hits set *Hot Shots*, which featured both of those classics, went 5X Platinum, and remains one of the foundation albums in any Canadian rock fan's collection.

Also in Vancouver, Terry Jacks was looking at different projects. He'd lost interest in touring, closed down The Poppy Family, split with wife Susan, and just had one of the biggest-selling singles in history with "Seasons in the Sun." He plugged away with some singles and made another album, but what could match that monster hit? So his attention turned back to a group he knew well, the old Vancouver favorites The

Collectors. Only they weren't The Collectors anymore. Singer Howie Vickers had left, and the rest of the group had decided to carry on with a new name, Chilliwack. Jacks helped a bit on the group's first album in 1970, just called *Chilliwack*, but came on board in 1974 as a co-producer for their fourth album, *Riding High*, when they signed to his Goldfish label. After Vickers had left, Bill Henderson had to step forward as the lead singer and songwriter. Two albums in, Claire Lawrence left the group, taking with him the jazz influences, and Chilliwack refocused around Henderson's punchy pop.

It was something he did very well, with interesting, off-kilter singles that had some punch, but still enough sweetness to land on the hit parade. "Lonesome Mary" (1973) had been an interesting one, a boogie number not far from Southern rock, but had a mysterious chorus, and some fine twin guitar interplay. It was a solid rock song that got to number nine. Jacks spun his producer magic next, on the single "Crazy Talk," with a slinky groove, and a sly, mumbo-jumbo-talking woman. Chilliwack had a long streak of hit singles, but also had an equally long streak of bad luck. Every time it seemed like a big break was about to happen, they'd have to switch record labels, losing momentum. Through it all Henderson offered up hardy pop-rock numbers such as "California Girl," "Fly at Night," "Baby Blue," and "Arms of Mary." There was even the long-deserved number one in Canada with 1981's "My Girl (Gone, Gone, Gone)," also a U.S. hit. True to form, Chilliwack's record company in the U.S. promptly went under.

The late '70s saw rock music shifting and reacting to a couple of twin assaults at its usual position at the top of the music heap. Disco had gone from the clubs to the mainstream, and *Saturday Night Fever* was the new sales champ. On the critical side, the old rock heroes of the early '70s were taking a beating in the press from punk rock bands and their fans in the press. The old Woodstock-era groups such as CSNY were being mocked for being out of date and now part of the system they had once battled. Canada didn't really have a strong disco scene, with only occasional hits such as Patsy Gallant's "From New York to L.A.," a major international hit in 1976, going Top 10 from England to Australia, and Norway to South Africa. She spent several years in Paris in the 1990s, yet another star of *Starmania*. Single pop hits could be found from a variety of artists, as well as lots of new and different rock bands, but few dominating new stars emerged in the late '70s in the country. Dan Hill certainly exploded into the public's view with the huge, sentimental hit "Sometimes When We Touch" in 1978. He'd started out in 1975 from the stage of the still-operating Riverboat in Yorkville, and had a couple of medium-level national hits, but the big ballad from his third album went to number one in Canada and number three in the U.S. Despite a long and continuing career, it proved to be the kind of number that was hard to match, or live down, depending on your point of view.

Back on the rock side, more guitar bands came along to do battle with the encroaching disco machine. Toronto's Triumph were one of the hardest, with guitar hero Rik Emmett. Formed in 1975, the group came to wider success on an interesting path, through Texas. The band's 1977 album *Rock & Roll Machine* hit first in San Antonio, leading them to tour the Lone Star State, and build up to Platinum-levels of success through the '80s. Max Webster was another Toronto group, which dated back to 1973. Always a hometown favorite, eventually the band would attract significant national attention by the end of the decade. They were best loved for the 1977 album *High Class in Borrowed Shoes*, and the always-surprising approach of songwriters Kim Mitchell and Pye Dubois. Dubois wasn't a member of the group, but the main lyricist, a job he would continue after Mitchell went solo after the band's collapse in '81. Longtime supporters Rush were huge admirers, and Max Webster served as the opening act on several Rush tours in the '70s.

Streetheart traced their roots back to the 1960s in Regina, Saskatchewan, but finally came together under that name in 1977. The group's biggest success was a 1979 cover of The Rolling Stones' "Under My Thumb," and had a strong following for their albums, earning four Platinum albums before breaking up in 1983. Two of the early members of the group, guitar player Paul Dean and drummer Matt Frenette, had left in '79, before the bulk of the group's success, but they would do all right in their next outfit, called Loverboy. Prism was launched in Vancouver in 1978, and although a modern, pop-metal group, came together in an old-school way. Producer Bruce Fairbairn put the group together, wanting to mold a group from the start. He brought in various local players in a shifting lineup, but featuring Jim Vallance as the main songwriter, although he used the phony name Rodney Higgs much of the time, and also drummed for the group. Other early members included the brothers Tom and Jack Lavin, who would go on to form the successful Powder Blues Band. The carefully assembled group had a hit right away, "Spaceship Superstar," their first three albums went Platinum, and Fairbairn was soon where he had hoped to be, an in-demand producer. He worked out of Vancouver's world-renowned Little Mountain Sound Studios, producing hit after hit for Loverboy, Bon Jovi (*Slippery When Wet*), Aerosmith (*Pump*), INXS, KISS, and more. His protégé at Little Mountain Sound was Bob Rock, a member of the group Payola$, who went on to produce a few hits himself, for everyone from Metallica to Michael Bublé. Jim Vallance left the Prism project early on, but was asked to come back in 1979 to contribute a few songs for the group's third disc, the double-Platinum *Armageddon*, which earned the band a Juno Award for Group of the Year. This time, Vallance brought his new writing partner, the very young and still unsigned Bryan Adams. Fairbairn's Prism project turned out to be very influential.

There was a punk scene in Canada, largely unheralded at the time but influential and quite respected. It didn't get the notoriety of London or New York and didn't get outside the very major centers of Toronto, Montreal, and Vancouver much either. As well described in Men Without Hats' landmark hit "The Safety Dance" later in 1982, punk and New Wave wasn't very well thought of in most clubs in most cities, and it often wasn't safe to dance or be seen as a punk. The southern Ontario triangle of Toronto, Hamilton, and London supplied The Viletones, Teenage Head, and The Diodes, and the short-lived scene around Toronto's first punk club, The Crash 'n' Burn. Teenage Head's glorious first two albums, the self-titled debut in 1979 and 1980's *Frantic City*, were brilliant updates of '60s garage rock, with a very bad attitude. Frontman Frankie Venom was perfect, a scowling, dangerous-looking but charismatic frontman, a real and original punk. "He's not kidding, he really means it," said guitarist Gordie Lewis. "I've seen things that would have buried me ten times over, I've seen him get up, dust himself off, and move on. He's the real thing, and there's not many of them." Lewis still keeps the faith in Hamilton, running the band in memory of the late Venom, who died from cancer in 2008. The Diodes were one of the very first to embrace punk in the country, formed in 1976 at the Ontario College of Art, and played their first gig as the opening act for Talking Heads. Guitar player John Catto had soaked up some of the early NYC punk influences as well, hanging out with The New York Dolls. The Diodes scored another first when they became the first Canadian punks signed to a major label. "The A&R guys from CBS Canada had been to their worldwide convention in June 1977," said singer Paul Robinson. "They saw The Clash live, came back to Toronto, and said, 'Boys, we have to find our own punk band.'" With few places willing to let them play in Toronto, the band created its own club, The Crash 'n' Burn, which brought in outside groups such as The Dead Boys and The Nerves, and played host to some visiting Ramones, putting the scene on the punk radar. Plus, The Diodes had one of the great songs of the time, or any really, with "Tired of Waking Up Tired."

The Viletones were the other member of the Toronto troika, and along with The Diodes and Teenage Head, appeared at a Canada showcase at New York's CBGB in 1977. From London, Ontario came The Demics, where they were the only punk band. They recorded the grand anthem "New York City" in 1979, and by that time punk/New Wave had become popular enough to even get them some airplay. The chorus "I wanna go to New York City," should be taken as ironic, a jab at another hometown band who thought London wasn't good enough.

The most influential Canadian punk group, and certainly the longest active, is Vancouver's D.O.A. After a group known as The Skulls broke up, Joey "Shithead" Keithley put together D.O.A., nothing out of the ordinary for punk groups of 1978. But by 1981, they had stayed together, a rare thing for punk bands then, and they had ignored New Wave and post-punk, instead opting to go even further into the heavier side of punk. When they named their second album *Hardcore '81*, they gave a name to the new genre, and helped create a scene that not only kept punk alive, but saw it grow to its zenith in the early 1990s with the grunge groups. D.O.A. finally seemed over in 2013 when Keithley took the band on a farewell tour; then, he announced a reunion in 2014.

Neil Young had an adverse reaction to the success of *Harvest*, and was not about to pay any attention to the public's desire to have another acoustic hit like "Heart of Gold." Instead, he purposefully introduced all those new fans to his dark and troubled side. The tour after the *Harvest* album saw him playing jarring and sloppy new songs such as "Last Dance" and "Time Fades Away" or creaky ballads at the piano such as "Journey Through the Past" and "Don't Be Denied." Young was troubled, as his Crazy Horse buddy Danny Whitten had become a heroin addict, and Young had to fire him before the tour began. Whitten immediately overdosed and died. The band was combative and often drunk, and Young has called the resulting live album, *Time Fades Away*, which he perversely released as the follow-up to *Harvest*, as the worst of his career. It's actually brilliant in its very sloppiness, mired in gloom, part of the much-admired "Doom Trilogy" with *On the Beach* and *Tonight's the Night*. Whatever he was hoping, Young had managed to kill much of his career momentum, and surprisingly quickly. He didn't really have to worry that much about money, though, as he reunited with CSN for a huge stadium tour in 1974, the first time such massive venues had been used for a full tour. Young wasn't about to let success go to his head, though, or allow his bandmates to reap any more rewards. Young scrapped a proposed new album, and later, left a Stills-Young Band tour in the middle, with no explanation.

His albums were for the most part strong through this time, including 1975's Crazy Horse reunion *Zuma*, featuring "Cortez the Killer," and '77's *American Stars 'n Bars*, with "Like a Hurricane." In 1978, he even went back to some of the acoustic and country sound of *Harvest* on *Comes a Time*, which featured his version of Ian & Sylvia's "Four Strong Winds," one of his favorite songs since hearing it at the 4-D folk club back in Winnipeg. But then there was the punk thing. Young was certainly one of the targets of punk rock's anger, with CSNY mentioned as one of the dinosaur bands that the more vocal punk bands hoped to see wiped out by the new, angry sounds. That's just the kind of opinion that attracts Neil Young, himself really a punk in attitude more than most who wore the right clothing. Young's response was to turn up his guitar and create a conceptual tour around a new song, "Hey Hey, My My." He'd first come up with it while working with the group Devo on his typically bizarre film *Human Highway*. The major line, "rust never sleeps," gave a title to the subsequent album, recorded live with overdubs done at Young's studio. It featured some of the most explosive playing of his career and out-punked the punks for volume. Plus he called out their leader, by telling Johnny Rotten it was better to burn out than to fade away. Young had made the album for himself, but with it, he had stood up for all the old rockers, the ones with value anyway, and pointed out there was a lot of life left for the '60s musicians. In a decade that had started out with Young making the quietest music of his career, he ended it with the loudest, and revitalized his career by doing so. It was yet another great gamble, but it returned him to Platinum status for the first time since *Harvest*, the album of the year in *Rolling Stone* magazine. There would be more gambles, most of them unsuccessful, coming in the '80s.

ROCKIN' IN THE FREE WORLD

New Wave, CanRock, and the Video Era

I t was the best of rock, it was the worst of rock. What a way to start a chapter. But we are talking about the '80s, that most confusing decade, featuring a new wave of exciting pop music, a brand-new video revolution that turned us from listeners to viewers, the introduction of the two biggest stars in Canadian music history, and the reintroduction of an old hero, almost forgotten. It was also the decade of fashion crimes, horrible hair, a focus on style over substance, dated production, too many synths, and the worst music of the careers of two other Canadian heroes. As always, though, with music you can simply choose to revel in the highs and laugh at the lows, and amidst all those awful videos there was plenty to enjoy.

Punk rock's first era didn't have a dramatic effect on Canadian music, but its cleaner, seemingly safer cousin, New Wave, was much more successful and immediately influential. Initially viewed with scepticism and even some of the old hostility aimed at punk, by the start of the '80s several Canadian New Wave groups were enjoying hit records. But it did take some convincing. Toronto's Martha & The Muffins couldn't get a record deal in the homeland at first. The group had come together at the Ontario College of Art in 1977, based around a mutual interest in experimentation. With a sax player and a couple of keyboard players named Martha, the group moved from free jazz to funk to pop, mostly just for the sake of art, and fun. With little attention in Toronto, a demo tape was sent to Andy Warhol's *Interview* magazine in New York, and the music critic offered to help out. He was a good helper. He played it for King Crimson leader Robert Fripp, an early fan, got the band a gig at Hurrah in NYC, and set up a meeting with Virgin Records from England. In no time, the band was off to London to record its debut.

"The British press had never seen a band like ours," said guitarist Mark Gane. "It's hard to imagine now, but we were greeted with great curiosity because Canada was considered a wasteland, with folk singers and outdated heavy metal stuff. Even back then you were getting this surprised condescension—like, who's this weird band from the colonies? Once it was doing well in the U.K., then Europe, Australia, and everywhere else, then Canada was into it as well." The song that broke them was "Echo Beach," about getting away from your boring existence, and getting to your own personal piece of paradise. There was never a real Echo Beach, but it turned out everybody had their own idea of what that might be like. The song was a Top 10 hit in both England and Australia and charted in many countries around the world, and soon after became a hit in Canada as well in 1980, winning the Juno Award for Single of the Year. It was perhaps a little too modern for the U.S. market at the time, one of the few English-speaking countries where it did not chart.

Other groups took notice of the shift toward more electronic and modern music. From Burlington, Ontario, Gordon Deppe and his friend Sandy Horne had formed a prog-rock band in high school, but their influences quickly changed. "When the New Wave thing came in in the early eighties, there was so much variety in electronica and drama,"

Deppe explained. "I said, wait a second, maybe we could get a shot at this, maybe we could slip in there because we were so quirky. Just by making a few little changes, it strangely fits. So that's how it began, a nerdy progressive band that jumped on the New Wave bandwagon." Cue the drum machine. Spoons' "Nova Heart" took off at a couple of forward-thinking radio stations, and the new college radio circuit as well that was developing across the country. The divide between music nerds and Top 40 and rock fans was growing wider, and the kids who liked to play DJ at their university stations were mostly part of the first group. It became an important way to introduce the growing field of alternative rock, with bands such as Blue Peter, Pointed Sticks, Images in Vogue, Strange Advance, and The Box gaining airplay across the country.

Of all the new music groups of the early '80s, the most outrageous, and one of the most popular and successful, was Rough Trade. Although associated with the New Wave years, the group actually goes way back to, yes, Yorkville Village. That's where mainstays Kevan Staples and Carole Pope first met in 1968 at auditions for a band that never was, but the pair became partners in groups from then on. Sensational, edgy performances in art spaces and gay clubs, with Pope often in bondage gear or revealing costumes, put their name around Toronto, and by the mid-'70s they had formed Rough Trade, now a more musical outfit. A debut album, *Rough Trade Live!* became the first rock album ever recorded direct-to-disc, offering greatly increased fidelity. A limited, numbered release, it was produced by none other than Jack Richardson, still helping put Canada on the map with recording techniques. The duo continued with theatrical shows both in Toronto and New York, and was becoming known for their envelope-pushing songwriting. A follow-up record deal was hard to find, with most labels leery of the content. "Record companies always had a hard time with us," Staples said. "Not that they didn't get it, they were afraid of us; a lot of people didn't want to deal with a woman who had what Carole had to say. It was the content, too much social-sexual politics and feminist viewpoints."

One high-profile job the duo landed was writing songs for the 1980 Al Pacino movie *Cruising*. Two were featured, but several were left over, including the provocative "High School Confidential," a lesbian lust song. Now it was another old Yorkville veteran to the rescue, as Bernie Finkelstein thought it was the best thing he'd ever heard. Once he signed the group to his True North label, the band released the *Avoid Freud* album, which featured other notable numbers such as "What's the Furor About the Führer?" and "Fashion Victim," the A- and B-sides of the first single, and a minor hit. It was all to pave the way for "High School Confidential" though, which took the country by storm, making number twelve on the national charts, despite its controversial language and subject matter. "They [radio] had a hard time with 'cream my jeans,'" confirmed Staples. "We weren't trying to be shocking or provocative, that wasn't our intention. To us, it was social satire, sexual politics, and social commentary. We certainly didn't think about it when we were writing it." The lyric eventually got beeped out for airplay, which only added to the controversy and attention. The once too-outrageous-for-the-mainstream Carole Pope soon won the Juno for Female Vocalist of the Year.

The punk and early New Wave movements had opened the pop world to larger statements than love songs and guitar heroics. Now bands were being formed with more in mind than just playing for fun. The Parachute Club were a big noise on Toronto's newest scene in the early '80s, Queen St. West. "We were (a) political; (b) danceable; and (c) celebratory," explained lead singer Lorraine Segato. "We were trying to break new ground in whatever we could, politics and music. We were four women, three men, and we wanted to show that women could be players, in music and the world. And we wanted to show that politics could be danceable, too." With a Caribbean rhythm, inspirational lyrics, and a big groove, the band's "Rise Up" became an instant hit, rising up to Top 10 in Canada. The purposefully inclusive lyrics didn't hurt, either. "A lot of people claim it as their own," explained Segato. "The gay movement, the women's movement, every group. We went to England, and they were playing it on Christian radio as a gospel song. The Obama thing started it again. Little waves that come up, and every time, I'm completely shocked. It was just a call to equality." It won the Juno Award in 1984 for Single of the Year, and The Parachute Club won Most Promising Group of the Year. For his work on the song, the relatively unknown Daniel Lanois was nominated for Producer of the Year. He was, however, about to become very well known.

If you'll recall, a lack of quality recording studios in Canada had been one of the major stumbling blocks in developing a music industry in the country in the mid-'60s. With several of them around a decade later, it made all the difference in the world to up-and-coming bands. The Kings were longtime bar-band regulars on the southern Ontario circuit, itching for a record deal. They knew they needed a quality demo, so they saved up enough money to go for the best. "Nimbus 9 was where Jack Richardson had recorded The Guess Who and Bob Ezrin had done Alice Cooper," said the most excellently named Mister Zero, the group's guitar player. "We knew the history, but we didn't know Bob was around. He was back after doing *The Wall* with Pink Floyd. One of our managers got to talking with him, and he took our tapes home to listen. His kids liked our stuff and so did he. So it was a Cinderella story when he went to Elektra in L.A. and got us a deal." The band had two songs, "Switchin' to Glide" and "This Beat Goes On," which everybody liked, but there was a feeling the two were incomplete. In a moment of inspiration, the band combined them, and it was this medley that really caught on. Radio stations that had turned "Switchin' to Glide" into a minor hit pounced on the new, longer arrangement. The group's Ezrin-produced debut album went Gold. The beloved number remains a radio favorite to this day, and the group jokingly called their DVD biography *The Anatomy of a One-Hit Wonder.*

In Montreal, synthesizer wizard Ivan Doroschuk turned New Wave into protest music. He was a fan, and wanted to go to clubs and dance, but New Wave was still a hard sell. He had an epiphany on a trip to the nation's capital. "It came out of a direct experience," Doroschuk said.

> It was in Ottawa. We would go to clubs, and the New Wave and punk music—they weren't playing much of it. It was still pretty much disco and heavy rock. Every time they'd play a punk or New Wave song, we'd start dancing and pogoing. We'd usually get kicked off the dance floor and thrown out of the club by the bouncers, or told by the management to tone it down. So I went home and I wanted to tell people, don't let these bouncers say we can't dance to New Wave if we want to.

The result was "The Safety Dance," the synth-heavy number with the gruff lead vocals, that first got the group Men Without Hats a hit in the U.S., number one on the dance chart. That circled around and made the song a hit in Canada. Then one of the most colorful, odd, and memorable rock videos of all-time made the song a phenomenon. It was made in Bath, England, had a medieval theme, lots of costumes, traditional Morris Dancers, Punch and Judy, a maypole, and Ivan dancing around with a jester, played by well-known dwarf actor Mike Edmonds. "The Safety Dance" became a Top 10 hit in the U.S., England, and several other countries, but only reached eleven in Canada, where there wasn't a full-time video channel in 1982.

The biggest band of the New Wave days in Canada helped bring a city to the fore that had always felt overshadowed by Toronto, and everything east in general. Vancouver, thanks to its isolated status way out west and behind a big wall of mountains, had an independent music streak, often feeling more akin to the U.S. West Coast. The huge U.S. band Heart was actually started in Vancouver by a draft dodger and some friends from across the border in Washington State. They made their debut, *Dreamboat Annie*, in Vancouver, were with a Canadian label, and became a hit locally well before releasing the album in the U.S., even considered CanCon during those Vancouver days. Chilliwack was a much bigger band in British Columbia, and going as far back as the '60s, Terry Black was a teen idol when much of the country didn't know his name. But some significant moves were going to make Vancouver the major player in the country in the early to mid-'80s, and a world leader in talent, management, recording, and label ownership to this day.

Payola$ had formed on Vancouver Island in the late '70s by some high school friends, who soon crossed over to Vancouver, joining the early New Wave scene. One of the group members, Bob Rock, was also talented on the technical side, and he got a job at Little Mountain Sound Studios, working with producer Bruce Fairbairn. It was a great arrangement, because Rock could record his own group on the side. A first single, "China Boys," featuring Paul Hyde on vocals, got them the attention of A&M Records, which was looking for New Wave acts to break. An EP did well enough, and an album was given the green light. Produced by Rock, it failed to chart. Around this time, former David Bowie guitar player Mick Ronson of The Spiders from Mars had told A&M he was available for work, so the young group was soon back in the studio, now with one of their heroes. This time, Rock and Hyde had come up with the missing ingredient, a hit single. With Ronson playing and producing, and Rock engineering, the song "Eyes of a Stranger" was one of the top-selling songs of 1982, reaching four on the national charts. It was actually based on the worst pickup line Hyde could think of, the opening words of the song, "Can I touch you to see if you're real?" That qualified the duo to win the Juno for Best Songwriters of the Year, another for Best Single, and a third for Most Promising Group.

The band lived up to the promise with another hit album in 1983, *Hammer on a Drum*, which included the East-meets-West duet, "Never Said I Love You," with Carole Pope. A number eight chart placement confirmed New Music's move to the mainstream.

Vancouver was doing very well turning out hit bands. Somewhere between New Wave and old bar band R&B was Doug and The Slugs, one of the most intense and fun groups to ever grace a college town's biggest bar. Led by charismatic frontman Doug Bennett, the group's first single, "Too Bad," was an instant hit, massive in Vancouver where the group was a party favorite, and Top 20 across the land. Doug and The Slugs were unconventional on the business front, forming their own label from the very start, promoting their own dances in Vancouver, and financing much of their career. Along in that plan was the group's manager, Sam Feldman, a former doorman and a booking agent. He was partners with manager Bruce Allen, and soon became one of the most important agents and managers in modern music, representing Joni Mitchell, Norah Jones, James Taylor, Diana Krall, Bryan Adams, Michael Bublé, and many more.

A group of musical vets looking for a base for their new group decided Vancouver was a better option than Calgary. When they had left Streetheart, guitar player Paul Dean and drummer Matt Frenette had returned to their home city, and Dean met singer Mike Reno, who had recently left the group Moxy. The pair had set their sights on the big time, and with some decent credentials already in hand with their previous bands, relocated to Vancouver and started approaching major record labels. There was no interest in the U.S., but the Canadian division of Columbia took note. The group went into the best local studio, which was, of course, Little Mountain Sound, with the usual team, producer Bruce Fairbairn and engineer Bob Rock.

Fairbairn had done well with his Prism project, but it was time to move on. He'd won the Juno Award of Producer of the Year for the group's third album, 1979's *Armaggedon,* and was just finishing up work on the fourth, *Young and Restless,* when Loverboy came calling. It was a perfect match, as everyone involved wanted the same thing, a commercial hard-rock hit. Loverboy delivered, with the group's self-titled debut a hit in Canada first, which then prompted CBS to come on board in the U.S. First single "Turn Me Loose" offered up an updated hard-rock sound, with a synthesizer on top of the guitars and drums the whole way through. Oh, and Mike Reno's headband, that was catchy too. The song went Top 10 in Canada, and placed even higher in Australia and New Zealand, plus broke into the Top 40 in the U.S. Follow-up "The Kid Is Hot Tonite" kept the ball rolling, and hard rock radio stations helped propel the album to major sales figures, at number seventeen in Canada and a surprising thirteen in the U.S. It sold a million copies in Canada alone, and doubled that in the U.S. "Turn Me Loose" took the Juno for Single of the Year.

The Dean-Reno team had lots of material ready, and "the difficult second album" proved no such thing. Called *Get Lucky*, the album featured a pair of red leather pants on the cover, and a major hit song inside, "Working for the Weekend." A classic party anthem, the song hit the Top 10 in Canada and twenty-nine in the U.S, but more importantly scored again at rock radio, sending the album into the Top 10 in the U.S. and Canada, selling four million copies. *Get Lucky* won the Juno for Album of the Year in 1983, and at the 1984 Juno Awards, Loverboy took home Band of the Year, beating out two other Vancouver acts, Payola$ and Chilliwack. Vancouver would no longer worry about the rest of the country acknowledging its talent.

That doesn't even include the biggest Vancouver star. He'd been slowly working his way up, building credits and a solid team. When Jim Vallance had left the Prism project, his next order of business was to start working with a kid he'd just met, shopping at the instrument store. His name was Bryan Adams. "I was twenty-three when I met Bryan,"

Vallance recounted. "He'd just turned eighteen. It was the first week of January 1978. I was at Long & McQuade with my friend Ali Monroe. Ali knew Bryan and she introduced us. Bryan said, 'Hey, we should get together and do some writing.' A day or two later, Bryan came over to my house, and we spent the next eleven years together, almost every day. He had confidence bordering on arrogance. Just a real sense of 'I'm gonna make it, and nothing's gonna stop me.'"

Adams had already had a small bit of fame at sixteen, having joined the Vancouver band Sweeney Todd in 1976, after original lead singer Nick Gilder had quit. Gilder got the better end of that deal, with Sweeney Todd scoring a number one hit in Canada with "Roxy Roller" during Gilder's time, but nothing with Adams. Gilder then hit even bigger solo, with a cross-border number one, "Hot Child in the City" in 1978. Adams wanted a piece of that.

The Adams-Vallance partnership had a less-than-auspicious debut on the charts, with the 1978 disco number "Let Me Take You Dancing," a minor hit, mostly on the dance charts. It has been expunged by the Adams camp, long deleted, never issued on CD or featured on any of the many best-of compilations. Better luck was found by offering up their early works to some of their friends. Adams contributed three cuts to Prism's 1979 hit *Armageddon,* and another number went to Bachman-Turner Overdrive that year, while Vallance contributed four to the same album. In the meantime, Adams was hard at work on his own debut album. Self-titled, it arrived in 1980 to no great acclaim, but enough backing from A&M Records to keep working on the formula. They knew what they were going for: "We always tried to write something that sounded like it belonged on the radio or on a record," explained Vallance. "If you're writing for radio, you're trying to write anthems. That's what hit songs are—anthems. Just because you try doesn't mean you're going to succeed, but that's often what we were trying to achieve, quite unashamedly." The next album, 1981's *You Want It, You*

Got It, fared better. It made some inroads at radio in Canada and the U.S., and Adams started opening for some major artists, including a national Candian tour with Loverboy, where his energetic show earned him a lot of converts.

It all paid off in 1983. *Cuts Like a Knife* started out softly, but with a big hit, the power ballad "Straight from the Heart." It's the song that truly launched his career, making number ten on *Billboard*. The depth of tracks on the album showed the attention to the craft that Adams and Vallance were pursuing. It had a big arena rocker in the title cut as the second single, and a feel-good pop song as the third, "This Time." And by the end of the year, it had sold two million copies in the U.S. and Canada. Adams and Vallance won Composer of the Year at the Junos for the song "Cuts Like a Knife," and the release was named Album of the Year. It was also just a start.

Reckless from 1984 dwarfed *Cuts Like a Knife*. It sold six times more, ending up at 12 million worldwide. It was number one on *Billboard*'s album chart, Canada's chart, and either number one or Top 10 in several other countries. It sold five million copies in the U.S. alone, and it became the first Canadian album to ever sell more than a million copies in the country. It had seven hit singles, led off by the dark rocker "Run to You," followed by the stadium anthem "Kids Wanna Rock," the easy-going "Somebody," and the power ballad "Heaven." There was more in reserve, though, and Adams then hit everyone with "Summer of '69," the nostalgia-laced coming-of-age number that, while not his greatest chart hit, has become his most popular song, and his own favorite as well. "Without a doubt," Adams confirmed. "I love it too. The song was originally called 'Best Days of My Life,' and it was kind of a mixture of ideas about growing up and nostalgia. The main thing about the story was I wanted to be able to sing about something real, like I did buy an electric guitar at a five-and-dime in Ottawa, and the characters in the song, Jimmy and Jody, are people I worked with at the time." Vallance added: "Whenever I've seen Bryan in concert—Canada, England, wherever—this is the song that gets the biggest reaction from the audience." It's hard to imagine Adams being able to surpass this monumental album and beloved hit single, but there was a big world out there, and Adams was soon showing Canada and the U.S. that everywhere you go, kids wanna rock.

The early '80s had seen an explosion in record sales, thanks to blockbusters such as Michael Jackson's *Thriller*, Prince's *Purple Rain*, and Bruce Springsteen's *Born in the U.S.A.* Spurring on those mega-sales figures was the new marketing tool, the music video. When a Springsteen or a Bryan Adams would put out seven singles from an album, there would be a brand-new video to accompany each, another three-minute advertisement for the record. MTV had gone on-air in the U.S. in 1981, but it took until 1984 for MuchMusic to launch in Canada, the first all-music network in the country. But the music TV concept did go back further than that in the country. In 1979, well before MTV, CITY-TV in Toronto had launched *The New Music*, an hour-long magazine-styled show that included interviews, concert footage, and videos, and took on major topics in music, using a journalistic approach rather than simply playing the latest hits. Owned by CHUM, this was the part of the team that later developed MuchMusic. Hosting the program from 1979 to 1985 were entertainment journalist Jeanne Beker, and CHUM DJ J. D. Roberts. Musicians were treated seriously, especially if there was a cultural angle to pursue. The Clash were interviewed backstage in 1979 after a rowdy show, talking about trying to bring back real rock 'n' roll energy to North America. U2 sat down after playing the El Mocambo club on the group's first trip to North America in 1980. And just about every new Canadian band was given the opportunity to have their say with some all-important national exposure.

Another precursor to MuchMusic was *City Limits*, the all-night weekend video show on CITY-TV. It was hosted by musician and actor Christopher Ward, who earned the honor of being the country's first VJ. One of the frequent guests on the program was a member of the Toronto branch of the Second City comedy troupe, Mike Myers, and during this time he developed his heavy-metal-loving Wayne Campbell character, later of *Saturday Night Live*'s "Wayne's World" sketches. When MuchMusic was given the go-ahead in 1984, Roberts and Ward were two of the inaugural VJs. Roberts stayed with the video channel until 1987, when he switched to become a CITY-TV news anchor, and moved to the U.S. full-time in 1992, where he has held anchor and national correspondent jobs with CBS, CNN, and Fox News. It's always amusing when people in the U.S., familiar only with John Roberts, the news reporter, discover clips of J. D. Roberts, host of MuchMusic's heavy metal show, *The Power Hour*. Christopher Ward went back to his music career in 1987, but an EP that year didn't gain much success. It was his songwriting that would be noticed instead.

Instead of a tight playlist of hit songs, MuchMusic tried to present a little of everything to every Canadian. There were lots of hours of regular video rotation, but also there were several shows that focused on individual genres, such as *The Power Hour*. There was a Francophone segment, alternative music, *MuchEast* and *MuchWest*, which took the programming outside of Toronto to the Atlantic and Pacific Coasts, dance music on Friday nights, a rap and hip-hop section, and a live-audience concert and Q&A series produced right in their broadcast facility, *Intimate and Interactive*, which regularly spilled onto the streets. Most important though was the steady diet of Canadian videos the station played. And they had to play them; like radio, the video license required CanCon play, and another boost was given to the Canadian music and film industries, from a twenty-four-hour-a-day network looking for quality product.

A new batch of groups emerged, with video-ready looks, and record company budgets. Toronto's Platinum Blonde started recording in 1983, with a pop New Wave sound, and when Much went on air, they already had videos prepared for the songs "Doesn't Really Matter" and "Not in Love," complete with feathered haircuts, headbands, and leopard-print jackets. High rotation on Much spread the name, and by the group's next album, 1985's *Alien Shores*, the cut "Crying Over You" went to number one. The production values had increased notably in the video, and so had the Duran Duran postures. Honeymoon Suite were from Niagara Falls, Ontario, the honeymoon capital of the world, and arrived just in time for Much in 1984. "New Girl Now" saw the group sporting leather pants, vests with no shirts, and at least one headband. Glass Tiger had a smash debut in 1986, "The Thin Red Line," produced by Jim Vallance, with included the number one Canadian and number two U.S. hit, "Don't Forget Me (When I'm Gone)." The song was given the official seal of approval by guest superstar Bryan Adams, singing a couple of lines at the end. A follow-up, "Someday," also entered the Top 10 in both countries.

Handsome guys seemed to do well on Much, and an already-established star jumped to new heights with his video single. Montreal's Gino Vannelli had first hit both the U.S. and Canadian Top 30 in 1974 with "People Gotta Move," and 1978's smooth "I Just Wanna Stop" was a smash, number one in Canada and number four in the States. He had taken time off, from 1981 to 1985, but when he returned it was with an explosion. "Black Cars" reintroduced Vanelli in the video age, with great hair, great clothes, great moves, and a very catchy hit, landing at number six nationally. Gowan's first album in 1982 hadn't done a whole lot of him, but a follow-up in 1985, *Strange Animal*, featured the Top 5 hit "A Criminal Mind," and a futuristic video with comic-book graphics and big shoulder pads. Italian-Canadian singer Zappacosta broke hearts in 1984 with "We Should Be Lovers," and broke the bank in 1987 when his song "Overload" was included on the *Dirty Dancing* soundtrack, which sold more than 30 million copies. Not to be outdone in the one-named singer ranks, Montreal's Luba represented women with the brightly colored videos for "Storm Before the Calm" and "Let It Go." She won three consecutive Juno Awards for Female Vocalist of the Year in the mid-'80s. It was actually her third attempt at a recording career in her third language, having previously released songs in Ukranian and French.

If there was one song that seemed to be played constantly in the first few months of MuchMusic's existence, it was another Montreal newcomer's first hit, "Sunglasses at Night" by Corey Hart. The nineteen-year-old had been sent to England to make his debut album, *First Offense*, the idea being to capture the hip and stylish sounds then coming out of London. The album was actually done, but Hart was toying around with a new song after he had returned to Canada. He liked it so much, he went back to his label, pleaded his case, and was sent back to London to record the track, even though they'd already spent the entire budget for the album. It was a smart move. "Sunglasses" was actually a hit in the U.S. first, and a bigger one there than in Canada. It hit number seven in *Billboard* in August of 1984, the same month MuchMusic launched. The U.S. success finally forced Canadian radio to play the track, which took it just to twenty-four, but MuchMusic had it on heavy rotation, and the album made it to number six. His next release, 1985's *Boy in the Box*, went to number one, and sold a million copies in Canada, following Bryan Adams into the Diamond club. The ballad "Never Surrender" also hit number one in Canada, number three in the U.S., becoming his biggest-ever hit, but thanks to the constant video play, it's "Sunglasses at Night" that remains the one forever associated with Corey Hart.

A French-language version of MuchMusic, called MusiquePlus, was also launched in 1986. As with English Canada, there were plenty of new visual stars with videos to play. Martine St. Clair was another singer tied to the success of the rock opera *Starmania*, as Luc Plamondon cast her in a starring role in the 1980 Canadian version. Her several cuts on the *Starmania Made in Québec* album led to her winning the Felix Award for best new performer in 1981. That same year she had a huge single with the older singing star from Paris, Gilbert Bécaud, called "L'amour est mort." Plamondon wrote the lyrics for her debut album, and her third disc in 1986 made her the top performer of the day in Quebec. "Ce soir l'amour est dans tes yeux" was the title track from the album, one of five hits, the best-selling single and the pop LP of the year.

Daniel Lavoie's fame in Quebec came in a very indirect route. He was born in Dunrea, Manitoba, part of the Francophone community in that province, and won talent contests and started a recording career in the 1970s. He didn't get much attention in Quebec, but when he moved to France, his background helped gain him a lot of attention. He became known as The Man of the Plains for his Prairie roots, and was a star in that country before being recognized at home. By 1979, he was a star in both Canada and France, and two decades of hits followed in both countries. But the biggest was still to come. In 1998, he was cast in the latest Luc Plamondon production, this time a musical based around the ever-popular works of Victor Hugo, called *Notre-Dame de Paris*. Lavoie appeared in the production for seven months in Paris, and then went on tour in France, Quebec, and England. The song "Belle" from the cast album, which he sang alongside Patrick Fiori and Sherbrooke, Quebec's Garou, sold three million copies, was a number one hit for eighteen weeks, and is the third-biggest selling hit of all time in France.

It was another Francophone from outside Quebec who broke a record on France's album charts. Again, there was an acting connection. Roch Voisine had grown up in tiny Sainte-Basile, New Brunswick, and like most '60s kids, wanted to be a hockey player. That dream ended after an injury, so he did the next best thing—he played one on TV. Voisine was already an up-and-coming singer in Quebec when he took a role in the highly popular series *Lance et Compte*, about a hockey team. Soon after, he released his third album, called *Hélène*. The title track became an immediate hit in Quebec, reaching number one, and crossing the Atlantic, it had the same results in France, where it stayed at number one for nine weeks. The album joined it at the top as well, and when the numbers were counted, it had sold a milion copies, making it the first Canadian Diamond-status album in France.

It would not be the last. The biggest star to ever come from Quebec was already well known in the province, well known in Europe as well. Celine Dion had released nine French-language albums in the 1980s, some that had come out in Europe, with some pretty significant hits as well. She had won the Eurovision Song Contest, and all this while still a teenager. She had been discovered when her brother had sent a tape of her to René Angélil, the former member of the '60s band Les Baronets. He was managing artists by then, and was so impressed with Dion's voice, he started working with the twelve-year-old singer. French Canada had quickly fallen to her charms, and she had won a couple of Felix Awards for Song of the Year, "Une Colombe" from 1984, and "Incognito" from 1987, which was also a major Eurorpean hit. But Dion and Angélil had another dream, which they were working on at the end of the decade, and the 1990s would see the Quebec artist achieve a level of fame that would only ever be rivaled by one other Canadian.

MuchMusic did play lots of the non-Canadian hits as well as all the locals, including those of an old favorite from the New Music days, U2, fast becoming the biggest group of the day. The 1984 album *The Unforgettable Fire* had drastically changed the group's sound, and "Pride (In the Name of Love)" was hypnotic, intense, and important. There was also a Canadian connection, somewhat mysterious at first. Listed as producer of the album, along with the avant-garde hero Brian Eno, was Hamilton, Ontario's Daniel Lanois. He'd last been heard from when he produced The Parachute Club's hit "Rise Up," and the band Martha & The Muffins, which featured a new member, Lanois's sister Jocelyn.

But somehow, Lanois had gone from decent-sized Canadian hits to the most important producing job in rock music, as there was little doubt U2 were about to become huge, unless they made some crazy mistake, like hiring a left-field, artsy producer and his unknown sidekick.

Not many Canadian music fans would have heard about Lanois's progression in the production world. He had started out by building a home studio in his mother's house in Ancaster, beside Hamilton, along with his brother, Bob. Local bands did demo recordings there in the '70s, folk favorite Willie P. Bennett had Lanois engineer his best-loved *Hobo's Taunt*, and even beloved children's entertainer Raffi made a record with them in 1977. Both were also musicians, and Daniel had earned his stripes the hard way, playing the Yonge Street Strip in Toronto, by then a seedier version of the '60s scene, with many of the old haunts turning into strip clubs. But Lanois was a hard worker and strove to learn his crafts, whether it was playing pedal steel and guitar in between strip shows, or learning the intricacies of microphones and mixing consoles. Most of all, he was obsessed with sound and all its possibilities. The Lanois brothers moved out of Mom's place and into their own Grant Avenue Studios in Hamilton, and Lanois's first major production credit was Martha & The Muffins' *This Is the Ice Age* album in 1981. Around then a copy of some of Lanois's work had been passed on to Brian Eno. Eno was in the middle of a series of recordings known as his *Ambient* albums, made of complex soundscapes and field recordings, sound collage as much as music, the emphasis on atmosphere rather than melody. Eno was intrigued with the sounds Lanois was finding and creating at Grant Avenue, and paid him a visit. Soon Lanois was enlisted as a co-conspirator on the latest *Ambient* album and several more projects, Eno himself setting up camp in Hamilton. "It just goes to show that if you do good work, eventually it will be heard," says Lanois. "It doesn't matter where you live."

For U2's album, Eno handled the ideas, while Lanois did more of the actual technical production. The success of that album soon led to other big-name projects. Peter Gabriel let him loose in his Real World Studios as the pair produced the soundtrack to the film *Birdy*. That worked out so well, Lanois stayed on to produce Gabriel's 1986 album *So*, an international smash featuring the number one single, "Sledgehammer." Lanois was now one of the most in-demand producers in the business. U2 wanted to see how the team could progress on a new album, and Lanois and Eno were back for 1987's *The Joshua Tree*, a more focused effort than *The Unforgettable Fire*, which resulted in even greater success, and a string of hits. That same year, Lanois produced fellow Canadian Robbie Robertson, on his first album since leaving The Band a decade before. It was a triumphant return, Lanois drafting in Gabriel and U2 for guest appearances. The decade ended with perhaps Lanois's most surprising job yet, producing the enigmatic Bob Dylan on the album *Oh Mercy*. Dylan's '80s albums had been more miss than hit, but this was regarded as an artistic success by fans and critics, and helped Dylan regain some missing respect.

Lanois wasn't the usual producer, standing behind the glass in the studio control room. His artistry was such that he became another player in the group, contributing sound and musical ideas, always handy with a guitar or his beloved pedal steel, as well as his audio tricks. He had rarely been a writer, though, until his clients started encouraging him. That led to his own albums as well, starting in 1989 with *Acadie*. A highly personal release, it told stories of his family and the move from Quebec to the Hamilton area, his French-Canadian heritage, his spiritual connection to nature, and a mysticism that he found in his travels, from Ireland to New Orleans. Now Lanois's path would include his own works as well as his productions, albums that explored everything from dub music to new ambient journeys to reexamined uses of the pedal steel, as well as more hugely successful releases for U2, Dylan, Emmylou Harris, Neil Young, Willie Nelson, and more.

What Lanois was to critically acclaimed rock in the '80s, Victoria, B.C.'s David Foster was to mainstream pop. The former member of the group Skylark had only had one success with that band, the 1973 Top 10 hit "Wildflower," but he managed to parlay that into a growing reputation as a keyboard player and arranger. His first major credit was for one of his heroes, getting to play piano, organ, and synthesizer, and do string arrangements on several cuts on George Harrison's 1975 album, *Extra Texture (Read All About It)*. He continued to build his reputation into the early '80s, adding songwriting to his arsenal, helping create hits for Earth, Wind & Fire, Boz Scaggs, and Chicago. As Chicago's producer, he was regarded as the wizard who had brought that group back to prominence. In 1985, Foster finally had another Top 40 hit, "Love Theme from St. Elmo's Fire (For Just a Moment)," for which he had produced the soundtrack, and written the number one single for John Parr, "St. Elmo's Fire (Man in Motion)." From that point, Foster would have a string of A-list superstars at his door, including Barbra Streisand, Celine Dion, Whitney Houston, Madonna, Andrea Bocelli, Michael Bublé, Josh Groban, Rod Stewart, and Stevie Wonder. He started his own label, where he signed Bublé and Groban, and in 2012 was named chairman of the classic jazz label, Verve. Not bad for Ronnie Hawkins's former bus driver.

Foster was the choice to guide Canada's music community in the global charity effort for famine in Africa. What had started in England with Band Aid's "Do They Know It's Christmas?" to raise funds for the crisis in Ethiopia had spread to the U.S., with U.S.A. for Africa's "We Are the World." That was produced by industry vet Quincy Jones, who had worked with Foster on Michael Jackson's *Off the Wall* album. He called and asked Foster to organize a similar effort from Canada, which could be included on the *We Are the World* charity album. Foster happened to be in the studio at the time with none other than Payola$. He'd been hired to take the band over the top, and hopefully provide them with the final magic needed to break the group outside Canada. All hands were on deck for this effort; Jim Vallance and Bryan Adams had helped with one song, Foster had cowritten the first single, "You're the Only Love," and a name change had been made to take the focus off the old payola scandal references at American radio (payola was the corrupt practice of paying off DJs to play certain songs). The group was now called Paul Hyde and The Payolas. None of this worked, and it was one of the very few bombs in Foster's long career. At least they all got one hit out of it. Foster, Hyde, Rock, Vallance, and Adams were all cowriters (along with Rachel Paiement, former member of the Quebec group Cano, and Vallance's wife) of "Tears Are Not Enough," credited to the one-time only supergroup Northern Lights. Featured on the song and in the cameo-filled video were Neil Young, Joni Mitchell, Gordon Lightfoot, Burton Cummings, Anne Murray, Mike Reno, Geddy Lee, Corey Hart, Bruce Cockburn, Hyde, Carole Pope, Lorraine Segato, Robert Charlebois, Claude Dubois, Zappacosta, and a host of others. Even the backup singers were celebrities, including Pauls Anka and Shaffer, John Candy, Catherine O'Hara and Eugene Levy from *SCTV*, and the greatest Canadian jazz man, Oscar Peterson. It was the number one single and video of the year in the country.

While the mid-'80s had been thrilling for some, there were others who seemed to have been cast adrift in a market so drastically influenced by new technology and the visual image. Neil Young had certainly tried to move with the times. His 1982 album *Trans* had featured Young singing through a Vocoder, which electronically manipulated his vocals, causing his regular fans to run away in droves. It was a noble experiment, and there were some decent songs on it once you got used to the synths. However, his next project couldn't even claim that. Young had angered his new record company Geffen, and the boss, his longtime friend David Geffen, by offering such strange album projects. After rejecting a country album, Geffen begged Young to simply give him a rock 'n' roll record. That was like holding up a red flag to a bull. Young gave him exactly that, a ten-song, twenty-five-minute- long rockabilly album, *Everybody's Rockin'*, just like they used to make them, only in 1958. It had some old covers, and some songs that sounded like they'd been written back then, only sung in a very shaky voice. The short running time was actually a blessing. And people wonder why Geffen sued Young for delivering noncommercial music. When his country album, *Old Ways*, was reworked and delivered in 1985, it was received far better, and Young said at the time he was finally getting to the music he loved, and might settle down as a country performer for the rest of his career. Riiiiiight. A return to rock with *Landing on Water* and then *Life*, followed by an all-blues album, only continued to confuse and alienate his audience, and caused many to question his future relevance. But as we have already discovered, one should never make assumptions about Neil Young.

Things weren't going much better for Joni Mitchell. Like Young, she had enjoyed a time at the top of charts, and at the top of the celebrity world. *Court and Spark* (1974) had provided the biggest pop hits of her career, "Help Me" and "Free Man in Paris," and the album was her all-time best seller as well, topping two million. It also featured a larger group of musicians, and she was now using some jazz-fusion players as her band. Because of her many different guitar tunings, this was especially effective. Over the next several years and albums, the jazz influences increased, and predictably, her sales figures shrank. Not that these were weak albums; 1976's *Hejira* is considered by many the peak of her career, but they were getting more esoteric, and further away from the ear-pleasing poetry of "Both Sides, Now." *Mingus* (1979), a project with the dying jazz master of the bass, divided even jazz fans. Her next studio album didn't come until 1982, and like Young, Mitchell also was lured to her friend Geffen's new label. Unlike Young, she was willing to provide him with a rock album, *Wild Things Run Fast*. While it was certainly more accessible, Mitchell's audience had largely given up on her new material, and weren't convinced to return for her cover of an Elvis tune as a single, "(You're So Square) Baby I Don't Care." *Dog Eat Dog* (1985) saw Mitchell experimenting again, but on the pop side, working with synth wiz Thomas Dolby, singing with Doobie Brother Michael McDonald, and making videos. Joni Mitchell sounded like most everybody else in the mid-'80s, which was not a good thing. On 1988's *Chalk Mark in a Rainstorm*, the guest stars were attractive, with such folks as Tom Petty, Willie Nelson, Peter Gabriel, Don Henley, and Billy Idol all involved. Pollution and the environment were among the themes, with Mitchell penning new lines to the old Sons of the Pioneers song "Cool Water." There was no indication if she knew it was written by a guy from Winnipeg and New Brunswick. Despite the star power, once again the record failed to make the Top 40.

It seemed the old Canadian stars, the initial wave that had moved to the U.S. in the '60s for success, were now out of fashion. Zal Yanovsky was running a restaurant back in Ontario. Denny Doherty was acting in Halifax. The Band was back together, but without Robbie Robertson, there was only limited interest. Leonard Cohen was still active, but also at the lowest point in his career. In 1984, he readied his latest album, *Various Positions*, for Columbia Records. While Europe and Canada prepared for its release, head office in the United States was less than enthusiastic. Not that they didn't appreciate the material; it's just that they felt there was no market left for him in that country. The album was turned down, left for a small independent label to pick up. What CBS had turned down were such future favorites as "Heart with No Companion," "Dance Me to the End of Love," and a work that had taken Cohen many drafts to complete, and had at one point included many more verses, called "Hallelujah." "That took twenty years to be a hit, and nobody mentioned it at the time," marveled Cohen in 2007. "Except Dylan! Dylan started performing it."

But it wasn't Dylan who returned Leonard Cohen to prominence, it was an old friend and employee, who was actually better-known in the U.S. than Cohen at the time. Jennifer Warnes had first toured with Cohen in the early '70s as his backup and co-vocalist, and had sung on several of his albums, including all the songs on *Various Positions*. While her own career included the number one hits "Up Where We Belong" with Joe Cocker, and "(I've Had) the Time of My Life" with Bill Medley, Cohen was her favorite duet partner. She realized a long-held dream in 1987 when she released her tribute album, *Famous Blue Raincoat*, with the full appreciation and help of Cohen, including a brand-new song of his, the surprising "First We Take Manhattan," a very modern rocker. It had a fantastic video, featuring guest Stevie Ray Vaughan, an incredibly sexy Cohen, and Warnes in the best sunglasses since Corey Hart. The album went Top 10 in Canada, and sold better than any Cohen album had in over a decade. He had become a star again for a new generation, without opening his mouth. "That single-handedly resurrected my career," confirmed Cohen. "I liked that album a lot." The new Leonard Cohen was no longer a dark and depressing figure, as so often he'd been portrayed, and no longer played a nylon-stringed acoustic guitar. On his 1988 album *I'm Your Man*, Cohen brought out a bank of keyboards, composed to drum beats, and took on a new role, as the hip, senior statesman of pop.

There was hope for the '60s generation after all. Leonard Cohen was a rock star, and a few months later, Daniel Lanois helped Bob Dylan rebound from a decade of disappointment. Neil Young came back to prominence in 1988, when his video "This Note's for You" created quite a bit of controversy when it was banned by MTV. It mocked Michael Jackson's current Pepsi commercial, and the beer slogan "This Bud's for You," with Young loudly proclaiming he'd never sell out to corporations. Young had the ear of the public again, and by 1989, he captured the times perfectly with "Rockin' in the Free World." Again, he courted controversy by mocking President George H. W. Bush's "thousand points of light" speech, and with the searing intensity that would soon be popularized by the grunge movement, Young attacked a political agenda that let citizens starve and die on the street. For the first time in a long time, Young was in tune with the times, and five days after the fall of the Berlin Wall, "Rockin' in the Free World" was released as a single. It was his most popular music in a decade, since *Rust Never Sleeps*. Joni Mitchell still hadn't found a comeback route, but her time would come in the '90s, a decade full of previously unheard of highs for Canadian women.

Far away in time: In 1980, Martha & The Muffins had the world wondering where Echo Beach was. (Photo by Peter Noble/Redferns/Getty Images)

LEFT: k.d. lang went from the reincarnation of Patsy Cline to the Tony Bennett–approved vocal sensation. (Photo by Stuart Mostyn/Redferns/Getty Images)

BELOW: Brother-sister act: Margo and Michael Timmins of Cowboy Junkies led the roots movement of the 1980s. (Photo by David Tonge/Getty Images)

Before Alanis Morissette made the biggest-selling rock album of the '90s, she was a teen dance-pop star in Canada, with two albums and a Juno Award to her credit. (Photo by Paul Bergen/Redferns/Getty Images)

TOP: Nickelback had the biggest rock song of the decade from 2000 to 2009—"How You Remind Me." (Photo by Gabriel Olsen/FilmMagic/Getty Images)

LEFT: Avril Lavigne's 2002 debut *Let Go* has sold twenty million copies worldwide, going to number one in the U.K. and Canada, number two in the U.S. (Photo by Chung Sung-Jun/Getty Images)

Some of the revolving cast of characters who make up the Toronto collective Broken Social Scene, including founders Brendan Canning (third from left) and Kevin Drew (center). (Photo by Wendy Redfern/Redferns/Getty Images)

Always looking great, Michael Bublé proved swingin' never goes out of style, with his mix of standards, pop hits, and originals. (Photo by Neville Elder/ Redferns/Getty Images)

Leslie Feist counts the members of Broken Social Scene as friends and sometime bandmates and knows how to count to four as well. (Photo by Wendy Redfern/Redferns/Getty Images)

The Butlers did it: Brothers Win and Will moved from the Texas suburbs to Montreal and established Arcade Fire. (Photo by Jeff Kravitz/FilmMagic/ Getty Images)

CANADIANA

Canadian Groups Lead the Roots Revival

The Americana radio format was developed in the early 1990s for radio stations in the U.S. that had found a new market existing in the cracks between country and rock, mainstream and alternative. There were people out there, and a lot of them, who weren't kids, didn't want DJs and electro, grunge or metal. They also didn't want modern country music, which was led by Garth Brooks and had become closer to Journey than Hank Williams. What they liked was more traditional country, like Emmylou Harris made, or Rosanne Cash, or Johnny Cash, or his friend, Bob Dylan, that kind of music too, whether it was his folk or his rock. Rock like Bruce Springsteen, he fit in as well, especially that acoustic album, *Nebraska*. But *The River* worked nicely as well. All those acts on *Austin City Limits*, they were popular too, people like John Hiatt and John Prine. John Fogerty, when he did that Louisiana swamp-rock thing with Creedence Clearwater Revival. Also Louisiana music, including Zydeco and Cajun and New Orleans, with Doctor John and Allan Toussaint and The Neville Brothers. Lucinda Williams was from Lake Charles, Louisiana, where else could she get played on the radio?

Steve Earle, he'd been kicked off country radio, he needed a new home, and so did Lyle Lovett, and somebody had to keep the memory of their old mentor, Townes Van Zandt, alive. This Americana sure meant a lot of different styles.

It had been called *No Depression* as well, after a magazine obsessed with new alternative-country groups started publication. It was influenced by the favored Uncle Tupelo from Illinois, which had covered the old Carter Family number "No Depression in Heaven" on their 1990 debut. That group splintered into Son Volt and Wilco, and out of Minneapolis came The Jayhawks and that was the younger Americana sound. Those bands could go off the rails when necessary, and throw a little punk energy into the scene. Then people were calling it roots or old-time or y'allternative. Heritage artists from all sorts of other genres were part of the club, such as gospel/soul singer Mavis Staples and Nashville newcomer Robert Plant. Americana got its own association and awards show, and moved into the Ryman Auditorium, the old home of the Grand Ol' Opry, country music's sacred spot. You can see such disparate types as bluesman Taj Mahal, country legend Loretta Lynn, Tex-Mex accordion player Flaco Jiménez, and California star singer-songwriter Jackson Browne, all being honored for contributions to this catch-all music category. So what exactly is it, this Americana music? Many Canadian musicians looked across the border, and thought, "Oh, that's what we do."

While that is a generalization, it does point to a connection to folk and roots music that has always been a driving force in Canadian popular music, and has played a more prominent part in the country's pop/rock history than in other territories. In both English and French, the singer-songwriter has usually won the most acclaim, and any attempts at defining a Canadian style usually have something to do with our writers, and the connection to nature, vast distances between cities, and lots of clichés about snow. There's no one Canadian theme, just many common connections, but folk music, writing good, solid, plain-spoken and moving songs of the people, seems to always be in fashion and the most admired style. Perhaps it goes back to lumber camps and camp-fires, kitchen parties and speakeasies. One form of this or another has certainly been in the background of most of the musicians I've inter-viewed in the pop-rock era.

There was a significant change in the Canadian music world that happened first in the underground in the mid-'80s. You could feel the seismic plates shifting, and find the bands if you looked hard enough, but it hadn't made it to the surface as yet. It was a reaction to all the technology that had taken over for a couple of years, when videos were more important than an actual song, and haircuts and headbands were discussed at higher corporate levels. These particular values did not sit well with certain musicians in Canada, including many who were con-sidered the best songwriters, or ones who would be soon enough. One of the groups you would certainly call alt-country, except that phrase hadn't been uttered yet. You might even have called Blue Rodeo Ameri-cana, except they were Canadian, and it was 1987 when they arrived, way before the format was named. Maybe we'll just call it Canadiana for a little while. At least the story starts in New York.

Greg Keelor and Jim Cuddy had met in Toronto in the '70s, and at first only Cuddy played guitar. Then the pair spent some time together in a classic Canadian setting, in an Alberta resort town by the mountains, even around a campfire. "I was greatly inspired by Jim and his friends," remembered Keelor. "We were all out in Lake Louise one summer, and everyone would sit around and play guitars and get high and sing. It just seemed like the greatest thing in the world to me, so I wanted to be a part of that." Back home in Toronto, once Greg had learned to play, they formed a group called The HiFi's. They went the way Toronto was going in the early '80s, New Wave. But they weren't having much luck in 1981 finding gigs, as the bars had switched to cover bands at the time. So off they went to New York, changed the name to Fly to France, and hit another wall. With few prospects, Keelor had an epiphany: "I was listening to *Gord's Gold* (a Lightfoot greatest hits album) in a bar in New York with my headphones on. It just sang so deeply to me. I remember deciding that I wanted to move back to Canada."

The move happened, but it also involved a change of genres. "We decided we were done with all attachments to the current music," said Jim Cuddy. "We were going to take Gordon Lightfoot's greatest hits, *Gord's Gold*, as our template and just strum the songs together." When they returned to Canada, they had the new name of Blue Rodeo thought up, and about half the songs written. Keelor was less than impressed with how Toronto had changed since they had left four years before. "You were surrounded by Honeymoon Suite and Loverboy," he remembered. "That was radio at the time. A lot of people I hung out with liked the sound we were headed toward, the singer-songwriter-with-a-guitar type." And, there go the seismic plates. A backlash music community was growing there, people who weren't so much worried about being played on MuchMusic as they were about just playing. As Cuddy descibed it, "All the punks and New Wavers had learned to play their instruments, were into hollow-body guitars and had new bands." A one-off performer named Handsome Ned was playing straight country music at the Cameron House, and the Horseshoe Tavern was open to the new twang as well. A label, Risque Disque, was started out of the Horseshoe, and Blue Rodeo was signed up. The new songs were getting some attention in the club. "We didn't think it was that big a deal, but the song 'Try' got such a strong reaction," said Cuddy. "We played in the Horseshoe, and we had to play it twice. People would make us do it again in the third set. We realized we had something, we didn't know what it was, but we knew we had a song that got people's attention."

It got Warner Music's attention as well, which did a deal with Risque Disque, and put out the band's first album in 1987, *Outskirts*. Oddly, the title cut was chosen as the first single, and it did very little for the group, barely cracking the national country charts. It was actually the hot new media that made the group famous, just when they thought it had gone sour, because of the failure of "Outskirts." "It was a bomb," declared Keelor. "We were taken out by our marketing manager and told this record wasn't going to happen. But then John Martin on MuchMusic played 'Try.' He loved the song, but hated the video. Still, he kept on playing it and playing it. 'Try' was a hit, so that opened the door for us." It's a powerful ballad with an exceptional vocal by Cuddy, and managed quite the feat at Canadian radio, conquering three formats, as a Top 10 song at both pop and adult contemporary, and number one at country, awarded a Gold disc. Blue Rodeo has never relinquished its status as one of the country's top recording and touring groups, with each of their new albums going either Gold or Platinum, the favorite being 1993's *Five Days in July*, at six times Platinum.

Another Toronto band rewriting the roots rule book in the mid-'80s was Cowboy Junkies. Formed by three siblings—Michael, Margo, and Peter Timmins—and friend Alan Anton, the group was part of the Queen St. West crowd, and attracted to hypnotic, slow blues. The band's first album, *Whites Off Earth Now!*, was released in 1986, and featured mostly covers of well-known classic blues players Lightnin' Hopkins, Big Joe Williams, John Lee Hooker, and a remarkable, snail's-pace version of Robert Johnson's "Crossroads," completely transformed from the Eric Clapton–fireworks version most people knew. Almost hidden on the album was a version of Springsteen's "State Trooper," with scary guitar lines from Michael Timmins, and a haunted vocal from his sister Margo. It was not the normal set list for any new group.

For the Cowboy Junkies' second album, they set up in Toronto's Church of the Holy Trinity, to capture the unique acoustics of the space. Then the group did something radical, for 1988. They all played in the same room, at the same time. Live, off-the-floor recordings had gone by the wayside in the days of overdubs and precise sound; when groups would actually listen to each other and adjust the performance as they went, the whole idea of being in a band that had been lost in the technology race. The church added a dreamy atmosphere, and it was all recorded on one microphone, capturing a special setting. Called *The Trinity Session*, the album became known for its unique mix; there were old country numbers, more blues, traditional tunes, several more originals this time, and most widely heard, a radically new take on The Velvet Underground's classic "Sweet Jane," taking that piece of underground Lou Reed swagger at about half the pace, foggy and somnambulant. In the 2000s, producers and bands became known for adding layers of atmosphere and ambiance to songs, something the Junkies did with just one microphone and one church. When music fans first approached the album in 1988, it was confusing and curious; nobody did country beside Lou Reed, a traditional song with a new rock number, or did half covers, half originals. It seemed like several barriers were broken at once, and with the album reaching the Top 30 in the U.S. and Platinum status, it had a major influence on the up-and-coming roots rock movement.

Another singer was radically changing how country music was viewed in Canada. Before there was an alt-country, k.d. lang was definitely alt. The Alberta firebrand was as radical a singer as had ever been unleashed on the country charts, with her cropped hair, wild Western skirts, powerful and fantastic voice, and her claim that she was the reincarnation of Patsy Cline. To top it all off, she claimed her 1985 Juno Award for Most Promising Female Vocalist in a white wedding dress and cowboy boots, running down the aisle in perhaps the most memorable and entertaining moment in the show's history. She forced the previously countryphobic rock audience to reconsider the music, thanks to her Cline covers, rockabilly rave-ups such as "Bopalena," and the polka-inspired original, "Hanky Panky." Gradually, the more outrageous moments were left behind, as more and more people realized her great talent as a singer. In 1987, lang was asked to work with one of her heroes, Roy Orbison, to re-record his classic "Crying" as a duet for the movie *Hiding Out*, a major boost for her career, as it won the Grammy Award for Best Country Collaboration with Vocals.

As lang smoothed out the edges in the music side, she continued to ruffle feathers and push for her beliefs. It was no secret she was gay, and Canadian country radio, far more happy with women in cutoffs and halter tops beside their guy in the pickup, had to come to grips with her success. She was too popular to ignore. Then lang did something even more controversial, and somehow survived: she appeared in an ad for PETA, hugging a cow, declaring she was from cattle country and knew how meat was treated, and that's why she was a vegetarian. The outrage at home was one thing, but there was also a larger movement to remove her music from country playlists all over North America. What they didn't know at the time was that lang was about to remove herself anyway. In another career makeover, she returned in 1992 as a pop vocalist, with the album *Ingenue*. On that side of the radio dial, there was a lot more tolerance and a lot less controversy. The hit single "Constant Craving" won her another Grammy Award for Best Female Pop Vocal Performance, and took home the MTV Video Music Award for Best Female Video. lang is now considered one of the great voices of a generation, with Tony Bennett one of her biggest admirers. The pair recorded the album *A Wonderful World* together in 2002, which won the Grammy Award for Best Traditional Pop Vocal Album. In 2006, Leonard Cohen was inducted into the Canadian Songwriters Hall of Fame, and lang was there to serenade him with a version of "Hallelujah," which he calls his favorite of the many hundreds.

It seemed all roots and folk music in Canada surged in the mid to late 1980s, fighting back against the more soulless sounds popularized by mainstream videos and generic rock of the day. As much of the music became glossy and bland, new groups of young musicians turned their backs on that, instead going back a generation or two or ten for inspiration. On Canada's East Coast, the four Atlantic provinces were rich in musical heritage, but it had been in danger of dying out. There were still traditional fiddlers and Celtic players, Newfoundland's unique seaport Atlantic fusion, every type of singer-songwriter, Acadian kitchen parties, square dances and jigs and reels. More and more, '80s musicians were learning to respect their elders. Nova Scotia's Cape Breton Island was the hotbed of Celtic culture, and you could still find fiddling legends Winston Scotty Fitzgerald, Donald Angus Beaton, Buddy Mac-Master, and others playing dances at the local hall on Friday nights. Inspired and properly instructed, artists such as The Rankin Family, Natalie MacMaster, The Barra MacNeils, and Ashley MacIsaac began a Celtic wave that took fiddle and vocal music back into the Canadian mainstream. It was a singer-songwriter who provided the biggest spark, though, an unlikely hero for the entire East Coast music scene. Rita MacNeil struggled through her early life, abused by a relative as a child, going through low-income situations back and forth from Cape Breton to Ontario, a broken marriage, and little hope. Her dream was to write and sing, and through sheer persistence and talent, her songs started to become known, despite her decidedly nonstar appearance. Shy and soft-spoken, she was able to sing for the heartbroken, the ones who had little but faith, honesty, and goodness. Her song "Working Man" was written for the coal miners of Cape Breton, and became an anthem for that industry home and abroad. It reached number eleven in England's charts in 1990, and MacNeil also became the first female vocalist to have three singles on the Australian charts at one time.

Newfoundland's rich mix of cultures had created a fascinating music scene on the somewhat isolated island. With its major port St. John's, and hundreds of small fishing villages, it counted the sea as its main inspiration, but the traditions could come from a broad number of places. It had stayed a British colony until 1949, so the folk connection was a little stronger there, and the many ships that had come to the island had brought music from Portugal and Spain, France and Quebec, and especially the U.K, although more Irish than Scottish. An early move at a modern roots movement had started there in the '70s with popular bands such as Figgy Duff, The Wonderful Grand Band, and especially a trio of Irish ex-pats, Ryan's Fancy. They all helped bring traditional music into the modern era in Newfoundland, and the next wave of performers had an open ticket to take the old music, and make it modern. Great Big Sea, formed in St. John's in 1993, knew all the sea shanties and played everything from bouzouki to mandolin to bodhrán to tin whistle to bones to accordion to concertina to whistles and pipes. And, they rocked it up, rowdy and fun, taking it to campuses and bars, first in Newfoundland and then across the country. The band quickly became the hottest group on the East Coast, and turned trad on its head. They could cover an old hit by the British glam band Slade ("Run Runaway"), or find some Newfoundland party music that would rock packed hockey rinks. Great Big Sea proved that traditional could be just as popular as rock, and even more so when the band mixed the two.

The Wonderful Grand Band had a songwriter in its midst, Ron Hynes. When that group, which was a theatrical and comedy troupe, as well as a traditional band, broke up in 1983, Hynes went on his own, building on his reputation as an elite writer and performer. A magnificent storyteller, he has a catalogue of emotionally charged folk songs that have earned him the nickname of Man of a Thousand Songs, but there is one that stands out in his career. Written originally for The Wonderful Grand Band, "Sonny's Dream" was a true story from his family, about an uncle living in a tiny, remote village, where he and his mother are the last people left, the rest having moved on to bigger centers. As a boy, he walks the village road, wondering what it would be like to move away, but never does. It became an Island favorite, and some visiting Irish musicians took it back home, where it took on a life of its own, in the folk tradition. The great Christy Moore heard an altered version and recorded it, making it a hit in Ireland. Then Irish performers brought it over to the U.S., where it has been recorded by everyone from Chet Atkins to Emmylou Harris.

Often considered an East Coast folk artist, Stan Rogers was actually from Hamilton, Ontario, but had strong roots in Nova Scotia. His parents were Maritimers, and he spent summers visiting family back east, who first inspired him to play. Rogers became a traditional folk singer and then a writer, and had a unique ability to create brand-new songs that sounded two hundred years old. Some of the most favorite folk tunes enjoyed by Canadians today, which they believe are time-honored, actually come from the late 1970s and early 1980s. Rogers's best-known song is "Barrett's Privateers," about a sailor tricked into a terrible voyage that cost him his legs, a shanty that starts "Oh the year was 1778," and is sung a cappella. It is far and away the most favorite pub song in Halifax, and can be heard in any Irish pub in the country almost nightly. Rogers would also write modern lyrics about the fate of his beloved Nova Scotia, and changing times in the region, with plants closing and the fishing industry collapsing, young people forced to move to Toronto and beyond for work. In 1983, Rogers was on board an Air Canada flight that caught fire midflight, forced to land at the airport in Cincinnati. Twenty-three of the passengers, including Rogers, died from smoke inhalation or a flash fire in the cabin. His ashes were spread in the ocean off the coast of Nova Scotia.

Canada's first stars of the modern folk scene, Ian & Sylvia, would enjoy new success in the '80s and '90s, although not together. The onetime duo had gone their separate ways in 1975, and it had been an eventful, sometimes rocky journey to that point. The folk scene they had helped establish, touring college campuses and playing acoustic music, had largely died off by the Summer of Love, and in 1967 the duo had moved to Nashville, partly to make music, partly so Ian could do some horse ranching. They also had been moving in a new direction, debuted on the album *Lovin' Sound* that year, adding drums, keyboards, and a folk-rock feel, financed by a new record company, MGM, keen to widen their audience. The single of "Lovin' Sound" did well in Canada, but not much in the U.S. The albums *Nashville* and *Full Circle* followed soon after, and despite the Tysons having access to some of those magical Dylan/Band Basement Tapes through their shared management, "The Mighty Quinn," "This Wheel's On Fire," and "Tears of Rage" didn't work their magic for the couple.

Ian & Sylvia were at a crossroads, and their next move would be surprising and groundbreaking. It was also largely unheard, although that wasn't their fault. Looking to develop again, the Tysons went further down the country road, but in doing so, also kept a progressive and modern edge. They decided they wanted to get away from their old image as a folk couple and expand their sound to include more musicians on stage. They formed a band of like-minded players, calling themselves Great Speckled Bird, one of the first true country-rock outfits. One of the key members of the group was a young musician named Amos Garrett, who had been playing out of Toronto and Montreal. He had developed a string-bending style that made him one of the most respected players in guitar circles, best known for his brilliant solo on Maria Muldaur's "Midnight at the Oasis" later in the '70's. Buddy Cage was on pedal steel, another Toronto player, later to join New Riders of the Purple Sage. Folk purists had much the same reaction to seeing the pedal steel onstage as they did with Dylan going electric; they walked out, and Great Speckled Bird was not well received. An album of that name was recorded with none other than Todd Rundgren as producer. This strange match happened because Rundgren had recently signed up with Albert Grossman; it was well before his huge successes producing Meatloaf and Grand Funk Railroad. Rundgren actually did a fine job, and the self-titled *Great Speckled Bird* album is considered a classic of the genre. What really killed it was terrible distribution and start-up problems for their new record company, Ampex.

The Tysons kept the band going, though, and appeared in 1970's Festival Express tour, a wild ride across Canada by train, with stops in Toronto, Winnipeg, and Calgary. The all-star lineup featured Janis Joplin, The Band, The Grateful Dead, Buddy Guy, Mashmakhan, The Flying Burrito Brothers, Robert Charlebois, and an ocean of booze. Filmed at the time, a documentary of the event was finally released in 2003, and you can see Great Speckled Bird perform "C.C. Rider" with Jerry Garcia sitting in, plus a tremendous take on "Tears of Rage" is included in the DVD bonuses. Ian & Sylvia continued to be drawn back across the border, home to Canada. In 1970 Ian became the host of *Nashville North*, a TV series made at CFTO in Toronto, featuring Great Speckled Bird and weekly musical guests such as Gordon Lightfoot, Anne Murray, and Bruce Cockburn, and visitors such as Willie Nelson and Waylon Jennings. The name was changed to *The Ian Tyson Show* after the first season, and it ran until 1975, the same year the couple stopped performing and divorced.

Ian Tyson took his own advice, from back in 1963. He thought he'd go out to Alberta, largely because of his continued interest in ranching. "I was in Nashville for a while, and then I was in Texas off and on," he explained. "I had border difficulties. I chose Alberta as being the best alternative and came out here. I left the music biz pretty much for a couple, three years and was just riding, training horses, and working on the ranch. That was in '76, and I've been here ever since." Tyson didn't stay out of music for good, though. From being part of the ranching community, he soon found beauty and art among the cowboys on both sides of the border. "There was this renaissance, and there were scattered guys all over the West, way out at the end of gravel roads, doin' stuff, whether it was making beautiful saddles or writing poetry or painting or doing music, in my case. We were just doing it for ourselves, but it was too big, there was too much creativity at that time for just the grass level, and it spread. I invented the music, the new music. I'm not just blowing my own horn, I brought up a new form." Tyson started recording what he called renaissance music for contemporary cowboys, aimed at the people living that lifestyle in Alberta and the Western U.S. He wrote about modern cowboy heroes, such as the landscape artist Charlie Russell, in "The Gift," and, along with fellow Western singer-songwriter Tom Russell, came up with "Navajo Rug." Those two songs were featured on 1986's album *Cowboyography*, considered the best examples of Tyson's Northern cowboy music. Sylvia Tyson became a favorite broadcaster in Canada as well, hosting both CBC Radio and Television shows in the '70s and '80s, and continuing to record folk and country albums. In 1993, she became a founding member of Quartette, a folk group made up of four excellent singers, which also included Colleen Peterson, Caitlin Hanford, and Cindy Church. Peterson passed away in 1996, with Gwen Swick joining in her place, and the Quartette continues on.

The unique McGarrigle sisters, Montreal's Kate and Anna, were able to bridge English and French folk music, and anything else they wanted. From both French and Irish stock, they were artistic women who seemed out of step with modern music and culture, more in line with kinder and gentler, sophisticated times, parlor music of the late 1800s perhaps. They knew their way around the outdoors, too, able to strike up a lumberjack's tune as well. Yet they could also write pop tunes, and heartbreaking snapshots of modern relationships. The duo first came to fame in 1974 when Linda Ronstadt recorded Anna's "Heart Like a Wheel," and the duo's 1975 debut, *Kate and Anna McGarrigle*, was one of the most-praised albums of the year. The McGarrigles were always doing something interesting through the '70s to the 2000s, surfacing every few years with a new project, whether it was adding alternative textures to the *Heartbeats Accelerating* album of 1990, recording with Dire Straits guitarist Mark Knopfler on "Love Over and Over," releasing albums of entirely French performances, or convening special releases and concerts by their musical extended family, including Kate's children, singers Rufus and Martha Wainwright. Kate McGarrigle died of cancer in 2010.

One of Canada's favorite folkies, Bruce Cockburn, shocked a lot of longtime fans in 1984. Cockburn had crafted exquisite acoustic music through much of his career and was known as a world-class guitar player in addition to his songwriting and singing skills. He'd showcased electric guitar more toward the end of the '70s and into the '80s, and had even had a big pop hit, 1979's reggae-tinged, happy-go-lucky "Wondering Where the Lions Are," a number twenty-one song on the *Billboard* singles chart, which even got him on *Saturday Night Live*. The enduring image of Cockburn was with a smile. That's why the album *Stealing Fire* was such a surprise. Cockburn had always had a desire to help where he could, and this service led to an invitation to travel with OXFAM to Guatemalan refugee camps in Central America. What he saw and experienced inflamed a new passion, and he became outspoken, in interviews and on record. Several songs directly referred to the situation, mostly famously "If I Had a Rocket Launcher," a song of frustration aimed at the politicians, dictators, and soldiers. It wasn't a complete change, and Cockburn would still call on his folk side in the following and continuing years, but it was the birth of his activist side that has won him much respect and several humanitarian awards since, plus inspired more social, political, and environmental songs that stand among his best.

As usual with music, it's hard to pinpoint the moment a genre begins, or name the one artist who invented a style. Certainly lots of musicians across North America were reacting to the more soulless aspects of video and technology in the '80s by returning to basic songwriting, and fans on both sides of the border were expressing a desire to get out and see live music again, instead of watching it all on TV. When it comes to roots music, thanks to a long history of folk music and singer-songwriter traditions, Canadians led the way in establishing the new (North) Americana movement.

YOU OUGHTA KNOW

Canadians Set World Records in the '90s

n the 1980s, most of the new English Canadian stars had been guys with guitars. There were a few women singing lead for bands, such as Carole Pope, Lorraine Segato, Martha Johnson, and Margo Timmins, but the new female solo stars could be counted on one hand: Luba, k.d. lang, Lee Aaron, Sass Jordan, and Jane Siberry. In the 1990s, that would flip-flop, with Canadian women excelling at home and worldwide, with a series of remarkable firsts and sales records. The streak actually began in 1989, when a hard-working, very determined singer broke out with a huge debut album. Alannah Myles had spent most of the 1980s acting in commercials and TV shows, doing lots of modeling, working in nightclubs, everything she could to raise money for one goal: it all went into making demos for a singing career. She got some significant help, too, as MuchMusic VJ Christopher Ward started working with her. He'd had some success with his records before the VJ gig and was by then carving out a career as a songwriter. Myles got lots of rejection letters, but eventually her high-quality demos landed with the right people at Atlantic Records in the U.S., and she started to record a first album.

Ward had been assigned to follow a bunch of Elvis fans around Graceland by MuchMusic, and the trip inspired him to write a song about The King. Called "Black Velvet," Myles loved it and grabbed it for her album. Early attempts had it covered in big electric guitars, but Ward begged Myles and producer David Tyson to throw that out and strip it down to bass and acoustic guitar, letting Myles's voice dominate. It did the trick, the song becoming a huge, worldwide hit. It was a *Billboard* Hot 100 number one single, a feat equaled in Norway, Sweden, and Switzerland, and Top 10 in England, Australia, Germany, and several other countries. Its parent album, Myles's self-titled debut, included the hits "Lover of Mine" and "Love Is" and was a number one album in Switzerland, Norway, and Canada, and Top 5 in the U.S., U.K., and several more nations. It sold a million copies in Canada, a million more in the U.S., and over five million worldwide. She's the only Canadian artist to receive a Diamond award for a million in sales in the country with a debut disc. Her 1992 single "Song Instead of a Kiss" was another number one hit for her in Canada.

It was a blockbuster for Canadian women unmatched since the heydays of Anne Murray and Joni Mitchell, but Myles didn't have long to enjoy the throne. A plan a long time in the making was launched in 1990, turning a proven star into a global superstar. Celine Dion was a major force in French Canada and Europe, but wanted an English career as well. It would not be simple; she had grown up in large Francophone family, the youngest of fourteen kids, and had not sung in English much at all. Dion took time off to work on the language, and come up with a strategy to launch herself in a big way. Her *Incognito* album had been a huge hit in Quebec in 1987, and she continued to tour that music through to 1989. Then, a trial balloon was floated. A single by Toronto R&B singer Billy Newton-Davis, "Can't Live with You, Can't Live Without You" was released. It was a duet, and Dion was co-credited, the song and video promoted in English markets. A minor pop hit, it did better on the MOR (middle-of-the-road) stations. Barely out of her teens at the time, Dion would be marketed as an Adult Contemporary artist.

One of the big guns from that genre was brought in, another Canadian. David Foster produced half the album *Unison*, helping convince CBS Records it would be a smash. But it was another producer, England's Christopher Neil, who hit the home run. Neil, fresh off producing the number one hit "The Living Years" for Mike & The Mechanics, nearly turned the same trick with Dion's "Where Does My Heart Beat Now," as it charged into the Top 10 in Canada and the U.S. More importantly (and profitably), *Unison* achieved Platinum status in the U.S., seven-times Platinum in Canada, and ultimately, three million in sales around the world. That's when CBS discovered the depth of Dion's international appeal. Those fans overseas, from Europe to Japan, who had been interested in her singing in French, were just as thrilled in English. Truth be told, so were those at home in Quebec, the fans, anyway. The critics sniped, and there was grumbling about Dion abandoning her French audience. At the 1991 Felix Awards, she was chosen to receive the trophy for Quebec Artist Achieving the Most Success in a Language Other Than French, which screamed sellout. She refused to accept the award, and soon answered the criticism with proof of her intentions. The 1991 album *Dion chante Plamondon* was all in French, all songs from the prolific and beloved lyricist Luc Plamondon. It was the best-selling album of the year in Quebec, and another international success, with two million copies sold. And that became the pattern for Dion; while she continued with success after success in English markets, she would always return with another French album.

Trying to list all of Dion's accomplishments and records is worthy of a chapter itself, if not a book, but the peak certainly merits mentioning. Her *Falling into You* (1996) album saw the singer work with a total of fifteen different producers, not searching for a sound, but rather moving all over, expanding and experimenting. She brought in Jim Steinman, best known for writing the epic tunes on Meatloaf's *Bat Out of Hell* album, and used that same feeling for the power ballad "It's All Coming Back to Me Now." David Foster returned for that middle-of-the-road magic, and together they reworked the old Eric Carman weeper, "All by Myself." She even brought back Ike & Tina Turner's Wall-of-Sound original, "River Deep, Mountain High." There was everything for every Celine fan, and they all bought it, a stunning thirty-two million copies in total worldwide, over eleven million of those in the U.S. alone. On the all-time album sales rankings, it sits just below such acclaimed discs as Michael Jackson's *Thriller*, Pink Floyd's *Dark Side of the Moon, Led Zeppelin IV*, and Fleetwood Mac's *Rumours*. Surprisingly though, it's not even the top-selling Canadian album, nor the top-selling album by a Canadian woman.

That record was set the year before, by a former dance artist who had started out as a teen with very big hair. Alanis was no stranger to Canadians; she'd won the 1992 Most Promising Female Vocalist Juno Award, remember? She was just eighteen then, and had hit the Top 20 with the dance-pop hit "Too Hot" the year before. But the teen audience is a fickle one, and when Alanis's second album fizzled, the heartless MCA Records dropped her contract, knowing what always happened to former teen idols once they hit their twenties. Alanis had one thing still going for her, though; because she had been writing all those dance numbers, she had a publishing deal. They hadn't given up on her, and after Alanis graduated from high school, the publisher hooked her up with writer-producer Glen Ballard. He was big-time, the cowriter of Michael Jackson's "Man in the Mirror," part of the team on *Thriller* and *Bad*, the guy who broke Wilson Phillips and worked on the first, big Paula Abdul album. So, dance-pop kind of stuff, one might think.

Alanis, however, wanted to be known as an adult now. She reclaimed her last name, and Morissette and Ballard started writing a series of tough, straight-talking and edgy modern songs in his Los Angeles studio. She developed a new vocal delivery to match the caustic put-downs in some of the songs and didn't shy away from explicit language or tough topics. There was no question that she'd been mistreated by a jerk boyfriend and no question that she had just delivered a scathing rebuke. Called *Jagged Little Pill*, the album was unlike anything released before, a gold mine of empowerment. It wasn't just anger, it was about lessons learned, healing, getting over the bad and moving forward. The medicine hurt going down but was powerful. It was one of the most radical developments and makeovers in music history, and it made plenty of history, selling thirty-three million copies. Surprisingly though, it's not even the top-selling Canadian album, nor the top-selling album by a Canadian woman.

So there was Alanis in '95, and Celine in '96 . . . who could top them in '97? Once again it was a singer who would rewrite an entire genre, and set new worldwide standards. Eileen Twain had a rough upbringing in Timmins, Ontario, with violence and poverty in the family background, and having to sing late nights in bars as young as ten to support the family. She was a natural, though, a very hard worker who wanted to succeed as a singer and songwriter. She joined bands, worked the circuit, met some people with contacts, climbed a little further, went forward two steps and then fell back one, the usual rags-to-not-much-more-than-rags story for musicians. Eventually she did make it, as Mercury Nashville took a chance on her demo tape and her strong stage presence. A debut, self-titled album from 1993 didn't make a huge splash in Canada or the U.S., but there was something about her that convinced label execs to not give up hope.

Enter Mutt Lange. The superstar producer had done just about everything he could with rock bands. He'd produced Def Leppard's biggest albums, AC/DC, too. He'd provided The Cars with their biggest hits, and The Boomtown Rats with theirs as well. *Foreigner 4*, with

"Urgent," Billy Ocean's "Get Outta My Dreams, Get Into My Car," Bryan Adams's *Waking Up the Neighbours*; he wasn't pure gold, he was pure triple Platinum. He was also bored, or something. Lange had made it known he wanted to work with a country singer, somebody unknown, and Mercury knew just who. Twain and Lange started phone conversations and then started a decidedly nonprofessional relationship as well. It happens. Check out the TV show *Nashville* someday. Anyway, the deal was done, and Lange was Twain's new producer. Together they transformed country. Lange brought in his bag of tricks, with lots of vocal and instrument effects he'd use for rock bands. Only with country, he could cross the line, and make it all bigger and bolder, and obvious. There was a huge drum sound, the floor toms booming and reverberating. Twain's lyrics were just as over the top, with "Whose Bed Have Your Boots Been Under?" the first hit single from the 1995 album *The Woman in Me*. The singer was country, the music was rock underneath but countrified with fiddles and twangy lead guitar solos. But once the dance mixes started being released, it was obvious that the rules had been changed. Garth Brooks was watching over his shoulder. The album zoomed up to number one on the country charts in Canada and the U.S., and into the Top 10 pop charts in both countries as well. That, as it turned out, was nothing.

In 1997, *Come On Over* continued the success of *The Woman in Me*, and it just kept building. Each week, the album would sell more than 100,000 copies, and did so for over a year. Of the sixteen tracks on the album, twelve were released as singles. Again, some were aimed for the dance and club scene. Others were pushed more to pop than country. And outside of North America, the whole album was remixed, to tone down the country side and push up the pop. There was no precedent for any of this, and every move was a marketing masterstroke. Twain's videos were cross-promotion tools to the extreme, some geared to generate more interest in her concert dates once she hit the road. Taking a page from Morissette, Twain's heroes were strong and empowered, sometimes playing it for laughs ("Man! I Feel Like a Woman!"), other times offering advice ("That Don't Impress Me Much"). The idea of a man being a buffoon was itself a bit of a cliché in country that went back to Tammy Wynette and Loretta Lynn, but Twain did include a serious message as well ("If You Wanna Touch Her, Ask!"). The records tumbled again. Coming in somewhere around forty million albums sold around the world, it has the distinction of being the biggest-selling country music album in history, the biggest-selling studio album by a woman, the biggest-selling album by a Canadian, and one of the Top 10 best-selling albums of all time.

Twain may have bested Dion's album sales record, but there were still singles to consider. Dion landed the top prize in the business, a surefire number one. It was a good bet that James Cameron's 1997 film *Titanic* would be a blockbuster, and every blockbuster needs a big theme song. And nobody sang big, blockbuster theme songs better than Celine Dion. But no one knew how big the movie and the song would get. *Titanic* became the first film to earn a billion dollars in ticket sales internationally. The film stayed in theaters for months, and the song stayed on the radio, all the pop stations and adult contemporary, too. For some reason, it even became the number one Latin hit in the U.S., although it was about as Latin as "White Christmas." It also sold like "White Christmas." "My Heart Will Go On" ended up selling 15 million copies, the biggest Canadian hit of all time.

Of course, chart positions and sales records really aren't the proper way to judge the merits of music, and plenty more Canadian women had banner years in the 1990s. Joni Mitchell had gone through the previous decade experimenting with synthesizers and new recording techniques, making adult pop with electronic production. Her lyrics had shifted from personal to observational and included a lot of angry work, mostly about modern society, from politicians to pollution to consumer and corporate greed. As she entered the '90s, she decided to return to a more stripped-back sound, fewer instruments and musicians, more of her acoustic guitar again. The first flowering of this was 1991s *Night Ride Home*, a far more intimate album with her vocals and acoustic guitar the main instruments. It did better than her previous releases, skirted the edges of the Top 40 albums chart, and once again people were remarking about her lyrics; the songs "Cherokee Louise" and "Come In from the Cold" were singled out, the latter with a lovely picture of growing up in Saskatchewan in the '50s, having to keep a foot apart from her partner at the school dances, everyone desperate to get indoors from the brutal Canadian winter.

It set the stage for the success of her next album, 1994's *Turbulent Indigo*. With a better relationship with her audience, and that more accepted sound she had developed, she once again recorded a series of accusing and angry songs. This time, more people were listening, and being affected. Her "Sex Kills" includes all manners of modern horrors, including oil spills and referencing the AIDS crisis in the title. "The Magdalene Laundries" was about a young woman sent to a notorious Irish Catholic workhouse, because she was pregnant and unmarried. In a bit of a shocker, it won the Grammy Award for Pop Album of the Year, a sign that every once in a while, people in the music industry consider art before commerce.

Another Western Canadian, Alberta's Jann Arden, had established herself in 1993 with a first album, *Time for Mercy*, and a major hit single, "I Would Die for You," which had won her Juno Awards for Best Video, and Best New Solo Artist. But she was another in a long line of performers to find out that while that made her a star, she was still a cash-poor one. "People think that you make all these millions of dollars," she admitted, "But they don't understand that you owe the record company three hundred thousand." Those videos cost a lot of money, and it's the artists who get the bills. Arden was living in small basement apartment underneath the homeowner, named June. "June didn't like me very much, and she was threatening to kick me out. I could never pay my rent. I was kind of blissfully miserable at that time. I still hadn't made a dollar. I had this really sick cat that I'd adopted. So the sick cat and I were down in the basement apartment, and I didn't have any money to go anywhere." So she wrote songs instead, at the kitchen table in the basement apartment. The results were heard on 1994's *Living Under June* album, which insured the titular landlady would get paid. It included the hits "Could I Be Your Girl," "Insensitive," and "Good Mother," Arden nicely situated somewhere between a pop and singer-songwriter artist. As her popularity grew, she also became known for her grand sense of humor and personality, making her a frequent host for events and programs, a broadcaster, actor, and best-selling author.

Sarah McLachlan enjoyed a breakthrough year in 1993 as well, with the release of her third album, *Fumbling Towards Ecstasy*. She had already become a star in Canada, after being spotted playing in a high school band in Halifax, and moving to Vancouver to work with Nettwerk Records. Her 1991 album, *Solace*, had established her with the hit "Into the Fire," and the single "Possession" from the next album was even bigger. Eventually the album went Platinum in the U.S., and McLachlan had some sizeable clout with her sensitive music with dance beats. McLachlan built her audience through sheer hard work, touring for over two years to promote the album. During that time, she noticed something about the touring industry that bothered her. Women were often second-class citizens in the eyes of the concert business. They would never set up a show that featured two women, or on a festival date, you couldn't have one woman follow another. The thinking was that the audience didn't want that many women, but it was perfectly acceptable to have men follow each other. She heard the same thing on radio, where DJs would never play two women in a row.

To counter that, McLachlan came up with a concert concept, called

Lilith Fair. The idea was to show that not only was there a market for more than one woman on a stage, you can actually program all-women (or female-fronted) bands on a stage, and draw a big crowd. Beginning in 1997, Lilith Fair toured as a multistage, day-long event, with a rotating cast of all-stars and up-and-comers, playing the whole summer through the U.S. and Canada. It quickly proved McLachlan right, as it became one of the highest-grossing tours of the year. That first year, acts including Emmylou Harris, Sheryl Crow, Jewel, Suzanne Vega, Indigo Girls, and Tracy Chapman. At its other stages, Lilith Fair proved to be a boost for new performers as well, with Dido, Christina Aguilera, and Tegan and Sara among dozens of newcomers during the festival's tours. It certainly shot McLachlan to new heights as well. Her album for 1997, *Surfacing*, was a stunning success, selling a million in Canada and eight million in the U.S., with four Top 10 singles at home: the Canadian number one "Building a Mystery," a number two in "Sweet Surrender," "Aida" at three, and "Angel" peaking at nine, the latter two both Top 10 in the U.S. It included the most intense and emotional music of her career, with the slow burn of "Building a Mystery" and the forgiving, sympathetic "Angel." The Lilith Fair tours went until 1999, and were brought back in 2010.

In 1997, Manitoba Celtic and world music artist Loreena McKennit released her major hit album, *The Book of Secrets*. McKennitt was a self-made star if there was ever one. She'd always been an independent artist, raising the money for her first album herself in 1985, forming her own record label, Quinlan Road. Playing harp, accordion, and piano, she mixed traditional sounds with her own melodies and modern touches and recording techniques. McKennitt would go to great lengths for her albums, by traveling to different countries to study their culture and stories, becoming immersed in the traditions. She recorded in churches and cathedrals for the right ambiance, and ranged outside Celtic territory, bringing in Spanish and Morrocan, Greek, or Turkish influences. McKennitt was certainly one of the leading performers in world music at the time, her albums million-sellers, her audience found through Europe and South America as well as North America. Then she did something new for New Age; she crossed over, and had a hit on the pop charts. "The Mummer's Dance" was already a popular song from *The Book of Secrets*, but then the British duo DNA got hold of it. The noted remix producers were best known for radically altering Suzanne Vega's "Tom's Diner" into a big hit in 1990. They didn't have to do that big a makeover on "The Mummer's Dance," just adding a bit of rhythm and playing with the faders here and there, but it did the trick. The song became a radio favorite, making number eighteen on the *Billboard* Hot 100, and leading the album on to sales of four million. It also made the Top 40 albums charts in over a dozen countries, including number three in Canada.

For the first time since Buffy Sainte-Marie was on the charts, Canada had an aboriginal star. Susan Aglukark, an Inuk from Arviat, Nunavut, didn't even start singing until she was twenty-four, but quickly became a leading voice for Arctic people. She mixed some of the folk traditions of the Inuit with the old country music she had heard growing up, and performed across the North, and word of her talent spread via CBC Radio. Her first recording was an independent release, but in 1992 she was signed by EMI Canada, the company's president, Deane Cameron, calling her a beautiful singer and powerful songwriter, and one of the country's most significant cultural treasures. Singing in both English and Inuktitut, she was not locked into tradition, but instead told the stories she wanted people to hear, including those from the last fifty years of Inuit life, and the many changes that had come to the region. She had her first national hit in 1995, from the album *This Child*. "O Siem" was a number one country hit, and number three pop. The title means "joy in community," Aglukark expanding it from her own family to the whole nation. Another single, "Hina Na Ho" featured a furious, highly danceable rhythm over the Inuktitut chorus. Aglukark became the first member of the Inuit people to ever have a Top 40 hit.

French Canada hadn't had a problem developing female stars in the '80's, with Celine, Martine St. Clair, Dianne Tell, and more. That just continued right on in the 1990s. Lara Fabian was actually from Belgium, and had already started a popular singing career in Europe. In 1990, she did the opposite of so many, and moved to Canada to further her career. Fabian felt that establishing herself as a French singer in Montreal was a worthy career, would open that market for her, and she could continue her European success. And that's exactly how it happened. Fabian's first Canadian-made album in 1991, called just *Lara Fabian*, sold 100,000 copies, and set her on her way. In 1995 she won the Felix Award for Female Singer of the Year. Her plan had worked perfectly, as her success then spread back across to Europe, where she became one of the top French-language stars. To date, she's sold twenty million albums worldwide. As a twenty-year-old, singer Julie Masse launched her career in a big way. Her self-titled debut in 1990 was filled with hit singles, dance pop like "Prends bien garde" or dramatic ballads like "C'est zéro." That won her the Felix for Female Artist of the Year in 1991, and a big career seemed ahead of her. Her 1992 album *À contre-jour* did so well, it won her the Juno Award for Most Promising Female Vocalist, beating out all the English candidates. Perhaps that encouraged her next move, which was to record an all-English album, 1994's *Circle of One*. That was not a success, despite the involvement of Montreal star Corey Hart. That turned out better. Masse and Hart started a relationship and were later married. The couple largely retreated from public life. He surfaces every so often with a project, but aside from her 1996 best-of called *Compilation*, Masse has not released another album. Her recordings have been limited to guest spots on Hart's projects, including the 1998 French language duet single, "La-Bas."

With so many highlights happening for Canadian women in the '90s, it's important not to forget the ladies. Barenaked Ladies of course. The Toronto band hit the country as a breath of fresh air, having way too much fun for a regular rock band. They told jokes, improvised on stage, played crazy numbers about Kraft Dinner and Yoko Ono, and were unlike anything else around. When some local politicians didn't get the joke behind the name, and got them banned from a public New Year's Eve show, they were suddenly famous right across the country. People wanted those funny songs, and the band's latest homemade tape, forever named *The Yellow Tape* in honor of its color, sold through the roof; at shows, and record stores desperate for any product from the hottest band in the land. It became the biggest-selling independent cassette release ever, with sales somewhere around 100,000 copies, or Platinum status in Canada. Nobody had more fun onstage, spitting out pop culture references that had the audience laughing at the same time they were trying to dance. The one everyone knew was "If I Had $1000000," which poked fun at just about everything you could buy if you won the lottery, from fur coats to K-Cars. When all other bands around them were being grim, BNL had brought a laugh back to rock 'n' roll.

Hip-hop, by 1990 well established in many other countries, had taken much longer to enter the mainstream in Canada. There were artists, and scenes, but it was largely ignored by radio and record labels. So, hip-hop did the same back, and ignored those media. The artists aimed for club play, and did get support from MuchMusic, always closer to the cutting edge than most broadcasters. That's where Wes Williams set his sights. Known as Maestro Fresh-Wes, he knew that airplay on Much would be a better boost than radio could give him, and could expand his audience out of Toronto and into the markets in Montreal and Vancouver. He cobbled together enough money, $5,000, to make a low-quality video for his debut, "I'm Showin' You." Much, according to Williams, was more than supportive, playing it in rotation even though the quality was weak. It was valuable exposure; Williams signed a deal with a label in New York, and for his next video, the production values shot way up. The cut, "Let Your Backbone Slide," topped the Dance/ Urban charts, and then grew so popular via MuchMusic that in February of 1990, it broke through into pop, eventually hitting number one on the singles charts in *The Record* (which was by then considered more accurate than *RPM*). It was the first and biggest-selling hip-hop hit in Canadian music. Unfortunately, it didn't start any trends. Every so often, another artist would break through and score another hit, but it was always one at a time, and a trickle. Canadian hip-hop had to fight hard for any exposure for the next twenty years, and "Let Your Backbone Slide" stayed the top-seller in the genre.

Bryan Adams had done exceptionally well in the 1980s, but he was not one to settle. He had gone from an opening act in hockey rinks to an arena headliner with *Reckless*, but also knew it wasn't wise to repeat himself. So when an offer came in to record a film song, it seemed like a smart move. The film was the Kevin Costner vehicle *Robin Hood: Prince of Thieves*. Adams wrote what he considered a simple ballad, called "(Everything I Do) I Do It for You." The song was launched before the movie, and in England, it connected immediately. While it was number one in most countries, something about the song grabbed the British public. It grabbed so hard, it held on to number one for a record sixteen weeks. It was only number one in Canada a mere nine weeks. It sold ten million copies, and along with the *Waking Up the Neighbours* album, took Adams from superstar to world star, and now only the giant sports arenas could handle his shows.

Another of the big Canadian stars in the 1990s was already well known as a member of the band Red Rider. Tom Cochrane was the singer and chief songwriter, and the group's first album, *Don't Fight It*, came out in 1979. The single "White Hot" gained fans from both the New Wave and Top 40 camps, and the album did very well for a debut, going Gold. The band could always be counted on for solid, memorable songs through the decade, including "Lunatic Fringe," "Young Thing, Wild Dreams (Rock Me)," "Boy Inside the Man," and "The Untouchable One." By then the group had become Tom Cochrane and Red Rider, and he had become the focus for the group on the all-important videos. The group's *Victory Day* album of 1988 became their most successful, going double Platinum and scoring three hits: "Big League," "Good Times," and the title track. Tellingly though, the front cover featured only Cochrane's photo. After a well-received album with the Edmonton Symphony Orchestra, *The Symphony Sessions*, Red Rider was no more. No one doubted Tom Cochrane's future, though.

In 1989, Cochrane had made the first of his trips to Africa for the charity organization World Vision. Visiting Ethiopia, Somalia, and Mozambique, he was exposed to the daily hunger and poverty of the region, and felt he had to pass on something in his songs to help. The trip had taken its toll on him, mostly mentally, and he felt exhausted. Wanting something to pick him up, he realized that was the type of song he was looking for as well, something that would make him feel good, inspire other people, and bring a positive atmosphere to help better the situation in those African countries. He made sure to point all this out in every interview, and there were a lot of them. "Life Is a Highway," from his *Mad Mad World* album of 1991, was his biggest hit ever, an ear worm for the year, a number one Canadian hit and number six U.S. The album gave him one of those rare Canadian Diamond awards for a million in sales, and a total of four Juno Awards, for Album and Single of the Year, and Songwriter and Male Vocalist of the Year.

Diamonds were all the rage in the '90s, and the next bunch to earn them were from Kingston, Ontario. The Tragically Hip got to a million in sales in Canada without the benefits some of the others had. Cochrane, Alanis, Shania, Bryan Adams, and other big names watched their albums climb up the U.S. charts as well. That meant Canadians were seeing them on talk shows and in U.S. magazines, getting all the pop culture buzz that pours over the border, only this time for our artists. So while David Letterman was happily repeating the lyrics to "Life Is a Highway" every night on his show, and eventually having Cochrane as a guest, all his Canadian viewers were taking the hint and buying up more albums. It only makes The Hip's success more surprising. Americans never got the band, despite them actually being signed originally to a U.S. deal. The push right from the start was for them to make it in the States, but as one critic said, "We already have our own R.E.M." That was an unfair shot, the two bands not being that similar, aside from enigmatic lead singers.

The Tragically Hip has stayed the same since 1986, with Gord Downie on vocals, Rob Baker and Paul Langlois on guitar, Johnny Fay on drums, and Gord Sinclair on bass. They came up at a time when the pressure was on in Canada for another big hit band. Canadian record labels had seen what could happen with international stars such as Adams and Loverboy. While they were certainly proud of being Canadian, these groups weren't exactly catering to an all-Canadian crowd. The word in the music industry, at least at the big labels, was that Canadians could sell, as long as they didn't seem too much like Canadians. There's a long list of video-ready, generic CanRock bands from the mid-'80s who had a lot easier time getting signed than The Tragically Hip. One rep from BMG wanted to sign them, but only on the condition they become a country band. They did demos and talked to companies for over a year. Finally a rep from Los Angeles for MCA Records heard the band play the Horseshoe in Toronto, and offered to sign them right after the set. He just thought they were good and could develop into something great. A mini-album came first in 1987, and then the 1989 album *Up to Here*, with its breakthrough hit for the group, "New Orleans Is Sinking," a breakthrough in Canada at least. It turns out the Canadian rock audience had moved on from hair bands and wanted something real, and The Hip were the real thing. They were tough to pigeonhole at first, too alternative for radio to play but too old-school rock for the alternative crowd. They were just immensely popular. They did get on radio, mostly because fans insisted on hearing them, and when stations did play them, the songs went over big. *Road Apples* from 1991 continued that with "Little Bones," and some well-appreciated Canadian name-dropping in the song "Three Pistols" mentioned painter Tom Thomson. Audiences were getting the point that this was a Canadian band to cheer for.

Fully Completely (1992) put everything together, cementing the bond between the band and fans. Gord Downie's Canadian lyrics weren't flag-waving, they were simply good stories he knew and wanted to tell, such as the one in "Fifty Mission Cap," about former Toronto Maple Leaf Bill Barilko, who had scored a winning goal in the Stanley Cup playoffs, and then took off on a fishing trip in the off-season. He died in a plane accident, and the Leafs didn't win another cup until the year his body was finally found. Downie tops it all off by telling the listener he read all about it on the back of a hockey card. The song "Courage" was subtitled "For Hugh MacLennan," the great writer who had died in 1990, the winner of five Governor-General's Awards for Literature in his lifetime. "Wheat Kings" had as its inspiration the story of David Milgaard, a man wrongfully committed of a rape and murder in Saskatchewan who was released after twenty-three years in prison. It rocked, it made you think, and it made you think about Canada.

More bands were springing up with a new, positive attitude about the home and native land, and showing you could exist just fine within the now-established Canadian music industry. Toronto group The Rheostatics went out of their way to insure people got the point they were proud of their birthright, especially on the 1991 album *Melville*. They had been advised over and over again in the late '80s that you couldn't be serious musicians if you let people know you were Canadian. They were told they'd never get anywhere writing about their lives in

Canada. So they went the opposite direction; they covered Gordon Lightfoot, and "Wreck of the Edmund Fitzgerald," as a near-punk-rock tune. They called another song "Saskatchewan," and then sang it completely in French. Another one addresses the problem head-on: "Chanson les Ruelles" explains that he (author Tim Vesely) decided to write this song in French, because it didn't matter, it's the melody that counts, but that it would probably hurt the song's chances in the United States. Cheeky.

Sloan from Halifax were initially made famous by a U.S. company. Geffen Records had heard about the group, and were looking for the next big thing, post-Nirvana. They loved the near-grunge sound of the band's debut, especially the single "Underwhelmed," a slacker anthem that was attracting lots of interest in the group. So the company threw some money at them, and expected more of the same. The band had had it with grunge, however. "We thought it was over," explained bass player Chris Murphy. "We wanted to get off that train before it crashed." Instead, Sloan took the money and spent it on a big, bright production with more '60s and '70s references, softer and sweeter songs, and showed what a brilliant pop band they were, calling the album *Twice Removed* and presenting it to Geffen in 1994. The company was not happy, and thought it would fail, so they told the group to change it or they wouldn't support it. Sloan wouldn't back down, and Geffen put the album out but refused to promote it. It died a quick death in the U.S. but became a critical and alternative smash in Canada, a college radio staple, and soon helped the band transition to MuchMusic favorites and hit makers. Not for Geffen though, the band announced they were going to break up rather than continue with their contract, so the label let them go. A reformation quickly took place. In Murphy's 2003 song "The Rest of My Life," he famously sings that he'll be spending the rest of his life in Canada.

Just about anything could and did happen in '90s music in Canada.

Blues had long been one of the bedrock sounds of the country, with lots of fans, but was mostly found in the bar world. Most Canadians had grown up with favorite blues acts from their drinking days, whether it was Dutch Mason and Matt Minglewood on the East Coast, Powder Blues out in Vancouver, maybe the great Downchild Blues Band, who helped inspire Dan Aykroyd's love of the music, and who then repaid leader Donnie Walsh by recording two of his songs on the million-selling Blues Brothers album. There were great players and great characters, such as David Wilcox and Colin Linden, the latter learning his craft as a young teen as an unlikely friend of the great Howlin' Wolf. British legend Long John Baldry settled in Canada in 1978, after being part of the same blues circle as The Rolling Stones, and having Rod Stewart and Elton John in his bands. This was a night of music for many of us for years, but rarely on the charts. Two hot guitar players were able to change that. Colin James's 1990 cut "Just Came Back," from his second album, *Sudden Stop*, hit number five, and won the 1991 Juno for Single of the Year. The blind phenom from Toronto, Jeff Healey, probably loved old jazz more than blues, but his guitar playing amazed them all. I remember him jumping up onstage as an unknown guest at an Albert Collins show in Toronto in 1985, with the blues legend shaking his head in wonder at Healey's unorthodox playing, with the guitar face-up in his lap. Collins's great student, Stevie Ray Vaughn, was at the back, equally impressed. Healey could light fires, or bring on the ballads with a tender voice, landing a hit with John Hiatt's "Angel Eyes," and the follow-up album, 1990's *Hell to Pay*, number five at home, and twenty-seven in *Billboard*.

And what would a decade be without a Neil Young update? He'd done very well at the end of the '80's, coming back to respectability with "Rockin' in the Free World." *Ragged Glory* (1990) was pretty success-ful too, as he was back with Crazy Horse, back wearing flannel shirts and knocking out feedback-drenched lead guitar on the following tour.

That was the image that soon earned him his nickname as the God-father of Grunge. But, being Neil Young, he dropped the noise, got off the Horse, and did what nobody thought he'd ever do; he did what everybody had always asked him to do, and revisited *Harvest*. It was his most acoustic and most accessible album in years, made largely with the same cast of characters he had used back in 1972. He even called them the Stray Gators again, and Linda Ronstadt and James Taylor were invited to sing along as well, repeating their cameos. In case anyone missed the connection, he even named it *Harvest Moon*. Now, the music wasn't completely like *Harvest*, it was more in the spirit of *Harvest*, but fans ate it up anyway. Especially rewarding was the lovely title cut, a waltz-time romance showing a happy and fulfilled Young. Most of the album seemed a love letter to his wife, Peggy. It was the soft side of the Godfather. It won the Juno Award for Album of the Year, and sold over two million copies. And then he quit that, and went on the road with Pearl Jam. So, it was another typical Neil Young decade. The 2000s would only get wilder.

HALLELUJAH

A Feisty New Crop of Talent for the 2000s

I t was a small venue, in a small city, far away from the paparazzi and major press outlets, about as remote as a rock star could choose for his return to the stage. There were fewer than seven hundred seats available that night, and all had sold out long before. The atmosphere was electric, the tension high, the audience unsure of what they would see that night. What took place over the next three hours was nothing short of magical, one of the great comebacks in music of any time. As the star walked onto the stage, beaming a humble and honest smile, the crowd stood for a lengthy standing ovation, the first of several that night. Leonard Cohen was back.

"It's been a long time since I last stood on a stage," said Cohen early in the show. "It was fourteen years ago, I was just a kid with a crazy dream." It was a great joke, one he repeated at every show on a tour that just kept getting longer and longer. It was May 11, 2008, Cohen was then seventy-four years old, and no one had expected him to tour again, but there he was at The Playhouse in Fredericton, New Brunswick. He was visibly nervous, as was the band, but the warmth between the audience and performer quickly put everyone at ease. That, and the fact it was a spectacular concert. The opening show was part of a short series of concerts on Canada's East Coast, designed to allow Cohen a bit of privacy, and to let him see if he was capable of touring again. It was obvious from the first song, "Dance Me to the End of Love," that his charisma and talent were still very much intact. The tour quickly moved from soft-seat theaters to opera houses, cavernous arenas, and outdoor festivals, across Europe and back and forth to Canada. He played at castles, the Royal Albert Hall, the Glastonbury Festival, the Montreux Jazz Festival, and the O2 Arena. There were three different legs of the European tour, and by the end of 2008, he'd played eighty-seven concerts. Cohen was just getting started. He began 2009 in Australia, and then finally made it to the U.S., for the Coachella Festival, Madison Square Garden, Red Rocks Amphitheatre, and Radio City Music Hall. After eleven months of touring in 2009, he wrapped it up with a further four months in 2010. Then he made an album, *Old Ideas*, which came out in 2012, and spent two more years on the road, followed by yet another new release, 2014's *Popular Problems*. It was a pretty good third act.

It was not the retirement he had foreseen. Cohen had made one of the most successful albums of his career in 1992, *The Future*. It was a hit across Europe, and double-Platinum in Canada, winning him the Juno for Best Male Vocalist. He toured across Europe and North America through 1993, and then he quietly disappeared from music. He went to a Zen Buddhist monastery on Mt. Baldy, near Los Angeles, serving as a cook and assistant to his teacher, Roshi. It looked as if he might not return to music. But in 2001, the album *Ten New Songs* appeared, followed by 2004's *Dear Heather*. The albums were well received, but there was little excitement to the releases, and certainly no talk of touring. Shortly after that, Cohen did make headlines, but with sad news. It was revealed he had been robbed, and was nearly broke, as a former manager had taken millions from him, what Cohen referred to as his retirement fund. Despite winning in court, the money was now gone, a life's work and fortune.

Help arrived from an old friend, one of his old songs. Since CBS had initially refused to release the *Various Positions* album in 1984, the song "Hallelujah" had taken a remarkable journey. It was first notably covered by John Cale for the 1991 Cohen tribute album, *I'm Your Fan*. Then Jeff Buckley included a version on his album *Grace* in 1994. The hit movie *Shrek* in 2001 included Cale's version in the film, and Rufus Wainwright's on the soundtrack album. By 2006, the song's popularity was snowballing. More and more movies and TV shows were using it, and the song was starting to show up on *Idol*-type competitions. Buckley's version was getting airplay, and was released as a digital single in various countries. In England, it was the winning song for performer Alexandra Burke in the show *The X-Factor*, selling a million copies, and battling Buckley's version on the charts. By 2008, there were over three hundred cover versions of the song recorded, and millions of copies sold. Cohen was now a superstar, as everyone knew he was the writer, and in March of 2008, he was inducted into the Rock and Roll Hall of Fame. And two months later, on that May night in Fredericton, the crowd stood up again, giving "Hallelujah" the longest and loudest applause of the night. Cohen's retirement fund had been refilled, no doubt many times over, and in the process, millions of fans have been able to see him perform, and Cohen's creative streak has continued into his eighties.

The 2000s had started with more major new hit makers arriving, finding success at home and internationally. Nelly Furtado even came ready-made for an international career. She was born in Victoria, British Columbia, but her parents were Portuguese, having moved to Canada from the Azores in the 1960s. Furtado grew up singing in the local Portuguese community, and when she graduated from high school, went to Toronto where her sister lived. There, she was heard by Gerald Eaton and Brian West, members of the group The Philosopher Kings, a strong vocal R&B group then enjoying several Canadian Top 10 hits. With the duo's help, Furtado started making tracks that were hard to place in one genre. She had dance elements, there was hip-hop, Latin, R&B, and more, with confident and modern production, deep grooves, and multiple layers. With Furtado's soaring vocals as the final, winning piece, her album *Whoa, Nelly!* made an immediate impact when it came out in October of 2000. It featured one of the biggest debut singles in years, with "I'm Like a Bird" landing at number one in Canada and the Top 10 in various countries. Ultimately it won the Juno Award for Single of the Year, and the equivalent Grammy Award as well and another Grammy for Best Female Pop Vocal Performance. Since then, Furtado has continued to explore and expand her music, including recording the Spanish-language album *Mi Plan* in 2009, subsequently becoming the first Canadian to win a Latin Grammy Award.

Furtado was the story of the 2001 Juno Awards, but the winners of Best New Group were making their own kind of noise. The band Nickelback, originally from the small town of Hanna, Alberta, was playing out of Vancouver, and had released a couple of independent albums. They mixed hard rock with hooks, and their song "Leader of Men" sounded like cleaned-up Nirvana. Label Roadrunner signed them up and reissued their album *The State*, which won them the Juno. But later that year, the bomb dropped. The first album specifically recorded for their new label and big league status was called *Silver Side Up,* and came out in September. Nickelback unleashed a monster, the cut "How You Remind Me," a new kind of power ballad. It started out simple and gentle, and then took the old grunge formula of soft-loud, going into a thrashy chorus. So, two songs in one, the ballad and the bluster, and it proved unbeatable, ending up at number one in both Canada and the U.S., and a major hit in Europe as well. The numbers started to add up, with staggering results. It was the top song of the year in the U.S, and *Billboard's* top rock song of the decade, and number four overall for the decade. *Silver Side Up* became a ten-million seller, and that was just the start. The group has sold over fifty million albums worldwide, and was named the top rock act of the 2000s by *Billboard*.

One more from the Juno class of 2001: taking the trophy for Best Alternative Album was another Vancouver group, the polar opposite of Nickelback. The New Pornographers were a happy accident as a band, a collective of Vancouver folks who were making music for the love of it. Leader Carl Newman had pretty much given up on music being his career. He'd been in the alternative pop group Zumpano in the '90s, much loved by those who heard them, but that was not enough to keep them afloat. After two albums, Newman had quit and taken a job at a guitar company, figuring the steady paycheck was better then struggling. Finding he hated the nine-to-five world, he worked away on a handful of songs, including one called "Letter from an Occupant," which he thought was a sure hit. Among the pals he called on was singer Neko Case, who had moved to Vancouver from Tacoma, Washington, to attend art school. She also played in several local indie bands, and then started singing alternative country music, recording her first album, *The Virginian*, in 1997, aided by Newman. He also got her to record some vocals on his new material, including the full-on guitar pop of "Letter," but he couldn't raise any label interest.

Finally in 2000, the independent label Mint was putting out a compilation, and Newman offered them "Letter." The label loved it, and offered Newman a full album deal. So Case was called back, and Newman called on all his friends to complete the project. Joining him as a writer and singer was Dan Bejar, from the Vancouver indie band Destroyer, who contributed some of his own songs. Other local musicians rounded out the band, who then had a surprise hit on their hands. The album *Mass Romantic* became a critical darling, and Newman was back in the music business. Case would go on the road when she could, but her own career took off in the 2000s as well. Newman released his own solo albums, and Bejar's Destroyer got more popular. Still, the group has managed to record six albums since 2000, and continues to work whenever Newman has new material ready.

The realities of music industry economics brought some interesting changes during the 2000s. As income from music sales started to slip with downloading, and with live music always going through hot and cold periods (mostly cold), musicians had to come up with new ways to survive. In earlier times, being in a band was an all-or-nothing proposition, and members were discouraged from moonlighting. In indie circles, though, cooperation was becoming the key. There were shared bills and tours between groups to cut costs, and soon musicians were playing for two or three groups, wherever the need was. It was as much out of friendship as hardship, as it was just too expensive to keep a full band going for some. In Vancouver, Newman's New Pornographers was one model, and there was another scene growing in Toronto. Kevin Drew and Brendan Canning started this one, and called it Broken Social Scene. Canning was well known in indie rock, having been in the group hHead in the '90s, and then helping out in By Divine Right in 1999. With Drew, the first plan involved mostly instrumental and ambient music on an album called *Feel Good Lost* in 2001. It was the two of them for the most part, although another then-member of By Divine Right, Leslie Feist, did a bit of singing. When it came time to play live, the pair figured they didn't really have a show with that music, so they called in more friends.

Jason Collett was a carpenter and builder and also an alternative country performer who joined on guitar. Emily Haines played keys in the synthpop group Metric and had gone to school with Drew. So had Amy Millan, from the group Stars. Andrew Whiteman came out of the group Bourbon Tabernacle Choir. More and more friends came to shows, when they were needed or whoever could stop by. The lineup was fluid, and it worked so well that it was decided to make the next album a full band one. The ambient textures stayed, but now they had a big punch in front of them, and all sorts of variety in instruments and vocals. *You Forgot It in People* was one of the best-reviewed albums of the year, and won the 2003 Juno for Alternative Album of the Year.

Another collective rose from the ranks of Montreal's indie scene. Aside from Régine Chassagne, the rest of the members of Arcade Fire had moved to the city as students, but all had music backgrounds. Win Butler had come from Texas at the suggestion of his friend Josh Deu, and the two started the initial group, cowriting several songs. They met Chassagne at McGill University, and became a trio. More members were brought in, an EP was recorded, but the band's relationships were rocky, and most of the members left. Butler's younger sibling Will had followed his brother to Montreal, so he joined. Work continued on tracks that would become the group's first album, including contributions from friends in the band Bell Orchestre, and Richard Reed Parry and Sarah Neufeld joined up as well. Bass player Tim Kingsbury had moved to Montreal from Guelph, Ontario.

The band was big; they all played different instruments as needed and the sounds they made in the studio would be even grander. More players were invited in, including string expert Owen Pallett. Together they made wonderful, huge music, with rich orchestrations, horns and strings together with keyboards and guitars, bells and whistles. Will Butler said, "That's just how the music happened. The sound was maybe determined by the number of people in the band, and the number of people was determined by the number of grand people we knew who we wanted to make music with." It was the key to these collective bands, a shared friendship, and musical compatibility, with a desire to help make the best music possible. Released in 2004 in Canada and the U.S., and 2005 in England, the album *Funeral* kept gaining more and more acclaim and fans. The group's exciting live shows were the talk of the festival circuit, with key shows at Coachella, Lollapalooza, and the Sasquatch! Music Festival. A big-name supporter arrived, with David Bowie making some timely appearances and boosting the band's profile and hip status. England especially loved the group, making several of the cuts hit singles. It is regularly chosen at the top or in the Top 10 of lists of the best albums of the 2000s. The group's third album, 2010's *The Suburbs*, achieved a remarkable first. Along with massive critical acclaim, it was chosen for the 2011 Grammy for Album of the Year, the 2011 Juno Award for Album of the Year, and the 2011 Brit Award for Best International Album. In the meantime, the members of Arcade Fire have enjoyed several different side projects and solo works, keeping the idea of the collective alive and well.

Leslie Feist has an open invitation to return to Broken Social Scene whenever that group is working, and she has used it on occasion. But most of the time, she's just been too busy since first joining them in 1999. While Arcade Fire was on a roll with *Funeral* through 2004 and 2005, Feist was with them step by step, with her stand-out album *Let It Die*. Juno voters even gave her the Alternative Album of the Year award over the Montreal band in 2005. The collectives were really shining that year, with Stars also nominated in the category, featuring three of Feist's colleagues from Broken Social Scene, and Carl Newman from The New Pornographers a fourth nominee. Feist's album came out of time spent living and recording in Paris the previous two years. Her work had taken on a dreamy, yet danceable feel, with Feist now an elegant chanteuse. The music was gently sculpted, smooth curves instead of sharp corners, and a chic-retro vibe cemented the Euro connection. Split between covers and originals, it included her recasting of The Bee Gees' disco ballad "Inside and Out," and "L'amour ne dure pas toujours" by the Parisienne '60s icon Françoise Hardy. Feist's own songs, including "Gatekeeper" and "Mushaboom," continued the leisurely and lovely pace, and she brought a new life to Ron Sexsmith's "Secret Heart," the latest in a long line of cover versions of that Canadian classic.

While *Let It Die* brought her a significant presence in Europe and Canada, and strong notices in the U.S., it was Feist's follow-up, 2007's *The Reminder*, which not only made her famous but also changed the whole relationship between songs, mass media, and marketing. Feist's catchy single, "1234," had been chosen by Apple to use in the ad for its new iPod nano. Really, all they did was use thirty seconds of her imaginative and colorful video, placed on several nano screens. But the ad was everywhere, and so was the song. It immediately became a hit single, Top 10 in the U.K. and U.S., which then translated to huge sales for the album, especially where it counted the most in the new economic model of the music industry, the iTunes store. It raised a lot of interesting questions about musicians teaming with corporations, and even about who was using whom, given the mutual success. In the end what mattered most was that it was another strong Feist album, the edges sometimes rougher than on *Let It Die,* with more electric guitar. Standouts included the uplifting "I Feel It All," and a new cowrite with Ron Sexsmith, "Brandy Alexander."

Sexsmith had continued to be the favorite new songwriter of the nation, since his breakthrough with "Secret Heart" back in 1995. Famously, it was first noticed after Elvis Costello raved about it in the British magazine *Mojo*, where he said, "I've been listening to it all year, and you could all be listening to it for another twenty." Sexsmith's fan club became famous for being famous; his long list of admirers included Elton John, Paul McCartney, Chris Martin of Coldplay, k.d. lang, Emmylou Harris, Nick Lowe, and many more. Sexsmith is a throwback, a fan of great pop songwriting, from a century past, Tin Pan Alley or classic Canadiana, a devotee of Dylan, Lightfoot, and Harry Nilsson, Andy Kim and Michel Pagliaro. His albums always contain gems, inspired melodies matched with uncanny observations. Simple trips on public transit could conjure up stories that became memorable and beautiful songs, such as "Strawberry Blonde." He could also cut a mean soul song, evoking the smooth '70s with "Whatever It Takes." For all the attention and accolades, Sexsmith never seemed to make the commercial leap to the level his peers attained, despite the constant flow of cover versions from the likes of Rod Stewart, Feist, and Michael Bublé. But in 2011, his album *Long Player Late Bloomer* became his most successful release since his debut, and featured the surprising pairing with Vancouver producer Bob Rock. Best known for his Metallica albums, Rock wisely didn't go overboard with Sexsmith, but did succeed in helping him make a more commercial album that was particularly successful in England, number one on the Amazon U.K. Alternative & Indie Chart.

Michael Bublé has had number one hits, and lots of them, since his first album in 2003. The Burnaby, B.C. native has brought smooth jazz vocals back to the top of the pop charts, proving the clout of adult music fans, and also showing that some younger ones still like a solid singer and a good tune, no matter what the style. Bublé came to fame thanks to some heavy friends, those well-connected Canadians who had their breakthroughs in the music business decades before. Bublé had been asked to perform at the wedding of former prime minister Brian Mulroney's daughter Caroline, where he was introduced to famed producer David Foster. While Foster was impressed, he knew singing adult-jazz-pop wasn't the easiest sell. Paul Anka then came on board, offered his support, and a deal was struck where Bublé would record on Foster's own label. His self-titled debut was a hit in several countries including Canada and the U.K., featuring everything from old standards to more modern numbers such as Van Morrison's "Moondance." It was more of a slow build to break into the U.S. market, but with lots of touring and TV appearances, that happened with the next one, 2005's *It's Time*, a Top 10 album in the States and many other countries. By now he was crossing over from jazz to pop to adult contemporary charts, with hit singles such as "Home," which won 2006's Juno Award for Single of the Year, one of four he won that year, and eleven as of 2015, to go along with his four Grammy Awards.

Diana Krall, also from British Columbia, is more jazz than pop, yet the singer and pianist has a huge audience as well. She was a protégé of the great bass player Ray Brown, who had been a member of Canadian Oscar Peterson's most famous trio. Her first album, *Stepping Out*, was recorded in 1993 for the Montreal label Justin Time, and made an immediate impact, gaining the attention of top producer Tommy LiPuma. The pair teamed up for her next album, 1995's *Only Trust Your Heart*, which featuring Brown as a guest, and made the U.S. jazz Top 10. By 1997's *Love Scenes*, her interpretations of standards had now made her the top new jazz musician in North America, with sales of over a million copies, a very rare feat for traditional jazz. She reached a new peak in 2001 with *The Look of Love*, which topped the Canadian albums chart, selling 700,000 copies, and another 1.6 million in the United States, where it was again the top jazz album, and climbed to number nine in the albums chart. In the pop-dominated awards world, she won the Junos for Artist and Album of the Year. Krall has expanded her creative reach in her albums since, composing some of her own material, including songs written with her husband, Elvis Costello, and recording an album of more obscure, early jazz from the 1920s and 1930s, 2012's *Glad Rag Doll*.

It would be hard for anyone in Francophone music to eclipse the worldwide success of Celine Dion, and even with much of her career focused on the English market, she was still the dominant Quebec artist in the 2000s. But the downturn in music sales in the digital era was less significant there, thanks to the continued broader support of music, and there were lots of new performers joining the ranks. Kevin Parent started out fast in the mid-'90s. His first album, 1995's *Pigeon d'argile*, was full of hits, including the strong rocker "Boomerang," and the album went on to sell 360,000 copies, making him the best-selling French artist next to Celine. He won the Felix Award for Song of the Year from 1996 to 1998, with mature songs and thoughtful topics. His voice is distinct, with a rough edge thanks to his Gaspésien accent, having grown up in the coastal, rural Gaspé region of Quebec. Despite being hugely popular, there's never any doubt that Parent is a serious songwriter. His success continued through the 2000s, and he won the Juno Award in 2002 for Best-selling Francophone Album.

Garou's success came at home and abroad. Discovered by Luc Plamondon, he was whisked out of bars in Sherbrooke, Quebec in 1997, and onto the Paris stage of Plamondon's new musical *Notre-Dame de Paris*, where he played the role of Quasimodo. The play was a huge hit, and so was the music; the song "Belle," recorded by Garou with Patrick Fiori and Daniel Lavoie, spent eighteen weeks at number one in France, and selling three million copies worldwide. That created a huge interest in Garou's own future, and his debut album in 2000, *Seul*, sold two million copies across Europe and Canada. The queen herself, Celine, joined Garou for the duet "Sous le vent," a European smash.

Quebec has always enjoyed eccentric artists, and few could match Jean Leloup. Also known as Jean the Wolf, he's a bit of a mystery man, a controversial character with a shifting persona, several different musical guises, and an artistic bent. His gigantic hit "1990" was a dance rocker that mentioned his sexual prowess and the Gulf War. "Isabelle" was ska-influenced, with a black-and-white video that placed him in a Jean-Luc Godard film. The biggest French radio hit of 2000 was his mellow singer-songwriter number, "Je joue de la guitare." In 2003, he announced the retirement of the Jean Leloup character, and came back in 2006 as Jean Leclerc, only to reintroduce the Wolf in 2008. The rise of alternative music in the 2000s hit French Montreal as well, with Malajube joining raved-about artists Arcade Fire and Wolf Parade. In 2006, the group's hit "Montréal –40°C" paid tribute to the legendary cold winters with a good-hearted and happy tune and lyric, the memorable lyrics about it being so freezing, there was a polar bear taking the bus.

Although her name was French, Avril Lavigne sang in English, having grown up with a French father and English mother in Ontario. Proving yet again that everybody knows everybody in Canada, in 1999 at fourteen years old she won a radio contest that let her get up onstage with Shania Twain at a sold-out show in Ottawa and sing with the star. It wasn't long until others got interested in her stage presence and attitude, as well as her voice. Mark Jowett of Nettwerk management in Vancouver, the same person who had discovered Sarah McLachlan, got a videotape of her doing karaoke in her parents' basement, and started sending her to New York for songwriting sessions. One of those trips led to an audition for Arista Records head L.A. Reid, and the making of a pop-punk princess was underway.

When Lavigne's debut, 2002's *Let It Go*, came out, she was seventeen. The image of a skater was completely true, the attitude was all her, just the country singing was missing. Arista had teamed her with the production team The Matrix in Los Angeles, and songs such as "Complicated" and "Sk8er Boi" played up the teen punk image with edgy guitars and lots of pop culture, video-ready references. It took little time to explode, as teens all over had a new hero, a tough young woman who looked like she was having a lot of fun. *Let It Go* has sold over seventeen million albums since its release, a number one album in Canada, England, and Australia, number two in the U.S., and even topping the charts in some South American countries.

Lavigne's 2007 single, "Girlfriend," was another giant international hit, making it to number one in Canada, the U.S. and all over. It was very different from 2002, though, and very different from all the other historic highpoints of the Canadian music industry. In 1957, it was Paul Anka, selling ten million copies of "Diana." In 1974, Terry Jacks topped eleven million with "Seasons in the Sun." Bryan Adams conquered England and didn't do badly elsewhere in 1991, selling over ten million copies of "(Everything I Do) I Do It for You." Celine Dion dwarfed them all with "My Heart Will Go On," and 15 million copies sold. Lavigne's "Girlfriend" sold over seven million, but those weren't those quaint old 45s with a song on each side. Nor were they the long outdated cassingles that some of the Adams fans had purchased, and not CD singles, from Dion's time. Lavigne's audience didn't have to leave their homes; they just downloaded the song from iTunes.

There are still charts and hits and sales, but it's a vastly different music world. Comparing Avril to Anka is quite impossible, even though they were both teen idols. You can have stars such as Neil Young, who released an album a year, which for the most part sell modestly; but his touring revenue is huge, and his *Greatest Hits* and *Harvest* CDs still move decent amounts out of the few remaining retail outlets. The new model is Drake. The Toronto rapper has only been releasing music since 2009 (other than mixtapes) but has already put out over seventy singles. Some are hits, some not, some are starring Drake, more of them include him as a featured guest. The end result is that in 2014, *Billboard* announced that Drake had reached its Hot 100 chart seventy-three times, which placed him ahead of The Beatles, who did it seventy-two times. It's apples and oranges, the game has changed. It's tough to put these achievements into historical context, and equally tough to wonder if the new Canadian music stars will have a lasting influence, and hold the same sentimental memories. Carly Rae Jepsen's "Call Me Maybe" is one of the world's biggest hits of the digital era, selling 13.7 million downloads. Justin Bieber sold twelve million of "Baby." It's tough to think of them as this generation's Neil and Joni. Major record labels have spent most of their time negotiating the package deals for ready-made stars from reality shows for the past decade, and singers such as Eva Avila, a finalist on *Canadian*

Idol, and Marie-Mai, a winner of the French equivalent, *Star Académie*, performed at the closing ceremonies of the 2010 Olympic Games in Vancouver.

It's funny though, no matter how much music changes through technology, and commerce influences what gets recorded and we hear through mass media, Canadians always seem to come back to basic songwriting. Sometimes it takes a couple of years, but trends come and go, and a good song never goes out of fashion. The Juno Awards may not be the best barometer of talent in the country, but they try to be. Good art does get acknowledged, sometimes more than sales figures. In 2014, the Group of the Year and Pop Album of the Year Junos went to Tegan and Sara, identical twin sisters from Calgary, who play indie rock and pop. The duo have been slowly, steadily building a large following since 1999, when they first signed with Neil Young's Vapor Records. *So Jealous*, released in 2004, included the hit "Walking with a Ghost," later covered by The White Stripes. The album *Hearthrob* was the biggest success yet, number two in the Canadian album chart, number three in the U.S., and making headway in Europe for the first time. Embracing their inner pop selves, the sisters tweaked up the synthesizers and raised the pop percentage, best heard on the feel-good hit "Closer," which also won a Juno for Single of the Year. Artist of the Year and Songwriter of the Year went to Serena Ryder, who had the infectious hit "Stompa." Her hypnotizing voice invited us to clap and stomp our way through the best three minutes of the day, with a beat that shook mountains. Arcade Fire took Album and Alternative Album of the Year, for *Reflektor*, and good old Ron Sexsmith walked away with another, the Adult Alternative Album of the Year, for his latest, *Forever Endeavour*. The Breakthrough Artist of the Year went to a country singer, Alberta's Brett Kissel, who had actually grown up on a cattle ranch, and still went back during time off to help his father. The Breakthrough Group of the Year combined hip-hop and

First Nations music, chanting, drumming, and dubstep. A Tribe Called Red is made up of three DJs, all from Ontario First Nations.

In 2014, Rush celebrated the fortieth anniversary of the release of the group's debut album by taking the year off. It was a well-deserved hiatus. They had just spent a full year on the road, promoting their latest album, *Clockwork Angels*, a number one on the Canadian album charts, number two in the U.S. On that huge tour, with its steam-punk inspired set, the group had largely stayed away from the greatest hits, performing much of the new album. The fans ranged from kids to seniors, with plenty of air guitarists and a few air drummers and bassists in the crowd. The band members looked ageless, and played that way as well. It's a time when most rock bands of their vintage have to make the sets mostly about their glory years, bring out the tried-and-true set list, or play an entire classic album from start to finish. The Rolling Stones do that, so does Bruce Springsteen, all the Hall of Famers still working. Not Rush though. And they are finally in the Rock and Roll Hall of Fame, inducted April 18, 2013. They could have been placed in the Hall as early as 1999, their first year of eligibility.

Why the long wait, the fourteen years of the Hall refusing to acknowledge their fame? Let's just call Rush an example, a metaphor for Canada's rock 'n' roll history, outside the country and often inside as well. It's well known Canadians have an inferiority complex. It comes from being a colony first, and then living beside a more famous nation. Canadians don't toot their own horn much, even about music. Rush, and the rest of Canada's music world, move on at a solid pace, doing the job, and doing it really well. It's taken a while sometimes, but it's nice that Rush and Cohen, Mitchell and Young, The Band, Denny Doherty, and Zal Yanovsky get acknowledged. There are a lot more where they came from—and more on the way.

Recommended Reading

For more information on Canada's rich music history and some more in-depth studies of the major players, here are several worthy additions to your library. These books were consulted for accuracy during the preparation of this text. (Quotes from Ronnie Hawkins in chapter 2 are from www.ronniehawkins.com. Quotes from Jack Richardson in chapter 6 are from www.abcbuzz.com. All other interviews were conducted by the author.)

Before the Gold Rush: Peace, Love and The Dawn of Canadian Sound *by Nicholas Jennings, Penguin Books Canada, 1998*
> The definitive look at Yorkville, all the stars and the should-have-been bigger ones. The greatest collection of talent in three blocks.

Blood, Sweat and Tears *by David Clayton-Thomas, Viking Canada, 2010*
> The Voice, from being picked off the streets by Ronnie Hawkins to leading Blood, Sweat and Tears to international fame.

RECOMMENDED READING

Canuck Rock: A History of Canadian Popular Music *by Ryan Edwardson, University of Toronto Press, 2009*
> How music in Canada became Canadian music, with an emphasis on the ties between a growing nationalism and the development of the music industry.

Don't Be Denied: Neil Young the Canadian Years *by John Einarson, Quarry Books, 1992*
> From Omemee to Winnipeg, Yorkville to L.A., the definitive story of how Neil became Neil.

For What It's Worth: The Story of Buffalo Springfield *by John Einarson and Richie Furay, Cooper Square Press, 2004*
> An insider's look at the tension-filled band, why it should have been huge, and what went wrong.

Four Strong Winds *by John Einarson, with Ian Tyson and Sylvia Tyson, McClelland & Stewart, 2011*
> Folk's first couple tell how they met, got to Greenwich Village, married, divorced, reunited, and made five decades of fine and often groundbreaking music.

Have Not Been the Same: The Canrock Renaissance 1985–1995, *Michael Barclay, A. D. Jack, and Jason Schneider, ECW Press, 2001*
> The authors suggest this is the greatest decade for Canadian music, when it became cool to be Canuck. Blue Rodeo, Tragically Hip, Sloan, Rheostatics, all bands that liked their country.

I'm Your Man: The Life of Leonard Cohen *by Sylvie Simmons, Ecco, 2013*
> A packed life, from Montreal to Greece to "Suzanne" to "Hallelujah" to Mt. Baldy to the sexiest senior in rock.

Joni Mitchell: In Her Own Words, *Malka Marom, ECW Press, 2014*
> The writer has known her since 1966, and there's a trust, which

is important with Mitchell, who always wants a serious artistic discussion about her work.

On a Cold Road: Tales of Adventure in Canadian Rock *by Dave Bidini, McClelland & Stewart, 1998*
The Rheostatistician talks to his pals in the rock world about the unique challenges touring in Canada.

Soul Mining: A Musical Life by Daniel Lanois, *Faber & Faber, 2011*
The great producer and sound explorer tells how he got where he is today by working hard, being prepared, and always striving for the best art he can make.

Special Deluxe: A Memoir of Life & Cars *by Neil Young, Blue Rider Press, 2014*
Growing up, his musical influences and all those cars. What a guy.

Still Takin' Care of Business *by Randy Bachman and John Einarson, McArthur & Co., 2007*
Bachman's tale of the Winnipeg rock world of the early '60s that spawned The Guess Who, Neil Young, and BTO.

This Wheel's on Fire: Levon Helm and the Story of The Band *by Levon Helm and Stephen Davis, Chicago Review Press, 1993*
Levon and The Hawk move to Canada and change everything. Spoiler: Levon wasn't happy with Robbie Robertson.

Treat Me Like Dirt: An Oral History of Punk in Toronto and Beyond *by Liz Worth, Bongo Beat, 2010*
Teenage Head, Viletones, Diodes, The Crash 'n' Burn, and more.

The Top 100 Canadian Albums *by Bob Mersereau, Goose Lane, 2007*
A panel of six hundred musicians, music industry folks, and fans vote on the best-ever Canadian albums. Neil wins!

The Top 100 Canadian Singles *by Bob Mersereau, Goose Lane, 2010*

The same idea, only with singles, from "Diana" to "1234." The Guess Who does very well.

Whispering Pines: The Northern Roots of American Music from Hank Snow to The Band *by Jason Schneider, ECW Press, 2009*
Schneider examines the songwriting talent of Canada, the impact Canadian artists have had on modern music, and why their work has crossed borders so well.

Recommended Listening

This collection of albums would make a fine library, no matter what country you're from.

Acadie, Daniel Lanois, Opal, 1989
> The super-producer and sound craftsman shows his songwriter side, connecting with nature and his own roots for this bilingual beauty.

After the Gold Rush, *Neil Young, Reprise, 1970*
> Aching, lonesome, and gently beautiful acoustic tracks such as the title cut, with sporadic bursts of electric fire ("Southern Man").

American Woman, *The Guess Who, RCA, 1970*
> Cummings and Bachman at their songwriting best, with tremendous pop punch on "No Time," "No Sugar Tonight," and of course the enduring title cut.

Blue, *Joni Mitchell, Reprise, 1971*
> More fun than you might remember, with "Carey" and "All I Want,"

but it is the raw emotion of "River," "A Case of You," and "Little Green" that makes this so powerful.

Court and Spark, *Joni Mitchell, Asylum, 1974*
Jazz-fusion touches liven up the arrangements, giving Mitchell pop hits ("Help Me," "Free Man in Paris"), lots of lighthearted moments, and her most accessible album.

Everybody Knows This Is Nowhere, *Neil Young, Reprise, 1969*
Young really ends decades well. He introduces Crazy Horse, and three monsters, "Cinnamon Girl," "Cowgirl in the Sand," and "Down by the River."

Five Days in July, *Blue Rodeo, Warner, 1993*
Getting out of the studio and recording at Greg Keelor's farm was the key, as the relaxed group vibe allowed for this roots-rock classic.

Fogerty's Cove, *Stan Rogers, Barn Swallow Records, 1977*
At a time when folk was supposedly out of favor, Rogers made the greatest Canadian folk album ever, with songs both ancient-sounding ("Barrett's Privateers") and modern-themed.

Freedom, *Neil Young, Reprise, 1989*
Remembered as the home of "Rockin' in the Free World," but also includes his lovely "Wrecking Ball," and mysterious epic, "Crime in the City (Sixty to Zero Part I)."

Four Strong Winds, *Ian & Sylvia, Vanguard, 1964*
The duo's second album features Ian Tyson's beloved classic, and as solid a folk repertoire as any Greenwich Village act. Includes the tune their pal Dylan gave them, "Tomorrow Is a Long Time."

Fully Completely, *The Tragically Hip, MCA, 1992*
Canadiana never rocked harder, with a poetic lyricist and a locked-in band making nation-building music without the clichés.

RECOMMENDED LISTENING

Funeral, *Arcade Fire, Merge, 2004*
    Big, exciting, layered, textured, vibrant, and all about a bunch of their recently deceased relatives. There's even a celebration of a massive snowfall. A joy to hear so many nonrock instruments.

Gord's Gold, *Gordon Lightfoot, Reprise, 1975*
    It's hard to pick a single Lightfoot, but this best-of covers his '60s beginnings and '70s hits, including "Sundown" and "If You Could Read My Mind."

Gordon, *Barenaked Ladies, Sire, 1992*
    Fun, joyous, Canadian. They knew who they were, white boys from the suburbs, and just had fun with it, plus pop culture in all its silliness.

Harmonium, *Harmonium, Polydor, 1974*
    Lighthearted and vibrant, a new synthesis of folk, prog, pop, and jazz that only existed in Montreal at that time.

Harvest, *Neil Young, Reprise, 1972*
    His most beloved, with "Heart of Gold," "The Needle and the Damage Done," and "Old Man," every track is a classic.

Hejira, *Joni Mitchell, Asylum, 1976*
    Just two years after her commercial zenith, Mitchell dives deep into jazz, with complex but hugely rewarding stories such as "Amelia" and "Coyote."

Hit Parade, *Pagliaro, Unidisc, 2010*
    Lots of his French hits, some of his English; if you just choose one Pag album, best to have some of both.

Hymns of the 49th Parallel, *k.d. lang, Nonesuch, 2004*
    A tribute to Canada's great songwriters, incluing Neil, Joni, Leonard, Cockburn, Sexsmith, and Jane Siberry.

I'm Your Man, *Leonard Cohen, Columia, 1988*
> The rebirth, with synths instead of nylon, a wink instead of a seduction, and the creation of his latter-day persona of the witty observer with "the golden voice."

Jagged Little Pill, *Alanis Morissette, Maverick, 1995*
> EmPOWERment. The former Canadian teen star grabs control with the most in-your-face album ever. Every female artist since owes a debt.

Jaune, *Jean-Pierre Ferland, Barclay, 1970*
> A wild ride as the chansonnier becomes a rock star, the *Sgt. Pepper* album of Quebec rock. A carnival of sound, and it sounded great, too, a rare thing for Canadian studios to that point.

Mad Mad World, *Tom Cochrane, Capitol, 1991*
> The home of "Life Is a Highway," but it keeps on rockin' with the rousing numbers "No Regrets," "Sinking Like a Sunset," and "Washed Away" too.

Moving Pictures, *Rush, Anthem, 1981*
> A little New Wave, the usual prog rock, more keyboards, and "Tom Sawyer." Rush hits the sweet spot.

Music from Big Pink, *The Band, Capitol, 1968*
> The game-changer. Just as everything was getting crazy with psychedelia and electricity, The Band took it back a few decades, and created roots music.

Oh What a Feeling: A Vital Collection of Canadian Music, *various, CARAS/MCA, 1996*
> A charity compilation by the Juno Awards, this four-disc set is the best overview of Canadian rock and pop ever assembled, with virtually every important hit or artist. Out of print, but easy to find.

***Reckless**, Bryan Adams, A&M, 1984*
Adams and Jim Vallance join the master hit songwriters, with
"Summer of '69," "Heaven," and "Run to You." Adams goes from a
national to an international star.

***The Reminder**, Feist, Arts & Crafts, 2007*
The bright colors of the "1234" are the start, but it's the fireworks
seen in the "I Feel It All" promo that tell you where this is coming
from. Feist makes a joyful noise.

***Rust Never Sleeps**, Neil Young, Reprise, 1979*
Rock 'n' roll will never die, but it gets better with some rust on it.

***Songs of Leonard Cohen**, Leonard Cohen, Columbia, 1967*
The debut, with "Suzanne" and "So Long, Marianne," nylon-
stringed guitar and the bedroom voice. He immediately joins the
highest ranks of songwriters.

***Stealing Fire**, Bruce Cockburn, True North, 1984*
Our favorite folkie gets upset, with dynamic results. Cockburn
takes on the warmongerers with the powerful "If I Had a Rocket
Launcher."

***Surfacing**, Sarah McLachlan, Nettwerk, 1997*
Soul music, not the R&B kind but the healing kind. It almost
bypasses your ears and enters through your pores, healing and
soothing.

***The Band**, The Band, Capitol, 1969*
The follow-up, perhaps even better, on a song-by-song basis.
"Across the Great Divide," "Up On Cripple Creek," and "The Night
They Drove Old Dixie Down" lead the pack.

***The Last Waltz**, The Band, Warner, 1978*
It might have been more bitter than sweet, but they sure played

great that night. All the best are here, with a first-class guest list, including Canadians Young, Mitchell, and Hawkins.

Twice Removed, Sloan, Geffen, 1994

The album the band's record company didn't want, because it was modern pop instead of grunge. Canadian fans loved it, though, with its bright sound and hooks.

Index

265

INDEX

INDEX

INDEX

INDEX

INDEX

INDEX

INDEX

INDEX

INDEX

INDEX

INDEX

INDEX

INDEX

INDEX

INDEX

INDEX

INDEX

INDEX

INDEX

INDEX